D0170180

Passive Revolution

Passive Revolution

ABSORBING THE ISLAMIC CHALLENGE TO CAPITALISM

Cihan Tuğal

Stanford University Press
Stanford, California

Stanford University Press
Stanford, California

© 2009 by the Board of Trustees of the Leland Stanford Junior University.
All rights reserved.

No part of this book may be reproduced or transmitted in any form or by any means, electronic or mechanical, including photocopying and recording, or in any information storage or retrieval system without the prior written permission of Stanford University Press.

Printed in the United States of America on acid-free, archival-quality paper

Library of Congress Cataloging-in-Publication Data

Tuğal, Cihan.
   Passive revolution : absorbing the Islamic challenge to capitalism / Cihan Tuğal.
      p. cm.
   Includes bibliographical references and index.
   ISBN 978-0-8047-6144-4 (cloth : alk. paper)—ISBN 978-0-8047-6145-1 (pbk. : alk. paper)
   1. Islam and politics—Turkey.   2. Islamic fundamentalism—Turkey.   3. Islamic modernism—Turkey.   4. Capitalism—Religious aspects—Islam.   I. Title.
   BP173.7.T82 2009
   322′.109561—dc22   2008046633

Typeset by Westchester Book Group in 10/14 Minion

To Deniz

CONTENTS

ACKNOWLEDGMENTS

THIS BOOK IS BASED on research in Sultanbeyli, an urban district once under Islamist control. I first of all thank this district's residents for suffering the presence of an ethnographer among them for several years. I acknowledge, on top of all, my great debt to friends among the district's teachers and municipal employees who led me through the maze of religion and politics at the local level, opened their homes to me, and taught me the subtleties of Islamic mobilization and demobilization.

Michael Burawoy contributed to the structure and arguments of this book, read several versions, and thoroughly commented on them. The revisit of my ethnographic site that he suggested proved crucial to the book, leading to the two-phase design: the observation of the same district in two different historical contexts. Esra Özyürek also commented on several versions. Mike Hout enriched the book with his helpful comments. The analyses benefited from discussions with Ann Swidler, Dylan Riley, Peter Evans, Victoria Bonnell, Raka Ray, Laura Enriquez, Loïc Wacquant, Martin Sanchez-Jankowski, and Philip Gorski, as well as from their feedback on previous work related to this project. I discussed with Aynur Sadet my observations on a daily basis during both phases of the project, and the sociological and political insights we have developed together over the years has shaped the analyses in this book. I also immensely benefited from the input of my editor, Kate Wahl, and the two anonymous reviewers Stanford University Press provided.

During the first phase of the project, Fatma Müge Göçek helped me develop a more complete sense of Islamic schools of thought. She not only encouraged me to live in an unfamiliar setting but acted as my initial guide in interpreting this complex locality with a historical perspective. Howard Kimeldorf was an engaged, patient, and untiring reader. He made sure that I did not lose direction. George Steinmetz pushed me to develop the theoretical implications of my arguments. Fernando Coronil, Arthur Stinchcombe, Gary Fine, Georgi Derlugian, Charles Kurzman, Elif Kale, Asena Günal, Berna Turam, Burçak Keskin, Dicle Koğacıoğlu, Aslı Gür, Mücahit Bilici, Barış Büyükokutan, Yüksel Taşkın, Nick Jorgensen, Devra Coren, Irfan Nouriddin, and Darcy Leach read and provided detailed comments on my earlier analyses.

Nükhet Sirman both indirectly influenced this book by cultivating my ethnographic sensibility and discussed my observations and ideas throughout the research project. Çağlar Keyder, Ayşe Öncü, Nuray Mert, Zafer Yenal, Yeşim Arat, Koray Çalışkan, Murat Yüksel, Oğuz Işık, Wendy Espeland, Bruce Carruthers, and Ann Orloff also contributed their recommendations and criticisms.

The Committee on Research at the University of California at Berkeley funded the second phase of this project. The first phase was funded by the Social Science Research Council, the Population Council, and the Lebanese Policy Center, along with the Rackham School of Graduate Studies and the Department of Sociology at the University of Michigan. An Andrew W. Mellon Postdoctoral Fellowship at Northwestern University has been helpful in rethinking aspects of the first phase of my research.

My partner, parents, brothers-in-law, and parents-in-law made this book possible by generously sharing my enthusiasm, joy, and troubles during both phases of the project. The book would not have seen the light of day if it were not for them. I dedicate this book to my son Deniz, whose birth and first months accompanied its writing.

ABBREVIATIONS

Parties

Center Right

DP: Democrat Party (1946–1960)

DYP: True Path Party (1983–2007)

ANAP: Motherland Party (1983–present)

Center Left and Right-Wing Kemalist

CHP: Republican People's Party (Kemalist to center left to right-wing Kemalist, 1923–1981, 1992–present)

SODEP: Social Democracy Party (center left, 1983–1985)

SHP: Social Democratic Populist Party (center left, 1985–1995) (descendent of SODEP)

DSP: Democratic Left Party (center-left to nationalist, 1985–present)

Islamist and Ex-Islamist

MNP: Milli Order Party (Islamist, 1970–1971)

MSP: Milli Salvation Party (Islamist, 1972–1980)

RP: Welfare Party (Islamist, 1983–1998)

FP: Virtue Party (Islamist, 1997–2001)

SP: Felicity Party (Islamist, 2001–present)

AKP: Justice and Development Party (ex-Islamist, 2001–present; also AK Party)

Nationalist Right

MHP: Nationalist Action Party (1969–1981, 1993–present)

MÇP: Nationalist Work Party (1985–1993; descendent of MHP)

BBP: Great Unity Party (religious nationalist right, 1993–present)

Socialist Left

TİP: Labor Party of Turkey (1961–1971, 1975–1981)

Nationalist Left

HADEP: People's Democracy Party (Kurdish, 1994–2003)

DTP: Democratic Society Party (2005–present; descendent of HADEP)

Armed Political Groups

Dev-Sol: Revolutionary Left

İBDA-C: Islamic Great East Raiders Front

PKK: Kurdistan Worker's Party

Associations, Foundations, and Other Institutions

DİSK: Confederation of Revolutionary Worker Unions

Hak-İş: Confederation of Real Worker Unions

İHL: High Schools for Imams and Preachers

MGV: Milli Youth Foundation

MTTB: Milli Turkish Student Association

MÜSİAD: Association of Independent Industrialists and Businessmen

Türk-İş: Confederation of Worker Unions of Turkey

TÜSİAD: Association of Industrialists and Businessmen of Turkey

Passive Revolution

INTRODUCTION

OVER THE LAST DECADES, pious Muslims all over the world have been going through deep and contradictory transformations. Public attention has focused on some Muslims' turn to violence and their cry for military jihad, ignoring more widely shared changes among the population. A personal story of transformation exemplifies another experience. When I met Yasin in 2000, he was a forty-year-old radical Islamist shopkeeper. He had been one of the leaders of Islamist[1] street action in his poor urban district in the 1990s. This district, Sultanbeyli, was at the forefront of Islamization in Istanbul during that decade. Yasin frequently went to unregistered, radical mosques for Friday sermons. Visitors took off their shoes in front of his office (to keep the environment clean and ready for ritual observance). He performed daily prayers regularly, together with partners and customers. Yasin, along with his partners and friends, did not support the (mainstream Islamist) Virtue Party (FP), which he found too submissive, cowardly, somewhat nationalistic, and obedient to the state. He was deeply committed to global Islamic unity and saw the Turkish nation-state as an artificial impediment.

When I was a newcomer in his district, I told Yasin I had heard that there were many Nur students (or Nurcus)[2] in the district. He heartily laughed at this suggestion and said, "How can there be Nur students in a district where the Islamists are so strong?" Only an outsider like me could believe that there could be any followers of this pro-state, Turkish nationalist, pro-Western, and capitalist Islamic group in Sultanbeyli. My ignorance deeply embarrassed me.

When I visited Yasin again in 2006, he had started to attend the seminars of the Nurcus. He argued that this was the only Islamic movement that had a

1

"systematic" way of working and therefore would survive in the long run. Indeed, various Nurcu groups had become the most active circles in Sultanbeyli. Moreover, Yasin no longer went to radical, unregistered mosques, and he now said, "Confrontational environments are not good. We have to think with sound reason [akl-ı selim olmamız lazım]. This is better for every sector of society." Shoes were no longer removed outside his office and he had started to perform his daily prayers in the mosque across the street rather than in his workplace. He upheld the Turkish nation-state and said it served Islam better than any other state in the Middle East. He deeply regretted the past decade of activism and said:

> Back then, there was a movement against the system, but it had no real content. It was not based on science and knowledge. Now [pious] Muslims think much more systematically. They have a broader horizon. They also learned how to respect other people's rights. Imposing Islam is not right anyway. They have learned all of these and they are in a better position to rule the country.

He supported a recently established conservative party, the Justice and Development Party (AKP), an organization on much more favorable terms with the state than the FP. The AKP, which had come to power after the 2002 general elections, represented for him the emergent science-oriented, systematic, and tolerant Muslims. He also praised the AKP's economic policies, thanks to which his once humble business was booming. Yasin was still strictly observant. He did not miss his prayers. He still wore the loose pants that allowed him to pray during working hours. His clothes did not reveal the contours of his body, a sign of Islamic humility. He still had his rounded beard modeled after that of the Prophet Muhammad. Yet, he had spatially separated ritual observance and work. He spoke in a less excited tone, more calmly, especially about politics and religion. He emphasized political calculation over political correctness.

This rationalization and partial secularization is emblematic of the change Islamists in Turkey are going through. By analyzing the transformation of Islamists in a previously radical district and the relationship of this change to the AKP, I will demonstrate how this rationalization of religion was not simply the end result of an inevitable world-historical trend (as a Weberian might think)[3] but an outcome of contingent political struggles.

MODERATE ISLAM: SPONTANEOUS RATIONALIZATION
OR HEGEMONIC STRATEGY?

Especially after the attacks of 9/11, public opinion in the West identified Islamic politics with radical challenges against the world system. Analysts pointed out a long history of revolutionary mobilization within national borders, which after the 1990s globalized into a world movement (Kepel 2002). This history was characterized by authoritarianism, social protectionism, and at least a rhetorical anticapitalism (Abrahamian 1991; Burke 1998; Fischer 1982; Zubaida 1989). However, in many parts of the Muslim world, Islamic politics started with such radicalism but evolved in a market-oriented, at least partially democratic, and sometimes even pro-Western direction. Scholars and policy makers have taken note of this alternative trend and labeled it "moderate Islam." While some have taken this as a completely distinct phenomenon, others have recognized that market-oriented Islamic politics in most cases have their roots in radical Islamism. Scholars have tended to treat this transformation of radical movements into prosystem movements as a healthy evolution, a learning process, adaptation, rationalization, cooperation, secularization, and democratization (Çavdar 2006; Çınar 2006; Esposito and Voll 1996; Moaddel 2004; Nasr 2005; Robinson 1997; Turam 2007). Instead, I treat this process as the *constitution of hegemony* and the *absorption of radicalism*.

There are certainly traditions of liberal and modernist religion in the Muslim world, especially starting from the nineteenth century on (Kurzman 1998; Moaddel 2005). However, the contemporary wave of moderate Islam cannot be taken as just another step toward this religion's ultimate liberalization. It is not continuity with these traditions that has empowered moderate Islam in countries such as Turkey.[4] It is rather the mobilization of broad sectors under the banner of radicalizing Islam, the subsequent defeat of radicalism, and the radicals' strategic (yet internalized) change of track after the defeat. These ex-radicals might be the heirs of the liberal Islam of the nineteenth century, but it is their previous radicalism and past experience with populist mobilization that allows them to naturalize modernized Islam among the masses. Without this defeated mobilization, moderate Islam would neither have its loyal followers nor its ardent leaders today.

In this book, I use the Gramscian concept of "passive revolution" to study this process of absorption. Passive revolution is one of the convoluted, and sometimes unintended, ways by which the dominant sectors establish willing consent ("hegemony") for their rule. Different from classic revolutions (as in the French, Russian, and Chinese cases) where an emergent dominant class attempts to sweep away the old dominant classes and their institutions through mass mobilization, in a passive revolution popular sectors are mobilized with revolutionary discourses and strategies only to reinforce existing patterns of domination.[5] I contend that moderate Islam is the culmination of a long process of passive revolution as a result of which erstwhile radicals and their followers are brought into the fold of neoliberalism, secularism, and Western domination. Today, the effective leaders of moderate Islam are not those who have always been liberal Muslims, but they are those who have fought against neoliberalism, secularism, and U.S. hegemony for decades, only to deliver their experiences to the service of their past enemies in the end.

The analysis of moderate Islam also contributes to our understanding of transition to market economies. Critics of neoliberalism draw attention to the social sectors that it inevitably excludes. It follows that neoliberalization will lead to major clashes between the haves and have-nots, except when social conflict is violently repressed. As the regulation mechanisms of the twentieth century (such as the welfare state) are now discarded, what on earth can appease the wrath of the excluded? Some might pose identity politics as a way out (Harvey 2005). But what if whole populations were mobilized against neoliberalization only to be brought back under its spell? What if controlled popular initiative became the main political engine of neoliberalization? Passive revolution is indeed a viable, even if unstable, route to a market economy.

The goal of this book is not simply to analyze Islamic politics but to develop our understanding of sociopolitical radicalism in general. While the empirical material of this book is about a religious challenge against the system,[6] my more general interest is in how radical attacks against the reigning order come into being, how activists organize them in the process of changing their own and others' lives, and how the system survives after sustained challenges. In this regard, this is not a book solely about Islamism but about how revolutionary movements are mobilized and ultimately absorbed.

ABSORPTION OF AN ANTISECULAR CHALLENGE

Today, many in the Western as well as the Islamic world enthusiastically embrace the AKP. This party seems to be the only Islamic political actor that gets the approval of both the West and Muslims worldwide. U.S. newspapers such as *The New York Times* and *The Washington Post*, prominent German newspapers such as *die Welt*, and officials of the European Union point it out to other Islamic movements as a democratic example to follow.[7] At the same time, while the party's Islamic acceptance is not universal (Çavdar 2006), Malaysia's most remarkable Islamic activist Anwar Ibrahim, as well as the Palestinian movement Hamas, declare that they take the AKP as their model. However, what is at stake in the AKP experience is not simply a marriage of Islam and secularism, of religion and democracy, of East and West, but the absorption of a radical challenge against the system, which we can only understand in the context of Turkish Islamism's development over the last century.

The last decades of the Ottoman Empire witnessed an Islamic movement organized in political parties, newspapers, magazines, and associations. After Mustafa Kemal Atatürk established the Turkish Republic in 1923, all Islamic circles were disbanded. Let alone permitting any activism, the state suppressed basic Islamic education by unofficial actors in the 1930s and 1940s. In the 1950s and 1960s, Islamic activists started to organize again in communities, informal networks, magazines, publication houses, and fringe political parties. It was at the end of the 1960s that they decisively came together under the roof of an Islamist mass party.

After Necmettin Erbakan's election to the parliament as an independent candidate, Islamists established the Milli Order Party (MNP). Even the title of the party, along with the name of its ideology (Milli Outlook), expressed a deep ambivalence. In early Islamic usage, *millet* (the noun for *milli*), a Kur'anic term, designated Muslim and non-Muslim religious groups. It referred in the Ottoman social system to religious communities with distinct administrative structures and legal systems (Lewis 1988). As there was nothing in local language to refer to "the nation," nationalists appropriated the term *milli* in the nineteenth century and started to use it as an equivalent of the word *national*. The Milli Outlook movement, born in the late 1960s, utilized the ambivalence of this term to appeal to the religious feelings of its audience in a country where the only officially legitimate collective identity had become Turkish nationality. Were the Islamists reproducing the already hegemonic nationalist ideology, or were they making use of the multivalence of the word *milli* to establish a radical Islamist line? Was this a system party or a revolutionary one? In the following decades, these questions plagued not only the guardians of the secular state but also Islamic activists who had doubts about the party's ideological sincerity. The secularist courts closed the party down in 1971 and the party resurfaced under a new name, a pattern that was to be repeated several times in the next thirty-five years (see Table 2.1 for the Islamist parties' changing names and positions over the years).

In the 1980s and 1990s, the party again ambivalently and implicitly alluded to both Islamic traditions and modern social justice struggles with its new name, the Refah Party (RP). (Refah means prosperity or welfare.) Those who wanted to see Islam in the party read this word as a part of traditional Islamic vocabulary. Those who wanted to see in the party the promise of a new world—an exploding class of informal workers[8] and many converts from the Left—saw an insinuation of the welfare state in this new name. While for some the party's new platform (the Just Order, see Chapter 2) signified radical redistribution, for others it was a metaphor for Islamic law. While the party said it would develop a market economy, it also promised market regulation, redistribution, unionization, and the eradication of poverty.

Ambivalence had its misfortunes. Already in the early 1990s, pious entrepreneurs (represented by MÜSİAD, the Association of Independent Industrialists and Businessmen) raised eyebrows over what they saw to be impractical economic promises in the party's program, while some radical Islamist groups stayed away from the party, accusing it of a lack of clarity in its Islamic and egalitarian demands. Despite all this, the party appealed to broad masses during these decades. It had millions of members in the mid-1990s. Islamic lifestyles gained force with the party's ascent, as symbolized most of all with the increasing number of women who donned the veil.

After election victories in 1994 and 1995, the Islamist party had a chance to apply its program in the municipalities and a coalition government. The party's municipal efficiency increased its popularity. Although it is still questionable whether the party really constituted a challenge to the secular system, the secularist military interpreted its policies as a major threat and intervened to remove the RP at the end of the 1990s. After this intervention, the Islamist party underwent a few tumultuous years, at the end of which a new generation of leaders split the party to establish the AKP, while the old leaders founded the Felicity Party. The AKP leaders attempted to remove any ambivalence and market the party as a secular, pro-state, pro-Western, and procapitalist organization.

While the staunch secularists were still not convinced, liberal businessmen, intellectuals, and academics in Turkey—and many liberals in the West—became enthusiastic supporters. Interestingly, many informal workers and

Islamic activists believed, just like the rigid secularists, that there was continuity between the Islamist party and the AKP rather than a break; but they also gave up the demand of an Islamic state. Combining the power of the new secular supporters and the old Islamist supporters resulted in a major election victory in 2002 and a one-party government, which Turkey had not seen since 1991.

The economy boomed under the AKP government, and the party turned out to be the most successful privatizer of public companies. Unemployment and poverty peaked, but the informal workers remained unshakable supporters. Many scholars and journalists have interpreted this process as one of rationalization. However, the ambivalences in Turkish Islamism's history, the indecisive mobilizations, and the still persisting contradictions lead me to read this transition as a passive revolution. Islamism had mobilized activists and workers, and the AKP appropriated this mobilization to reinforce neoliberalization in Turkey.

During five years of AKP rule, Islamist street action came to an end. The ratio of people who said they want an Islamic state decreased from around 20 percent throughout the 1990s to 9 percent in 2006 (Çarkoğlu and Toprak 2006). At the same time, practicing Muslim men who had not been allowed to occupy high offices before became a part of the ruling elite. Such a thorough change in such a short period of time requires explanation. Why would street action stop just when it could be most effective by making use of the emergence of sympathetic elites? Why would Islamists abandon the demand of an Islamic state? This book will reveal the dynamics of this massive social change by studying how the AKP changed people's everyday lives and their relations to politics.

The AKP government poses yet more conundrums for scholarly analysis. The first three years of AKP rule were a liberal's dream. The party passed many democratic reforms, recognized the existence of minorities hitherto rejected by official discourse, and liberalized the political system. Consequently, the liberal intelligentsia remained enthusiastic supporters of the party well into 2005. The indecision of the intellectuals after that point is more readily interpretable, but the position of informal workers is confusing at first sight. While the AKP slowed down democratic reforms by mid-2005, until the last days of its first mandate it maintained market reforms. Despite increasing unemployment and poverty, there was no massive popular resistance to the government—street action remained restricted to leftist unions, which were already mobilized in the previous decades. The puzzle of this book is: Why did the activists and popular sectors, who had until that point supported the religious and anti–free market platform of the Islamist party, wholeheartedly embrace the AKP government?

I argue that the pious business community has established hegemony, that is, it has made its vision the vision of pious popular sectors and activists, through the AKP. Almost all Islamists have come to the conservative position of the MÜSİAD: support for unfettered markets, integration with the international business community, deregulation, privatization, and emphasis on a conservative morality (deemed to be universal). They no longer emphasize what differentiates Islam from other religions and secularism.[9] Yet, this is not only MÜSİAD's hegemony but also that of the existing dominant sectors in Turkey and abroad.

The crux of the AKP's passive revolution was its uneven appropriation of Islamist strategies, which it put to the use of non-Islamist causes. This argument is based on the theoretical framework built in Chapter 1, where I hold that hegemony is established on the interface between civil society and political society. Over the preceding decades, Islamists had developed communities, informal networks, and associations that they linked to the political party to mobilize and politicize millions of people. That is, in the terminology of this book, they had been successful in linking "civil society" (networks that regulate everyday life, social space, and people's relation to the economy) to "political society" (leadership that constitutes authority and unity), at least initially. Yet, they failed in making the final leap of either integrating civil society and political society to the state or capturing the state through the combined movement of radical civil society and political society. The AKP, in turn, learned innovative ways of linking civil society and political society from past Islamist experience, yet at the same time made use of openings in the system to integrate the pious masses to the secular state.

So, does the AKP's success mean that Islamic radicalism is dead after the passive revolution? Not really. Earlier, Yasin was introduced as an "ex-radical." Yet, my interactions with him on other occasions raised doubts. A couple of times, when the military cornered the AKP government, he shared his misgivings with me: "In the 1980s, Sayyid Qutb's[10] writings had convinced us that nothing could be done via the political party. Then with the AKP, we saw that this was wrong. But now, I again started to think that Qutb might have been right." Several days after this conversation, when the storm abated, Yasin was again assured of the AKP's path. Many other people in the district fluctuated similarly. Can radical Islamists make use of such oscillations in the future and again mount a challenge against the system?

Other observations suggest that one kind of Islamism stands little chance, but radicals are in the process of finding new ways. One spring afternoon in Yasin's office, several men collectively read an article about interreligious dialogue from an Islamist magazine. Each one read aloud half a page and then passed the magazine to the next reader. After they were done reading, they discussed the issues raised by the author. Toward the end of the discussion, Rasim (a forty-five-year-old publicly employed engineer with a thin mustache)[11] walked in. He had in his hand the brochure of the newly established Family Association, an organization that focused on strengthening Islamic culture among the youth. This association was affiliated with the X group (see Chapters 3 and 5), which had shifted from armed struggle to focusing on associations after the 1997 military intervention.[12] The group still desired an Islamic revolution, but its members now thought that this could not happen for several decades. They supported the AKP, which they believed would strengthen associations, but did not join the party as members.

While Rasim was trying to get some funding from Yasin for the association, Vecdi started to criticize the brochure as soon as he saw it, for it did not "have enough Islamic references in it, and [was] therefore subservient to the system." Vecdi was a member of the now weakened mainstream Islamist organization, the Felicity Party (SP), which was composed of Erbakan loyalists critical of the AKP's liberalized Islamic politics. Twenty-nine years old, he was a fiery, round-bearded, tall, and plump economics student at a provincial university. He knew nothing about the association and its affiliation. Rasim was angry but expressed his anger in very soft words: "One needs to speak with information, but you're expressing only groundless suspicions [vehim]." Vecdi walked out angrily, hastily came back in, and asked whether Rasim was engaged in this activity under the banner of the AKP. This time, Rasim just laughed and dismissed him. After that, Vecdi sat with us and tried to understand what the association was up to, while intermittently propagating the line of his party.

As was usual with political debates in Yasin's workplace, the conversation went on for hours. In the evening, a bearded, middle-aged man from the SP came and asked Yasin whether he would become a member. Yasin laughed and said: "First explain yourself to me. I cannot be a member for nothing. What do you want to do politically?" The man went back to the party headquarters, came back with a membership application, sat down, and said:

Euzubillahimineşşeytanirracim. Bismillahirahmanirrahim.[13] This struggle
has been going on ever since Adam, peace be upon him.

Vecdi: No, don't stretch that far back in history, start with Muhammad.

Yasin (laughing again): You cannot form a unity even among yourselves,
how can you invite me to the party? First reach a decision about where
you want to start, and then come to me.

The middle-aged man was discouraged and left the room. In a second, the SP's
local president also came and shook our hands (a daily, ritualistic renewing
of links with district tradesmen that local politicians resort to) and then went
to the party headquarters. Vecdi followed the president. After they left, Rasim
criticized the organizational style of the SP:

> They are still trying to do it with emotions. But people will no longer
> come to these words. People expect concrete solutions to their
> problems. They want a scientific approach.
>
> Yasin: Everybody is curious about what politicians think about the
> economy. They want concrete solutions about the economy. You can
> no longer attract people only by religion. We are all Muslims anyway.

Here, the SP members and Rasim had clear positions. The former were carrying out old-style, solemn Islamic politics (which is heavy on emotions and
religious references), while the latter was engaging in what I will later analyze
as a "war of position" against the secular system. Yasin, no longer affiliated to
any organization but the AKP, disclosed many radical aspirations. But, despite his emphasis on being "systematic" (acting based on broad and long-
term projects informed by science and knowledge), he had no program or plan
for realizing these. Whether those like Yasin will indeed remain within the
fold or one day again rise up against the system ultimately depends on the
struggles between and within the SP, the AKP, and radical Islamic circles. In
this text, I analyze the historical determinants as well as the emerging parameters of these struggles.

AN ETHNOGRAPHY OF ISLAMISM

I studied the transition from Islamism to (economically) liberal and (culturally) conservative Islam in a squatter-majority district. Sultanbeyli, on the
eastern border of Istanbul, was an arch-experiment for Turkish Islamists.
Leftist movements have tried local experiments and diffused them as models
before. A particularly apt comparison is to the Brazilian Left's model commu-

nity of Porto Alegre. Just as Porto Alegre became the model to follow for leftists, Sultanbeyli set the example of an Islamist locality all over Turkey and beyond. Porto Alegre was a paragon of redistribution and participatory democracy, Sultanbeyli of Islamic purification and redistribution. Contrary to the trajectory of Porto Alegre, Sultanbeyli became the model of vice for pious Muslims as the pious traveled ideologically from populism to neoliberalism. While studying Porto Alegre reveals the gains and limits of participatory democracy for new leftist politics (Baiocchi 2005), studying Sultanbeyli uncovers the basic dynamics of the massive transition from Islamic radicalism to free market conservatism.

I first analyzed Islamic politics in Sultanbeyli between 2000 and 2002. Back then, Islamic politics were identified with the mainstream Islamist party FP, which had total control of the Sultanbeyli municipality. The AKP had neither come to power in Turkey nor established a functioning headquarters in the district. I taught at a secular primary school in 2000 and 2001, which allowed me to build contacts in neighborhoods, political parties, the municipality, and mosques. Even though I was honest about collecting data for my project, I also came to be known as a teacher of the district—*hoca* in the vernacular, which people in Turkey use to refer to teachers, imams, and spiritual leaders. Being a hoca allowed me to build trust, partially balancing the suspicions raised by my status as a student at a U.S. university.

My research at this time revolved around the question of how Islamists interacted with the urban poor. Through participant observation at the local municipality, the local headquarters of political parties, mosques, coffeehouses, religious teahouses, homes, associations, educational institutions (secular schools, clerical schools, theological seminaries [*medreses*], and Kur'an schools), rallies, street protests, and other Islamic activities in the district from the summer of 2000 to the summer of 2002, I collected material on religious beliefs, rituals, and interactions between Islamic activists and the people. I supplemented this ethnographic experience with fifty semi-structured, in-depth interviews.

By 2006, Sultanbeyli had become the ideal place for studying different patterns of Islamization over the decades (including the transition from Islamism to conservatism). In the 2002 general elections and 2004 municipal elections, which both occurred after my first visit to the district, the area's population shifted from support for Islamist parties to the AKP. Once the fortress of Islamism nationwide, it eventually ended up as just another conservative district. This was the local expression of a massive nationwide transformation (the entrenchment of democratic, pious Muslim rule), arguably comparable in significance to the change Turkey underwent in the 1920s.[14] This led me to revisit the district and collect data on politics and religion at the same sites to unravel the meaning of this transformation. In this part of the study, while focusing again on participant observation, I collected an additional forty semi-structured, in-depth interviews.

In line with the argument of this book, I have focused on the minute details of everyday life in their relations to politics and religion to study the establishment of hegemony. Therefore, participant observation constitutes the core of the text. Together with this theoretical lens that led me to participant observation, methodological discussions regarding the extended case method also inspired me to carry out an ethnography rather than a large-N study. The latter would allow generalizability rather than theory reconstruction (Burawoy et al. 1991), which is the goal of this book. The extended case method emphasizes researcher engagement over detachment, process and context over reliability and replicability, and theory reconstruction over representativeness (Burawoy 1998). It is based on observing how the same norms and rules are employed differently over time and in different situations, extending out from the micro to the macro, and observing how locals relate to outside forces and how external, global forces impose themselves upon the locals, who in turn resist and/or negotiate these forces (Burawoy 2000, 2003). The extended case method enables the researcher to draw conclusions about general processes even when the unit of analysis is only one case, as she starts with weak spots, gaps, and anomalies in theoretical knowledge and uses her field notes to reconstruct (rather than invent) theory (Baiocchi 2005, 165).

One such theoretical gap this book hopes to fill concerns the politics of absorption. My revisit to Sultanbeyli uncovered a sort of social change that is not adequately understood, either by scholars or by the larger public. To the unsuspecting eye, the de-Islamization in Sultanbeyli could appear as a "co-optation" of Islamists such as Yasin or their "rationalization." When people switch from radical to centrist ideologies, scholars and journalists usually resort to these tropes. However, the conversion from Islamism to conservatism I observed in Sultanbeyli was much more complex than that. True, Islamists no longer challenged the system head-on, but their participation also transformed institutions without overthrowing the existing elite and the secular system. Our political vocabulary can hardly make sense of this kind of change.

Therefore, public opinion (both in Turkey and in the West) was caught in a simple dichotomy: Are the Turkish Islamists hiding their real agenda or have they really changed and become regular conservatives?[15] The theory of passive revolution developed throughout this book will demonstrate that this is the wrong question to pose.

As stated above, the extended case method also emphasizes the uniqueness of cases rather than their representativeness. Sultanbeyli is informative not because it is a microcosm of Turkey (let alone the Islamic world) but because it was significant in the heyday of Islamism due to its role as a model, and it has now lost that status with the absorption of Islamism. Subsequently, the district has displayed different trends when compared to other Islamic strongholds such as Istanbul's historic district Fatih, the Central Anatolian city Konya, and newly Islamizing provincial cities in western Anatolia such as Denizli. Sultanbeyli contrasts with these cases by virtue of undergoing Islamization when the movement was expanding in the 1980s and 1990s (unlike the already Islamic Fatih and Konya and the erstwhile secular Denizli) and then de-Islamizing but remaining conservative when the movement started to emphasize conservatism over Islam (as opposed to Fatih and Konya where everyday life changed only slightly and Denizli,[16] which is now becoming more religiously conservative). The logic of focusing on this unique case is to reconstruct theory rather than tell a representative story that is meant to exhaust all Islamic experience.

OUTLINE OF THE BOOK

While the first and last chapters of the book put the transition from Islamism to conservatism in theoretical and comparative perspective, the chapters in between provide detailed historical and ethnographic accounts of this change. In Chapter 1, the theoretical models that scholars have generally used in analyzing Islamic politics are discussed. The shortfalls of these analyses have to do with the problematic theoretical tools used. I propose a hegemonic theory of politics as an alternative to modernization, political economic, social movement, and civil society approaches to Islamism. By discussing and rethinking concepts such as hegemony, civil society, political society, and passive revolution, this chapter points out what the theory of hegemony can gain from integrating theories of everyday life, space, and authority.

Chapter 2 contains an outline of the way the secular state and Islamic challenge in Turkey have historically developed based on the theoretical framework of Chapter 1. This chapter, as well as the other empirical chapters of the book, is structured as an analysis of how political society (with its political leadership, constitution of authority patterns, and visions of political unity) and civil society (with its regulation of everyday life, social space, and relations to the economy) change from one episode of the republic to the next, and from one hegemonic project to the other. The chapter sets the global, national, and historical context for the ethnographic analysis to follow.

Chapters 3 and 4 analyze the development of political society and civil society in Sultanbeyli in their interaction with Islamism's transformations, from the 1980s until 2002. Chapter 3 is an analysis of political society's role in the rise and fall of the Islamist movement. I study in this chapter the political leadership, authority structures, and visions of political unity that the Islamists counterposed to those of the secularists. The Islamist political party and the municipality under its control started to take over the tasks of the state (legal negotiation, welfare provision, etc.), thereby instituting "dual power" in the district—a situation where alternative institutions of power constitute an incipient second state alongside the existing one. Their partial success in this endeavor was based on an immense political organization (temporarily) interwoven with civil society and the zeal of the absorbed radicals. Yet, the Islamist leaders could not offer proper visions and practices of unity to the district's residents and could not overcome the Turkish-Kurdish divide. This proved to be Islamism's soft underbelly.

Chapter 4 focuses on civil society and traces changes in everyday life, use of social space, and relations to the economy in Sultanbeyli between the 1980s and 2002. It aims to demonstrate how Islamist associations, networks, and parties regulated people's lives, attempting to institute alternative lifestyles, places, and economic relations. The common theme of this chapter is "integral (*tevhidi*) religion," an all-encompassing Islam (which the Islamists wanted to render the "normal way of things," but failed).

The following two chapters discuss how neoliberal conservatism appropriated bits and pieces of Islamic political society and civil society after 2002 to reinstitute the linkages of economy, civil society, political society, and the state. Chapter 5 studies how the AKP destroyed the remnants of dual power in Sultanbeyli to peacefully relink society and state. The chapter demonstrates that both this relinkage, and the neoliberals' successful naturalization of capitalism, was an outcome of the absorption of Islamist cadres and strategies into the AKP. However, two challenges still troubled the passive revolution: (1)

the AKP could not build unity across the ethnic chasm, and (2) while some previous radicals had more or less quit Islamism, and those who hung onto old-style Islamism were quite ineffective, there were innovative radical groups that made use of democratization to rebuild "integral religion."

Chapter 6 is about the AKP's creative combinations of de-Islamization with Islamization in lifestyles, space, and the economy. These combinations successfully naturalized market relations among broad sectors. Emphasizing the role of political society, Chapters 4 and 6 stress that political leadership was quite active in civil society and interacted with it to regulate everyday life, space, and people's relations to the economy.

The Conclusion explores how the proposed model of hegemonic politics can be used to study other cases of Islamism. The theorization of passive revolution, embarked on in Chapter 1, is finalized through these analyses. The chapter compares Turkey with Egypt and Iran. It shows how variations in the way political society has developed can account for their different regimes. Due to differences in hegemonic strategies, only the Turkish Islamic mobilization culminated in a passive revolution.

CONCEPTUALIZING ISLAMIC MOBILIZATION

Part 1

1 TOWARD A THEORY OF HEGEMONIC POLITICS

THE CRISIS of the analysis of Islamic politics is the crisis of the paradigms that have been used to study Islamic politics. This chapter will situate the problems of the scholarship on Islamism within general sociological problems. The objective is not only to develop an alternative account of Islamic politics but to use the case of Islamism to revise the sociological theory of politics. A hegemonic perspective provides a more complete account of how politics work when compared to existing analyses of politics and society.

MODELS IN THE STUDY OF ISLAMIC POLITICS

This section illustrates why each conventional explanation in the study of Islamic politics is either problematic or only partially valid.

Orientalism and Modernization Theory

Culture-based explanations of Islamism point out the significance of the traumatizing influence of Westernization on traditional Muslim cultures (Aksoy and Robins 1994). Culturalist scholars—ranging from Orientalists to modernization theorists—base their claims concerning the popular support of religious movements on assumptions about the persistence of traditional religions. Some of them attribute the rise of religious movements, especially in the Muslim world, to the particularly political nature of Islam (Huntington 1996; Lewis 1993). Others define these religious movements as natural derivatives of popular religiosity in Muslim countries (Nasr 1998).

Explanations along these lines characterize both the Justice and Development Party (AKP) and its predecessors as hopeless resistances to modernization or as wisely adapting actors of jihad. According to one interpretation, this party is dissimulating its real ("fundamentalist") goals because the Turkish regime makes an openly fundamentalist position impossible (Rubin 2007). The AKP, culturalists argue, is a pragmatic Islamist party that aims to build a totally Islamic society in fifty years.[1]

My research reveals that the ideal types (traditional vs. modern, religious vs. secular, local vs. Western) put forth by culturalist explanations are misrepresentations of cultural complexity.[2] The last two decades in Turkish history exemplify how religion and secularism, Islam and Westernization, mix together to produce cultural composites, and this is particularly what has made the AKP possible: the coexistence of the Islamic and the modern in the AKP's practice and symbols is not an ill-conceived attempt to hide its real Islamist identity, but it is the creative making of an alternative modernity.

Political Economy

Other scholars have accounted for Islamic popularity by conjunctural and class factors (Abrahamian 1989, 1991; Ayubi 1991; Keddie 1991). They have focused on social sectors and classes (or national cravings) that secularist modernization has been unable to satisfy. University graduates without jobs, provincial businessmen who are not supported by the state, and rural-to-urban immigrants without secure employment are the primary factors underlying the rise of Islamism in their explanations. As to the question of why these grievances take an Islamic color, political economic explanations point to the property structure and the class balances in the Middle East.[3] The Islamic variety of populism has emerged because of the failure of former (nationalist) populisms, which has left Islam as the only untarnished cultural system (Burke 1998). Most political economic accounts tend to put less emphasis on (1) the multilayered religious and cultural work that actors have to carry out to lend any sociopolitical project credibility[4] and (2) how this religious and cultural work decisively transforms the project with which it is articulated.

In the Turkish context, Ziya Öniş (2006b) has argued that the AKP has been successful because it was able to combine the winners and losers of neoliberal globalization. The party has built a broad coalition of business sectors with the poor, while running on a pro–European Union and pro–International Monetary Fund ticket (Öniş 2007, 252). The split of the AKP from the Islamist mainstream, indeed, was facilitated by the emergence of a conservative business class, which influenced and moderated the Islamism of the poor (Öniş

2006a). The AKP is able to appeal to all these sectors because it sustains economic growth, comes from an Islamist tradition of municipal effectiveness, and carries out democratization (Öniş 2006b). The party also emphasizes social justice, seems to be committed to the poor, and is critical of corruption (Keyman and Öniş 2007). However, as the AKP's policies have not so far significantly improved the conditions of popular sectors, political economic approaches have to resort to explanations regarding the cultural and religious spheres, and this does not neatly fit in with their overall theorization. Öniş, for example, has stated that the AKP is able to get the support of the poor also by "*using* religion as an effective mechanism of mutual trust and bondage" (2006b, 212; emphasis mine).

While the political economy approach is right on target in its focus on the AKP's multiclass coalition, it does not tell us much about why Islam can become this cementing tool in the hands of an emergent neoliberal elite. While religion is of secondary importance in this account, winning the cultural and economic consent of subordinate classes is an integrated process that requires taking a microperspective on how the poor are mobilized. Therefore, the socioeconomic explanations of this literature have to be supplemented by accounts of how the economy is experienced and constructed in everyday life, how activists interact with authorities and followers in particular contexts to mobilize people, and how Islam shapes these experiences and interactions.

Social Movement Studies and Institutionalism

An emergent paradigm in the study of Islamic politics is social movement theory (Wickham 2002; Wiktorowicz 2001, 2004). Analysts of "resource mobilization" have focused on how activists mobilize people and how they frame their appeals—particularly the questions socioeconomic approaches leave unanswered. These scholars have attributed the popularity of Islamic movements around the world to successful activist tactics.

While correctly pointing out the importance of networks and resources, the social movement perspective on mobilization avoids analyzing the imaginative constructions of political projects. Instead, movements are defined as mainly technical operations. There is no analysis of why certain hegemonic projects have emerged, in what socioeconomic contexts, and in whose interests. The analysis is simply about how a project becomes able to mobilize people *after* it has emerged (Gamson 1975; Jenkins and Perrow 1977; McCarthy and Zald 1977; Morris 1984; Oberschall 1973; Tilly 1978).[5]

Another shape social movement theory takes, the study of opportunity structures, has also had an effect on the study of Islamism and of the AKP. Institutional ways of explaining political success overlap a great deal with this face of social movement theory. Institutionalists (Çarkoğlu 2006; Tepe 2006; Zubaida 1989) and analysts of opportunity structures (Hafez and Wiktorowicz 2004) account for the rise of Islamism by referring to divides among secular elites, the emergence of sympathetic elites, the availability of religious institutions in the absence of secular institutions of opposition, the declining capacity of secular states to repress dissent, the fragmentation of the political system, and the collapse of the center parties.[6]

While such factors are crucial to understanding Islamist success, these scholars do not embed these dynamics in social formations and sociopolitical imagination. They therefore are unable to explain the emergence and *transformation* of certain religious goals and expectations.[7] The social movement accounts of Islamism draw attention to the alternative Islamist elite and (in the case of the AKP) the increasing support of the secular liberal elites inside and outside of Turkey for this alternative religious elite. But, why was there an alternative elite among the old Islamists, and why would a wing of the global and national secular elite want to support them? Social movement studies leave these points unsettled.[8]

Modernity and Civil Society

Other scholars tend to see Islamism as yet another movement that unfolds in the complex drama of modernization, but they disagree with modernization theorists who restrict modernity to Western cultural forms. They argue that the Islamist movement leads to the incorporation of excluded religious people, institutions, and motivations in an ever-expanding modernity (Eisenstadt 2001; Göle 2000; Hefner 2001; Kasaba 1997; Singerman 1995; White 2002). This text draws on the works of these scholars in pointing out that the AKP has creatively blended Islam, tradition, supernaturalism, charisma, and informality on the one hand, and rationalism, tolerance, market relations, professionalism, and formality on the other to build an Islamic modernity. But it also underlines that the making of this Islamic modernity was embedded in a hegemonic project that produced and reproduced inequalities and domination.

The outlook of these scholars is also shaped by debates regarding civil society and the public sphere. They argue that a thorough modernization in Islam has strengthened civil society / the public sphere in Egypt, Indonesia, and Turkey and restricted the repressiveness of authoritarian secularist regimes (Hefner 2001). These scholars look at the AKP as the representative of an Islamic modernity and of civil society against the state, while they see the AKP's predecessors as immature and antimodern in their criticism of the state (White 2002; Yavuz 2003). They take Turkish citizens to be nonviolent builders of civil society who therefore vote for the AKP, which simply represents this civic orientation (Yavuz 2006, 7–8).[9] While this body of scholarship is the most tactful in analyzing the AKP, it neglects the role of the state in its making. I will argue that this party has not developed against the state, but it has formed in conjunction (and sometimes cooperation) with the state's attack against Islamism.

In the broader context of the Middle East, civil society scholars have argued that Islam has been a countervailing force against the state for centuries. Then, starting with the nineteenth century, modernization has been authoritarian and has sought to destroy the autonomy of the religious sphere (Kamali 2001; Kelsay 2002). This account ignores that religious scholars were in a majority of the cases under the control of states for centuries, and it simplifies the divisions and conflicts in the Middle East, reducing all of them to a tension between (Islamic) society and the (secular) state.[10] These problems with the civil society approach in the study of Islamism can be traced back to the problematic nature of the broader civil society literature itself, especially its tendency to locate the source of solidarity in society and domination in the state (Putnam 1995; de Tocqueville [1835/1840] 2000). Its sanguine self-justification ("countervailing forces against the state") aside, civil society is most crucial to the sustenance of a system based on inequality through the active participation of the subordinate sectors.

Toward an Alternative Account

There is something to be learned from each of these groups of literature. However, it is important to see how religion, economic dynamics, political institutions, the state, and civil society work in conjunction with each other. This is only possible if we look at the active work of agents who ultimately bring them together. There is no automatic logic that combines these different instances. A collection of actors has to integrate them. This integrating collectivity is not above history but comes to being through the work of integration. In this process of integration, each of the instances of the social takes a new shape by its interaction with the others (and thus cannot be an explaining factor in and of itself, as in the literatures cited above). Society, therefore, is not a self-sustaining entity but an outcome of the activity of integration. The term "articulation" refers to this active work of integration.[11]

Antonio Gramsci's concept of "organic crisis" is a useful corollary to the idea of articulation.[12] This concept can account for mass mobilization's context of emergence more sufficiently than anomie,[13] class realignment, political opportunity structures/institutional breakdown, or the desire of civil society to subordinate the state. Gramsci used this concept to refer neither simply to rapid urbanization, social-psychological crisis, and so on nor to only an opening in political structures. Organic crisis rather denotes a broader overlap and mutual reinforcement along several axes, including the factors that modernization and social movement theories have pointed out but also class-related and spatial crises.[14] After a certain point, the existing options of articulation can no longer hold society together, which will fall apart if a new agent (and model) of integration does not arise. "Organic crisis" refers to this situation. Unlike functionalist accounts, this book's approach emphasizes the centrality of the articulating agent who holds or fails to hold society together, and it discredits the idea of spontaneous breakdown or self-sustenance.

The concepts of articulation and organic crisis are only beginning points for developing an alternative theory of Islamic mobilization. The next section develops this theory fully.

REVISING THE ANALYSIS OF HEGEMONY

Islamic mobilization is the reconstitution of hegemony as a response to organic crises. Hegemony operates by linking society and state. Yet, in order to have a solid understanding of this operation, one must develop a better conceptualization than Gramsci of the mechanisms of this linkage. Revising Gramsci, I define "hegemony" as (1) the organization of consent for domination and inequality (2) through a specific articulation of everyday life, space, and the economy with certain patterns of authority (3) under a certain leadership, (4) which forges unity out of disparity. Hegemony is not the same as Weberian legitimacy or popularity in the political science sense: it is active support for a system of rule that actually changes people's lives. (An analysis of legitimacy, however, can be incorporated into the analysis of hegemony, as the following chapters will demonstrate.) So, hegemony involves taking part in changing one's life; it is partial power over oneself.

I will call the domain that links civil society and state "political society." Jean Cohen and Andrew Arato's (1992) and Linz and Stepan's (1996, 8–10) redefinition of political society along these lines is an advancement over Gramsci's use of political society as exchangeable with the state (government, military, civil bureaucracy, official education, and courts). Bringing in political society is also important because, as Perry Anderson (1976) has pointed out, consent in capitalist states is not solely established in civil society; the imagined equality of the rulers and the ruled, and therefore the citizens' link to the state, is an essential part of hegemony.

Unlike the conceptualizations put forth by Linz and Stepan, and Cohen and Arato, however, this book's conceptualization will focus on a very strong local component. Moreover, I redefine "political society," as the sphere where society organizes to shape state policies but also to define the nature of the state and political unity.[15] At the local level, political society includes the elected municipality, parties, other political groups, leadership, and local elections, as well as local official authority figures such as teachers[16] (when and if they link society and state). However, because not all the key offices of the state are open to elections and the control of elected officials on the local scene, the constituents of political society might not be able to exercise control on the state as in Linz and Stepan, and Cohen and Arato (who assume a democratizing political structure). In non- or semidemocratic national cases and local political settings, therefore, it can be expected that one of the primary goals of political society (or some groups in political society) will be changing this structure and subordinating state agencies to political control.[17]

Therefore, political society is the set of organizations (mainly political parties and other sociopolitical movement organizations) that form, control, and regulate (1) local and extra-local leadership and authority figures and (2) imagined political bodies, belongings, and collectivities, which together constitute people's experience and contact with the political. Political society is what integrates people into the state and makes them citizens. Without political society, the state is an abstract entity, a body of armed men (and occasionally women) accompanied by some people in robes (judges, professors, bureaucrats). It is through the work of political society that these people at the top become actual "rulers" rather than pillagers, thieves, and imposters. How does political society perform this magic of turning a gang into legitimate rulers? Its magic rod is the leadership it offers civil society. This leadership articulates various experiences of society into a hegemonic project. Weaving together three aspects of social life—everyday routine, the use of space, and economic experience—is the major challenge awaiting the leadership. After laying the groundwork for the analysis of political society, I will analyze each of these aspects and explain why they are fundamental to the making of hegemony.

Political Society

Political society links civil society to the state through political leadership, authority structures, and the imagination and exercise of a political unity. The mechanisms of this linkage are outlined below.

1. Political Leadership   The activities of an integrated political leadership are central to the construction of political society. Quite often, this leadership takes the form of a political party that brings together the morally engaged leaders of a locality (by recruiting them through newspapers, schools, conferences, associations, and so on), disciplines them, and unites them for a cause. The hegemonic leadership can also take the shape of a party system organized as the different wings of the same project (which was the case in Turkey, where hegemonic political society had a rigid secularist and a center-right wing, as the next chapter will demonstrate). The political world does not function through an automatic logic that brings like-minded people or groups with common interests magically together. There is no autonomous "multitude" that can constitute itself; it is always constituted.[18] Likewise, collective "dispositions" do not bring people together automatically (as in Bourdieu [1979] 1984), even though they are among the factors that ease coming together. An articulating organization is indispensable. Will the organization be able to interweave civil society and politics in its activities? This depends on the interaction between the political leadership and the imagined collectivity it is trying to constitute and the availability of an ideology that will incite people to action.

It will be my contention that in most capitalist polities it is only through the active intervention of political parties that all the processes and activities analyzed below come together to constitute a society.[19] Without this intervention, there would be no coordinated action at a mass level but many micro-coordinational activities on smaller scales. Parties *articulate* the actors' organizations of everyday life and of space and their relations to the economy and authority, and parties give these disparate relations and activities a certain direction.[20]

The party is a strong candidate for articulating all the aforementioned aspects of hegemony: everyday life, space, relation to the economy, relation to authority, and desire for unity. In the bosom of the political party, all these aspects of social life find a coherent expression. The party connects localities and individuals to the larger political unit as a whole and makes them members (subjects or citizens) of the state. In this process of connection, it both draws on and transforms their everyday life, their spatial experience, their material interests, and their relation to authority.

2. Authority   A revision of Max Weber's tripartite model of traditional, charismatic, and bureaucratic authority is useful for a revised theory of hegemony. This revision of Weber will be based on "decentering" authority,[21] emphasizing locality, and integrating the agency of the subjugated into the analysis while also situating authority in the general context of hegemony.

The modern nation-state attributes to itself the monopoly of legitimate violence. Yet, whether it actually monopolizes legitimate violence partially depends on local authorities. If local practitioners of authority do not link civil society to the state, legalistic monopolization would be empty talk. Top-down visions of state centralization and formation have neglected this essential dimension of the state. They have not taken the margins of the state seriously.[22]

While this text focuses on the margins of society and authority, national authority figures are also crucial to the production and maintenance of the local authority structure. Stories and myths about, and sculptures and portraits of, national authority figures are an ever-present aspect of local life. Their visits and other kinds of ties to localities also enable them to intervene in the authority structure. These ties integrate people into local institutions and organizations such as municipalities and political parties.

Consent for domination and inequality is built through the development of identification with local and national authority figures and the subsequent integration in local institutions. The limits of the love for and identification with local and national leaders are also the limits of the naturalization of their hegemonic projects.

3. Political Unity   The state poses an abstract unity. However, this is no guarantee that the citizens will experience each other as part of a single collectivity. This experience has to be made and remade continuously.[23] Activists, intellectuals, and politicians institutionally and discursively combine wildly conflicting or at least seemingly disparate groups and localities into cities, nations, and regional blocs.[24]

Unity—political unity of some sort—is important for most people.[25] They tend to give allegiance to whoever is able to connect the pieces into a viable unit. Leaderships that can deliver on the promise of unity have carte blanche for reproducing patterns of inequality. This is why quite often conservative parties have been able to appeal to the downtrodden even when their social agendas that maintain poverty become transparent. A lot of people are willing to sacrifice economic benefits for unity. Hence, building political unity is one of the foremost tasks of political society.

In the modern world, this political unity has mostly taken the shape of the nation. Especially in the periphery of the world system (but not only there), the nation form has the additional advantage of appealing to the economic interests and status-driven desires of people: nationalism promises to correct the injustices of imperialism; it is perceived as a fight against international exploitation and humiliation (Chatterjee [1986] 2001; Nairn 1997). Therefore, nationalism becomes not only the expression of the desire for unity but also a way of channeling internal class and status grievances to the international arena and delaying internal struggle.

However, even though the nation form is by no means disappearing, it is in a deep crisis. Different projects of political unity are now competing with it. Different attempts to build a state coextensive with the *ümmet* (the international Islamic community), what some Orientalists interpret as the inability of Muslims to mold themselves into nation-states, is actually one of these competing projects, rather than a remnant of medieval tradition.

All this said, note again that political society is not suspended in midair. If it is to satisfactorily link citizens and the state, it should be embedded in civil society. For when it is not, the whole polity undergoes sociopolitical crises. Hence, social theory should provide a framework for studying how political society is related to civil society.

Civil Society

Social integration and collective consent for domination and inequality depend on the linking of political society and civil society. A hegemonic project must couple leadership, authority, and visions of unity with civil society if it is to succeed. The understanding of civil society proposed here encompasses informal networks, movements,[26] and associations that regulate everyday life, the use of space, and people's relation to the economy. These networks, movements, and associations mediate between the economy and political society.[27]

1. Everyday Life   Theories of hegemony have generally neglected everyday life.[28] Yet, habits and everyday strategies are also crucial in the constitution of a hegemonic collectivity. Handled within the hegemonic framework, everyday practices are no longer the sites either of the spontaneous self-reproduction of society (as in Bourdieu) or of endless games and resistances (Scott 1985). Everyday life is rather one of the primary grounds of contestation among different hegemonic projects.

The approach to daily life most relevant to the hegemonic framework is Pierre Bourdieu's. Bourdieu explores everyday life in a structural context, which differentiates him from those who see it as almost completely shaped by the development of capitalism and/or state formation (Elias [1939] 2000; Lefebvre [1947] 1991) and those who attribute infinite malleability to everyday practices (de Certeau [1974] 1984; Goffman 1959; Scott 1985). According to Bourdieu, everyday practices result from embodied principles of division, which are inculcated in actors through socialization as collective dispositions (Bourdieu [1972] 1977, [1979] 1984).

Because this socialization is politically guided under the influence of social movement activists, intellectuals, political institutions, and politicians, a fusion of Bourdieu's work with hegemonic analysis is necessary. I hold that activists, intellectuals, educators, politicians, and so on establish consent for inequality through instilling certain patterns of behavior, rhythms of life, notions of time, uses of the body, classification systems, bodies of knowledge, and rituals. These everyday practices naturalize status distinctions, class differences, and power balances. Shared practices become especially important for sustaining consent in times of intensifying inequalities, as is the case with neoliberalizing Sultanbeyli (and Turkey).

Since in most contemporary and historical societies (with the exception of modern non-Catholic Western Europe) everyday life is fused with religion, any understanding of civil society requires a thorough analysis of religious life. Religion has an undeniable impact on patterns of behavior, rhythms of life, and uses of the body. The salience of religion in civil society, however, will depend on how it is articulated to other forces. In certain projects, moreover, it is rather the distance from religion that becomes a distinguishing feature. In other words, a religion's salience and the shape this salience takes are outcomes of the hegemonic project that articulates it. Religion cannot be conceptualized in a vacuum and must be studied in relation to space, the economy, and political factors.

2. Space   If everyday life is indeed a crucial component of hegemony, its location in space should also be conceptualized as essential to the making of consent.[29] Power relations are always inscribed in space. Consider, as Bourdieu did, the spatiality of distinction. Distance and hierarchy in social space are inseparable aspects of status inequality. The subordination of one social group to another is reflected in space; and the negotiation of this reflection reshapes social relations. Architecture and the layout of streets; imagined or real boundaries between neighborhoods, restaurants, cafes, and rooms in an apartment; and the strategic location of buildings, parks, places of worship, and other symbolic sites all speak the language of power.[30] Different hegemonic projects have different prescriptions for the way all these are organized.

Even though scholars have written on the structuring and structured nature of space, there is relatively less material on political projects that play on this structuration. Geographers and sociologists who have studied the political determinants of space have focused mostly on macrospace, that is, how different political projects redraw the boundaries of nations, cities, and transnational regions (Brenner 2003, 2004). How different hegemonic projects have different implications for the management of microspace (i.e., the surveillance and control of the boundaries in everyday life, interior design, architecture, the relational location of neighborhoods, etc.) has not been explored to the same extent.[31] However, the management of microspace is an integral part of the constitution of hegemony. Each hegemonic project has to concretize itself in a locality, where it shapes social space to naturalize inequalities and domination.

In rapidly industrializing and urbanizing modern societies, the relation between the urban and the rural, between the country and the town, between the destination and the hometown has become one of the central nexus around which the use of space is organized (Williams 1973). The question of who is urbanized and who is "not yet" is among the factors that determine the distribution of resources and (more so) recognition. This centrality of urban identity in patterns of inequality leads me to conceptualize it as one of the spheres of activity in civil society.[32]

3. Relations to the Economy   Speaking against the culturalist interpretations of the concept of hegemony, both Michael Burawoy (1979) and Adam Przeworski (1985) have drawn attention to the bases of consent in the economic sphere. Relations of production and exchange cannot be left out when theoriz-

ing hegemony. For sustainable relations of domination and inequality, the subordinate groups should have material stakes in the system. The dominant groups need to make some concessions.

However, the processes of production and exchange are themselves reconfigured through articulation to hegemonic projects. People are influenced by competing political projects as they engage in apparently nonpolitical activities like working, saving, and spending. The rhythm of life in the workplace, the way people use money, and so on are organized not only by and in the process of production but also by hegemonic projects. Hegemonic projects integrate economic relations with religion, gender relations, the desire for political unity, and people's love for their leaders.

In sum, analysts of hegemony have so far drawn attention to the way people associate together (i.e., build civil society) to respond to economic forces (such as the market). My analysis takes stock of this tradition but expands it to argue that associational activities are also responses to transformations in life patterns and social uses of space. Moreover, the construction of civil society cannot be fully analyzed without combining it with an analysis of political society.

People associate together, then, to respond to transformations in patterns of life, social space, and the economy. However, this coming together does not occur in a void. Political leadership regulates the way people come together. Therefore, regardless of what participants may think, associational activity does not lead to a total and self-conscious control of ordinary people on the economy and cultural forces. Rather, associational activity becomes a site of domination and inequality.

PASSIVE REVOLUTION: DYNAMICS OF HEGEMONY'S REPRODUCTION

If hegemony works as outlined above, how is it that the challengers of such an intricate system organize and topple (or fail to topple) it? How is hegemony reconstituted after the challenge? Political society proves essential to the reconstitution of hegemony too.

In times of organic crises, a revolutionary assault becomes possible. Even when there is no revolutionary attack, the hegemonic sectors feel the threat of a possible attack (especially if revolutionary movements are troubling other states) and respond by reorganizing hegemony. In order to understand the dynamics of this process, we have to look at how totalistic responses to hegemony operate. In a system that has become even partially hegemonic, a sociopolitical project cannot be implemented simply by taking over the state. A movement would have to slowly conquer all the ground that hegemony controls; it would have to unlink and relink civil society and political society. Only then could it take hold of the state and implement its project.

In contexts characterized by strong hegemonies, challenges that have not taken this protracted route have been quickly dismantled by the regimes or failed to appeal to the population. Cases of relatively easy regime repression include those directed against, among many others, the German RAF (Red Army Faction), the Italian Red Brigades, and other armed leftist organizations in Europe (Turkey, too) in the 1970s. Cases of marginalization include today's anarchist and autonomist movements in Europe and North America.

Because taking the protracted route itself is an extremely difficult strategy, most movements that take it end up realizing only bits and pieces of the transformations they desire. The strategies and institutions they develop do not result in a revolution. Rather, the extant hegemony absorbs these. Actually, because modern hegemonic regimes are quite strong, those movements that are not repressed or marginalized are absorbed by the regime rather than resulting in revolutionary transformation.

Gramsci (1971) has called this process "the passive revolution": incorporation of revolutionary movements in existing systems. According to Gramsci, western European states underwent a passive revolution during 1815–1870. This transformation mainly consisted of bourgeois empowerment without popular participation and economic loss of privilege for the aristocracy without its total extinction. The goal was impeding the French revolutionary model. This required the gradual absorption of antagonistic elements of society, which culminated in incomplete revolutions.

Even though Gramsci has laid the foundations for the idea of passive revolution, he has not written more than a few pages on the topic. The goal of this book will be rethinking this concept in light of the revisions to the theory of hegemony proposed above and empirical analyses of Islamic politics.[33] This theorization will be expanded in the Conclusion.

REPRISE: STATE, CIVIL SOCIETY, AND POLITICAL SOCIETY

Now that the conceptual framework for my analysis has been given, consider how hegemony works. The argument of this book is that hegemony is exercised by linking economy, society, and state. The analysis aims to lay out the complex mechanisms of this interlinking. Every hegemonic project builds both a civil society and a political society that intermediate between the economy and the state. Civil society consists of formal organizations like schools, dormitories, associations, and the media and informal networks such as neighbor networks, religious communities, mosque communities, and coffeehouse communities. These formal and informal associations regulate everyday life, the use of space, and people's relation to the economy. Political society is situated between civil society and the state. It consists of organizations such as political parties, parliaments, local municipalities, and sociopolitical movements (plus, occasionally, charismatic leaders). Civil society also organizes people's relations to political society, which works as a more solid link to the state. These formal or informal organizations institute patterns of authority, instill visions and practices of political unity, and mobilize the population.

Political society pulls together different strands in civil society and makes a coherent whole out of them. To the degree that this process is incomplete (it always is to some extent), hegemony is incomplete. Different cases of hegemony can be compared with respect to the success of political society in bringing together, melding, articulating, and suturing differing strands of civil society.

This activity of articulation does not need to take the form of imposition or even of publicly visible regulation. It can also assume the form of defining structuring logics across different spheres or creating a certain atmosphere.

Individuals involved in a certain kind of political society reorganize their relations to civil society as well, by avoiding certain nodes of civil society and strengthening others. The strength of an existing or emergent political society can be measured by looking at the extent to which its participants reshape their relations to civil society.

As civil society regulates everyday life, uses of space, and relations to the economy, and political society regulates the relation between civil society and state, we can posit that political society has a role of "super-regulation," that is, the regulation *of* the regulation of these spheres of life.

The goal of this book is to demonstrate how these connections work in a concrete setting, how they are challenged by a new project of connection, and how that project is ultimately tamed. While the Introduction provided a narrative outline of the book, the synopsis below indicates how the analytical flow is conceptually driven. The next chapter will outline the establishment of secularist hegemony in Turkey, the Islamist challenge directed against it, and the absorption of this challenge, by analyzing this country's economy, society, and state. The constitution of hegemony is a national project, but one that involves the organization of civil society through its connection to political society at multiple local levels. A thorough analysis of hegemonic politics needs to be comprehensive—it has to lay out how the national leadership responds to global and national changes (Chapter 2) and then look at how this impacts the hegemonic project's relations to people on the ground (Chapters 3–6). By definition, hegemony implies the involvement of the ruled in the system and only a bottom-up study can illuminate the terms of their mobilization. The macroanalysis will sketch the broad contours of the passive revolution, but only in-depth ethnographic analysis of this revolution-restoration can put flesh on the bones. Yet, the microanalysis is meaningless without the macroanalysis, as only the latter can give a sense of why there ever was a nationally organized challenge against the reigning hegemony.

Moreover, with an overall macrohistorical account alone, the changes in Islamic politics could appear as simple pragmatic maneuvers. As these changes result from deep and ongoing interactions between politics and society, an analytical scale shift from the macro to the micro is necessary. The four chapters following the macrohistorical one will therefore take an ethnographic approach and demonstrate how civil society and political society work in the context of hegemonic struggles within an urban district in Turkey.

Part 2 shows that there was a challenge, on the ground, to secular hegemony in the 1980s through the 1990s and that it failed, but it also prepared the ground for the passive revolution—the rearticulation of Islam and neoliberalism, as analyzed in Part 3. Part 2 is designed to show that the national organic crisis was experienced as an uncoupling of civil and political society at the local level. Chapter 3 underlines the role of Islamic political society in the making of this crisis. Chapter 4 shows how civil society was incompletely reshaped under the influence of the Islamist movement: Islamists had detached civil society from the secular state but, in time, civil society was detached from the Islamist project too.

Part 3 begins with the emergence of modern Islamic political society after 2002 (Chapter 5) and analyzes the way it was recoupled to civil society, the way it penetrated civil society, and the way it reconfigured civil society in its own image (Chapters 5 and 6). Interestingly, modern Islamic political society did not tightly control civil society (as Islamists desired in the previous decades) but was content with a loose integration characteristic of a passive revolution. The AKP's success partially lay in *not* trying to completely Islamize civil society. Nevertheless, the party's neoliberal vision, though the least discussed publicly among the residents, caused the most thorough transformation in civil society. In sum, these two parts explore the relation (and indeed the different relation) between civil society and political society in two different historical settings.

2 ISLAMIZATION IN TURKEY AS CONSTITUTION OF HEGEMONY

THE LAST CENTURY IN TURKEY has seen the consolidation of secularist hegemony, an Islamist challenge against it, and the absorption of this challenge.[1] Secularist hegemony was built on a specific party system, establishment of bureaucratic authority, the construction of the Turkish nation, the secularization of Islam, the making of urban identity, and the development of corporatism. It faced challenges in all of these spheres.

SECULARIST HEGEMONY AND ITS ORGANIC CRISIS

For most of the republic's history, the state had the strongest influence on the organization of consent. It aimed to create secular and urbanized citizens who were Turks before anything else and who downplayed their economic and other differences through their common allegiance to Mustafa Kemal Atatürk (the founder of the republic) and his legacy. Civil and political society developed secondarily, under the shadow of the state. Below, I analyze this state-led hegemony based on the matrix developed in the previous chapter.

Party Structure

The production, reproduction, and ultimate crisis of the secularist project outlined in the sections below depended on an unintended division of labor between the Turkish center left and center right. The terms "center right" and "center left" do not have the same referents in Turkish politics as in the West. In effect, they express the internal divisions within the "power bloc."

The "dominant sectors" within this power bloc (the rigidly secularist bureaucracy, the officially protected bourgeoisie, and rigidly secularist intellectuals and professionals) favored a regime of relative exclusion and repression. The subordinate sectors of the bloc (the conservative wing of the bureaucracy, the internationally oriented bourgeoisie, merchants, mildly secularist and liberal intellectuals and professionals, and some promodernization provincial notables) advocated inclusion. The latter frequently mobilized the popular sectors (workers, peasants, artisans, the semi-employed and unemployed, small/provincial merchants and businessmen, and religious intellectuals and professionals) in their struggle against the dominant sectors. The exclusionist center left in Turkey traditionally organized in the Republican People's Party (CHP), while several different parties represented the center right over the decades.[2]

The rapid fragmentation of this party system in the 1980s and the inability of the major parties to organize the population intensified an emerging organic crisis. The center right was discredited due to the Motherland Party (ANAP) government's failure to repress the Kurdish uprising and the ANAP's extremely pro-rich policies and discourse. The center left Social Democratic Populist Party (SHP) was a coalition partner, and it exercised municipal power throughout Turkey in the early 1990s. The SHP and its coalition partner, the True Path Party (DYP)—a party situated uneasily between the center right and the nationalist right—continued neoliberalization from where the ANAP had left off. Their joint economic reforms of April 5, 1994, further opened Turkey to global markets and at the same time impoverished the working classes. The SHP also proved incapable of solving the Kurdish issue. Another reason for the SHP's ultimate marginalization was its gradual shift back to the rigid secularist position of the early CHP, just when Islamic identity had started to gain importance. Such failures of center leftist and center rightist parties engendered a shift to the extremes and opened the door to a new political society.

From the Routinization of Atatürk's Charisma
to the Emergence of Populist Leaders

The secularist regime has established a bureaucratic mechanism based on the routinization of the founding leader Mustafa Kemal Atatürk's charisma. State offices, schools, and all public places in every town have been decorated by the statues, busts, and portraits of Atatürk. The carriers of the regime in the first decades—teachers, university and literary circles, lawyers, petty officials— have constituted the local authority figures, always in the shadow of the policies and images of Atatürk.

In the 1940s and 1950s, the Democrat Party (DP) united the market-oriented landed class, urban merchants, small peasantry, and religious communities against this authority structure. However, what united these sectors was not so much an alternative bureaucratic structure as patronage networks under the control of local notables (Sunar and Sayarı 1986). This rule of the notables within the Democrat Party was accompanied by the emergence of populist leaders, thanks to growing reaction against secularist rule. Though themselves not necessarily religious figures, center rightist leaders in Turkey have voiced the religious sectors' reaction against official secularism. The CHP's leaders and intellectuals, in turn, have blamed them with attempting to revive Islamic law and the prerepublican regime.

Even though the CHP has not always been successful in mobilizing people on its side, it has succeeded in instilling this specific take on "the Islamic threat" as common sense. The result has been, ironically, the frequent electoral successes of the center right. An alternative, popular reading of the paranoid secularist scenario, one that assumes center right politicians to be sincere Muslims rather than pragmatists, has made conservative figures such as Adnan Menderes (of the Democrat Party), Süleyman Demirel (of the Justice Party), and Turgut Özal (of the Motherland Party) into popular and religious heroes. Many religious people have believed that they were in fact religious combatants trying to revive the Islamic style of life. Such "conspiracy theories in reverse" have been central to the reproduction of conservatism in Turkey.

The 1980s and 1990s were marked by dissatisfaction with the top politicians. The same leaders had again and again occupied the top positions. Citizens started to hold the corruption and shortsightedness of these leaders responsible for Turkey's problems. However, rather than leading to popular organization, or to the bureaucratization of politics, this atmosphere led to a search for new saviors, new Atatürks.

Constructing the Nation

The young republic's identity was far from being based on an ideal typical ethnic or racial nationalism. The "Turkish nation" was ambiguously defined against non-Muslim subjects of the empire and their remnants in the republic. Policies like the Wealth Levy targeted the non-Muslim bourgeoisie and caused a transfer of wealth to Muslims (Aktar 2000). Moreover, non-Muslim populations were exchanged with Turkish Muslims living in Christian countries, and those who remained in Anatolia were harassed. Whereas this implicit Islamic definition of Turkishness enabled the state to assimilate several ethnic groups of various sizes, the sizable (Muslim) Kurdish minority retained its cultural distinctiveness.

The failure of assimilation manifested itself in several Kurdish uprisings in the 1920s and 1930s, which were all violently repressed. The Kurds began organizing again in the 1960s and 1970s, this time mostly under socialist and democratic demands. The military intervention of 1980 both repressed Kurdish organizations and intensified attempts at assimilation. As a response, almost half the Kurdish population threw its support behind the only organization that could escape the repression. This resulted in the most massive armed rebellion in Turkish history. The resulting guerrilla warfare claimed around thirty thousand lives. At the apex of this crisis in political society, the country badly needed a new political vision that could heal the wounds.

The Dialogic Development of Official Islam

The CHP (Republican People's Party) created an ideal citizen whose life was not deeply marked by religion. The citizen may or may not be pious, she may or may not worship God in the seclusion of her home, but in public the only legitimate religious interlocutor was the state. The citizen, if he was pious, was expected to join the religious rituals organized by publicly employed imams and get his religious education from the official sermons, public television, and religion lessons that were a part of the official curriculum.

This partial regulation of religion was combined with its partial disestablishment in everyday life.[3] For example, institutional measures such as the replacement of the Western calendar for the Muslim calendar were coupled with the reorganization of everyday activities around the clock rather than around prayer times. Radical changes in dress patterns were meant to de-Islamize everyday life (Göle 1996). The republic also sought to create secular national holidays and rituals that would be more integrating than Islamic rituals by being binding for the pious and the nonpious alike.

The rigid CHP monopoly over the state came to an end with the election of the DP (Democrat Party) in 1950. While some religious groups supported the DP in this decade because of its tendency to undo certain nationalist and secularist reforms, the new political elite also retained the secularist emphasis on the separation of religion and politics. Relations between the DP and the religious sectors of society brought with them certain concessions to religious communities, groups, or *tarikats* (religious orders),[4] but these concessions did not go as far as endangering the Westernist orientation of the power bloc. "Containing" concessions of this kind are inevitable for the exercise of hegemony.

The CHP leaders had already started to quit some of their unpopular policies and to make their own party more fit for a parliamentary regime (Tarhanlı 1993). The CHP had, for example, embarked on providing Islamic education in the late 1940s, whereas it had been fighting against Kur'an schools and other sources of religious education with fervor at the beginning of the same decade. The resulting official Islam, a joint construction of the CHP and the DP (and its offshoots), was characterized by the public use of religion for national cohesion, the struggle against communism, the making of compliance among the masses, and the glorification of capitalism and modernization.

In the 1970s, the strong challenge from the Left led the power bloc in Turkey to deploy religion in a way that changed this configuration. A military intervention in 1980 institutionalized religion so as to expand the hegemonic reach of the regime. Standard religion lessons were introduced to the curriculum of public education, while the emphasis on some scientific theories (such as evolutionism) was reduced. Certain religious communities (e.g., the Süleymancıs) gained public visibility under official protection. The constitution drafted after the military intervention included for the first time religious references in the definition of Turkishness (Parla 1995). The Motherland Party governments, following the 1980 military coup, further expanded religious education and the influence of Sufi communities, instrumentally using both to bolster neoliberalization. Nevertheless, this frequent deployment of religion created the necessary cultural environment for others with counterhegemonic purposes to speak in the name of religion with more confidence.

Urbanist Elitism and Populist Concessions: The Civilizing Project

Another goal of the new republic was the creation of ideal urban citizens. Just like nonsecular behavior had its proper place, so did nonurban behavior: it was not to be seen in public life. Yet, the rush of rural immigrants to cities and their subsequent status as squatters disturbed the imagined urban purity. From the 1950s to the 1980s, the state vacillated between repression and containment, assuming that industrialization would in time absorb the squatter population (Keyder 1999).

The 1980s gave rise to new balances. In conjunction with the global trend of self-help housing (Davis 2006), the Turkish state was supportive of squatter settlements, since decreases in real income had necessitated compromises to popular sectors in spatial organization (Keyder and Öncü 1994). In the 1990s, however, the media started to portray squatters as greedy pillagers, who were in fact not poor but attempted to create public sympathy by feigning misery (Buğra 1998b). The squatters were further attacked for displaying rural, uncouth manners, which harmed the beauty of "civilized" urban life. Finally, the increasing strength of Islamism in poor regions added to the fury of the authorities and the dominant media, resulting in increased control over squatting.

Despite these futile attempts at exclusion, the immigrants were no longer marginal rural populations. Immigrants attained influence mostly because of their localistic organizations (Erder 1997, 1999), another crucial node of civil society in Turkey. Beginning with massive migration from the countryside, informal organizations based on imagined kinship and place of origin (*hemşehrilik,* or co-locality) enabled immigrants to first find land and housing and then to acquire jobs. These co-local networks were based on people being from the same village or town in the provinces. In time, these informal organizations turned into formal associations. This became the nationwide pattern especially following the liberalization of the economy after 1980. Hence, one of the crucial problems for hegemony in Turkey is whether state and political society will be able to absorb the localistic associational activities of squatters, a problem traced throughout this book.

Neoliberalization

The corporatist model of capital accumulation in Turkey (which was the joint construct of the CHP [Republican People's Party] and the center right parties) ran into a wall with the global economic crisis of the 1970s.[5] As Joel Beinin (2001) has pointed out, the power bloc in Turkey did not respond swiftly to the crisis because of the entrenched patronage-driven nature of electoral politics on the one hand, and the high levels of labor organization on the other. Only a military coup could marginalize these mechanisms. The military intervention of 1980 restructured the economy along export-orientation lines, restricted union activity, and cut down on wages (Keyder 1987). It also brought under control the electoral populism reflected in the support of the small peasantry. The reduced state backing for agriculture also impacted the availability of auxiliary support structures that had until then eased the survival of rural-to-urban immigrants.

However, the Turkish economy was not totally reorganized around neoliberal principles, as privatization coalesced with the existing patronage

mechanisms to unduly advantage various elite families. As this became public, *yolsuzluk* (corruption) became a cornerstone of popular grievance. These
developments generated high levels of dissatisfaction with the existing system
waiting to be channeled into political action. As the non-CHP Left was
crushed by the military in 1980 and disoriented by the developments in the
Soviet Union, and the CHP (and its offshoots, the Social Democratic Populist
Party [SHP] and the Democratic Left Party [DSP]) had started to emphasize
its original modernizing mission to the detriment of its left turn of the 1960s
and 1970s, the "social justice" message of the Left was up for grabs.

RESPONSE TO CRISIS: ISLAMISM

The Islamist answers to this organic crisis developed unevenly along the axes
of hegemony specified in this book—namely, political leadership, authority
structures, visions of unity, everyday life, social uses of space, and relations to
the economy.

Islamist Power and the Military Intervention of 1997

The most organized force putting forth religious challenges to secularist hegemony was the legal Islamist party. This party, which was closed down and
which reemerged four times, consecutively took the names Milli Order Party,
Milli Salvation Party, Welfare Party, Virtue Party, and Felicity Party for the
following four decades (see Table 2.1 for the Islamist party's changing names,
positions, and offshoots over the years).

In 1970, Islamists established a mass political party for the first time in
Turkish history, under the name Milli Order Party (MNP). The new party's
base consisted of small businessmen, tradesmen, peasants, and provincial artisans. The military closed down the party in 1971. It reopened in 1972 under
the name Milli Salvation Party (MSP), with virtually no change in its program. The MSP received 11.8 percent of the popular vote in 1973, and it held
10.6 percent of the seats in parliament (Sarıbay 1985). Its votes dropped to 8.5
percent in 1977, whereby it held only 5.5 percent of the seats in parliament.

The MSP's program advocated heavy industrialization based on communally owned private enterprises under state regulation. Its coalition protocol
with the CHP (Republican People's Party) demonstrated how the left turn of
the secularists and the Islamists' populist socioeconomic program brought
them together,[6] casting a doubt on simplistic explanations that base their
analysis of Turkish history on an airtight dichotomy between Islam and secu-

Table 2.1. Changes in the platforms and leaders of Islamic parties
from 1970 to the present

Abbreviation/ Acronym	Party Name	Years	National Leader	Platform	Sultanbeyli Mayor
MNP	Milli Order Party	1970–1971	Erbakan	National-communitarian developmentalism, Islamism	—
MSP	Milli Salvation Party	1972–1980	Erbakan	National-communitarian developmentalism, Islamism	—
RP	Welfare Party	1983–1998	Erbakan	Social justice, communally regulated markets, Islamism	Koçak (RP-FP) (1989–1999)
FP	Virtue Party	1997–2001	Kutan	Islamism, democratization	Karakaya (1999–2001)
SP	Felicity Party	2001–present	Kutan	Islamism, nationalism	Karakaya (2001–2004)
AKP or AK Party	Justice and Development Party	2001–present	Erdoğan	Conservatism, democratization, market reforms	Ersoy (2004–present)

larism or society and state. At this point, the CHP advocated building a "popular sector" in contrast with the public sector and the private sector. In this third sector, enterprises would be directly owned and administrated by workers and local communities.

However, the coalition between the center left and the Islamists (established in February 1974) did not last long. The amnesty decision regarding the socialists and communists (imprisoned after the military intervention in 1971) caused some parliamentarians to desert the Islamist party. These parliamentarians, as well as some ordinary supporters of the party, had started to blame it for shifting to the left (Sevilgen 1979). The CHP also faced criticism from its base because of its partnership with the Islamists.[7] The coalition collapsed under these pressures in September 1974.

The MSP joined two more coalitions but as a less effective partner. These two "Nationalist Front" coalitions were formed by Turkey's rightist parties (first the Justice Party–Milli Salvation Party–Nationalist Action Party–Republican Confidence Party, then the Justice Party–Milli Salvation Party–Nationalist

Action Party) with the primary aim of repressing the leftist tide. However, the growing distance between the Islamists and other sectors of the Right rendered the sustenance of these coalitions precarious. This distance was expressed, for example, in violent attacks against Islamists by extreme nationalists of the Nationalist Action Party (MHP)[8] and the tensions between the Islamist students and nationalist professors and administrators of theology schools (Albayrak 1989, 92–94).

Radicalization in the Islamic world also had costs for the religious movement in Turkey. After the Iranian revolution, some intellectuals and cadres with radical tendencies distanced themselves from the main Islamist party (the MSP) to establish their own radical journal (*Hicret*). More important, the base of the party itself was radicalizing, as manifested in an MSP rally held in the central Anatolian city of Konya, the stronghold of the Islamists, in early September 1980. The rally was a response to Israel's occupation of Jerusalem. The Konya meeting featured slogans such as "Kur'an is the Constitution," "Either Şeriat [Islamic law] or Death," and "Rebellion against the Order." What is more striking, some people did not stand up while the national anthem was sung, which constituted one of the excuses for the military coup on September 12, 1980 (Albayrak 1990).

After the party reemerged under the name Welfare Party (RP) the youth started to push it again in a radical direction. Even though the top leaders of the Islamist party had kept their posts, a younger generation of Islamists, influenced by the radical ideas circulating in the Muslim world (through the distribution of translated texts mainly from Pakistan, Iran, and Egypt), started to have an impact in the party.[9] Inconclusive religio-political debates characterized the 1980s. The leading circles of these debates were composed of university students, teachers, young professionals, and young preachers who attacked both the mild Islamism of the former decade and the apolitical Sufi communities.

The RP came to be an unstable articulation of competing strands, with an emphasis on further politicization of religion combined with moderation. It co-opted many prestigious traditionalist[10] Sufi masters (*şeyh*s) and religious scholars (*ulema*). However, especially during its radicalization in the late 1980s and early 1990s, the movement loosened its ties with mystic communities, which usually shy away from attacking the establishment. The incorporation of radicals, meanwhile, resulted in an indecisive radicalization of the party but also in the moderation of the radicals—as in the case of the Girişim circle, whose leader Mehmet Metiner became the most prominent Islamic liberal of the next decade. Moreover, the RP appealed to conservative (and majority) Sunnis by continuing to differentiate its line from the (Muslim heterodox) Alevis. For example, it took an active, though not organizational, role in the massacre of more than thirty Alevis in 1993.[11]

The broad coalition the RP built enabled it to assume offices in most key localities after the 1994 municipal elections. Islamist municipalities channeled more services to urban poor regions and distributed free coal, food, and clothes to the poor. Moreover, as the RP had largely curtailed municipal corruption, the quality of urban services increased incredibly. The ideological impetus of the party had enabled it to stay free from corruption (at least until 1994) in the post-1980 ideology-free environment, where actors of different political colors were united in their pursuit of corrupt wealth generated by Turkish-style neoliberalism.

These moves of the RP increased its popularity, and it came out of the 1995 national elections as the leading party. The RP managed to form a coalition government with the DYP (True Path Party), with the RP leader Necmettin Erbakan as prime minister. The RP gave signs of severing Turkey's ties with the West: it worked toward a "global democracy" based on the cooperation of Muslim nations inside and outside of the Middle East under Turkey's leadership (Özdalga 2002). However, the RP failed to use governmental power to fight corruption, and the party supported the DYP, which was deeply immersed in corruption, to sustain the coalition government. At the same time, signs of corruption also started to appear in the ranks of the RP itself, which had lost some of its ideological fervor after it came to power. Concomitantly, the activities of religious communities and organizations also lost their ardor, as now most turned their attention to savoring the benefits of power.

Yet, even the now-restricted militancy of the RP did not fail to arouse the anger of the power bloc. During its governmental term, some Islamist municipalities and civil organizations organized meetings to declare sympathy for Islamist regimes and organizations worldwide. Erbakan frequently talked about the need to open more High Schools for Imams and Preachers (İmam-Hatip, henceforth İHLs), the salience of which is among the primary concerns of the secularist generals. He also hosted a dinner where prominent şeyhs were invited. Such a public dinner was a first in the history of the republic, and the secularists interpreted it as the formal recognition of religious orders and communities that were in effect banned by early secularist reforms. These developments led to protests by secularist, middle-class civil organizations that implicitly called for a military intervention.[12] The military did not overlook their demand in the mid-1990s for increased repression and tightened the ropes. Hegemonic civil society and state struck back.

The military intervention of February 28, 1997, restricted itself to giving "recommendations" to the coalition government instead of disbanding the parliament as the military did in 1980. It asked the government to increase obligatory secular education from five to eight years, restrict Kur'an schools and İHLs, and control religious orders. There was no way the RP could carry out these policies without estranging its base. The government resigned. The impact of the military intervention was sustained by acts such as the closing down of the RP (January 1998) and the banning of its leader, Erbakan, from politics (Koğacıoğlu 2004).

The Virtue Party (FP), which replaced the RP, toned down its criticism of the establishment but also ventured to elect a veiled woman to the parliament. The ideologues of the FP had started to reframe the veiling issue as a matter of democracy and human rights, which led them to expect the European Union (EU) to intervene on their behalf. The veiled Member of Parliament (MP), Merve Kavakçı, had to leave the parliament before she could be sworn in, under the pressure of nationalist and center leftist parties (Göçek 1999). This was one of the incidents that led to the closing of the FP. Center right and center left, the old foes were united in their support for the military intervention and its ongoing repercussions. The differences within (hegemonic) civil and political society were suspended to fight counterhegemony. After this counterattack by the system, the Islamist party plunged into a deep crisis. As several ways of challenging hegemony failed, a sizable part of the Islamist leadership opted for joining the elite.

The Marriage of Mass Politics and Charisma

The Islamist movement built a mass party based on ideological convictions over three decades. Unlike the entrenched parties, it constructed a huge and efficient bureaucracy that was nevertheless interwoven by a messianic spirit (Arat 2005). This party bureaucracy also engaged in redistributing resources, though this was not simply clientelism (see Chapter 3).[13]

Erbakan's charisma facilitated all this. Activists of the party attributed messianic qualities to him. They described him as "a figure with a round, gleaming face that emanated peace" (paraphrased from Arat 2005, 54) and in other similar terms. However, just like some of the center right leaders, Erbakan actually had his roots in the elite. Over time, news and rumors swarmed with details regarding his luxurious life, which apparently contradicted Islamic modesty. Later, the media revealed that he had become wealthier during his career as a politician. Religious sectors retrospectively attributed his luxurious lifestyle to his social background, and he was thoroughly discredited as just another elite politician. Erbakan's fall from grace prepared the ground for the emergence of new charismatic figures among the Islamists.

Islamists and the Nation

How did the emergent Islamic political society respond to the hegemonic vision of unity? While small radical groups were straightforward in their rejection of the hegemony of nationalism (see Chapter 3), the mainstream Islamist party combined elements of nationalism with Islamic internationalism. Ideological booklets that the MSP (Milli Salvation Party) distributed (e.g., Özdamar 1977) would start by pronouncing the central aim of Islamist ideology as rendering Turkey a great nation. Yet, the central aim would be redefined later in the same booklets as serving no one but God. These ideologues combined nationalist, religious, and internationalist discourses by holding that an Islamist Turkey would serve the whole world by bringing prosperity, popular rule, and justice to Muslim as well as non-Muslim populations.

The Welfare Party (RP) initially moved toward a more internationalist position without giving up the claims of Turkish leadership for the whole world. This internationalization of the party's ideology had to do with the globalization of its networks. For example, many immigrants to Germany, who had become more religious in their new homes, generously channeled funds to the movement for more than two decades. Money traveled out too, as pious people even in poor regions (like Sultanbeyli) used their savings to support Muslims in Bosnia, Afghanistan, and Chechnya. Most of these transfers were conducted through Islamic banks, themselves products of globalization. The relaxation of financial regulation had made it possible for religious entrepreneurs to recruit funds from pious people who had heretofore avoided investing in secular banks, which they found risky and un-Islamic. This growing cross-national solidarity, as well as the increasing number of Islamist regimes over the world, had made the Islamists believe that constructing an Islamic political pole within the wider globe was possible.

The RP's pragmatism, however, made it gradually give up some of the cornerstones of its agenda. For example, one of the central claims of the party was that it was going to resolve the Kurdish question through Islamic solidarity. Yet, during the fifth congress of the party, Erbakan's presidential speech glossed over the Kurdish question. This disturbed the Kurdish members of the party, but they did not voice their complaints formally.[14]

Moreover, toward the end of the 1990s, Islamist regimes in Iran and Afghanistan became embarrassments. Global flows of money could not rescue the Bosnians from massacres that bordered on genocide. Worse, international Islamic banks and credit institutions also became involved in corruption. Some of them, including one major bank in Turkey, went bankrupt, casting doubt on the belief that religion by itself could be an antidote to harsh market forces.

The ensuing global disillusionment with prospects for Islamic unity manifested itself in Turkey in the turn of the Islamists to the EU and to the discourse of universal human rights and democracy, especially after 1997. This move discredited the Islamists in the eyes of nationalist-leaning religious people, while it gained them the sympathy of liberal intellectuals and professionals.

Integral Religion

In the 1970s, the Islamists mostly concentrated on waging a culture war. They occupied the public scene through the sensational announcements of politicians regarding alcohol, sculpture, and other allegedly un-Islamic practices that the republic had legitimized. The MSP (Milli Salvation Party) ideologues also defined one of their central goals as providing public employment to pious people, especially in the midlevel bureaucracy (Karib 1975, 102–4).

More significantly, the MSP succeeded in relaxing the pressure on İHLs (High Schools for Imams and Preachers). The students and graduates of these schools became the main activists and leaders in the movement over the next decades. In Turkey, İHLs are officially intended to educate prospective preachers (*hatips*) and prayer leaders (imams). However, as it is not possible for students to observe the precepts of Islam (such as praying) at regular public schools, religious families who did not necessarily want their children to become preachers and prayer leaders sent their children here (Özdalga 1999). In time, İHL graduates started to hold important public positions and constitute a religious middle class capable of competing with the secularist middle class in economic, cultural, and political realms.

In this decade, Islamists worked mostly on transforming everyday life (including behavior in public places and offices) and avoided any direct confrontation with the system. This was to change with the global radicalization of the movement starting at the end of the 1970s, when translated books propagated the idea of an "integral (*tevhidi*) Islam." This entailed the total Islamization of culture, the economy, and politics. "Traditional religion," integralists held, was insufficiently political, restricted to a narrowly spiritual sphere, and mired in superstition.[15]

There was a nationwide blossoming of Islamist publishing houses, magazines, and newspapers in the 1980s and 1990s, leading to the further empowerment of integral Islam. These two decades also witnessed the strengthening of Islamic dormitories, where the youth were politically trained through ideological debates and an Islamization of everyday life.

Throughout these decades, the Islamization of civil society and state was linked by the Islamist party (in its many incarnations). The CHP (Republican People's Party) had never succeeded in linking the secularization of civil society with that of the state to such a degree.

The Islamist Takeover of Urban Space

The relinking of society and state took yet another turn with Islamism's fluctuating positions with respect to urban space. The Islamist party triumphed in metropolitan municipal elections starting with the victories in Sultanbeyli and Arnavutköy of Istanbul (1989). Large metropolitan centers gradually became more pious. Religious symbols were introduced in key urban sites (Çınar 1997). The RP (Welfare Party) sought to reconvert Hagia Sophia into a mosque and open a mosque in the very center of the main entertainment square of Turkey, Taksim (two old projects of the MSP [Milli Salvation Party]). Official pressure thwarted these attempts. Nevertheless, the movement had broken the identification of cities with secularism (Çınar 2005).

However, different actors defined Islamism's urban project (which they called "conquest") differently. Some argued that after the conquest, cities would be more integrated with the world (Bora 1999). They pointed out that municipalities could use Ottoman history to attract more tourists. They also contended that inclusion of Muslim energies in the redevelopment of cities would make them compete better in world capitalism. Others, however, were less interested in market efficiency. They wanted to see the termination of the elitist exclusion that had kept the masses on the peripheries of cities.

These differences over the use of space in fact echoed the class tensions in the movement. On the one hand, Islamist strength in cities clearly became a function of squatter votes. On the other hand, though not as numerous as squatters, a new religious middle class was also emerging. Some of these professionals and intellectuals wanted the movement to develop along more bourgeois lines and therefore were more sympathetic to the salience of ex-provincial businessmen within the movement.

Moral Populism Versus Muslim Capital

Due to globalization, small- and medium-sized firms had acquired unprecedented relevance, gradually empowering the provincial businessmen who were more or less dependent on the Islamist political party in the 1970s. As a response to this shift, the new economic program of the RP (Welfare Party) emphasized private enterprises and an export orientation more than "heavy industrialization."

However, this seemingly neoliberal stance in the new program was balanced by promises concerning communal and/or employee ownership of and control over enterprises (Erbakan 1991). The religious intellectuals who came up with the model of the "Just Order," the party's new slogan, were influenced by (non-Marxist) socialist experiences and ideas.[16] The party's manual, "Just Economic Order," attacked the exploitation of labor, criticized class inequalities, and emphasized the unjustly low share of labor in national income (Erbakan 1991, 4–5, 9–10, 89). The relation of the program to neoliberalism was further complicated by its attack on *faiz* (bank interest) on the one hand and on taxation on the other, which could be construed as antiliberal and neoliberal, respectively (Buğra 2002). While the party conceded that prices would be determined by supply and demand, it also promised that the state would universally set wages and make sure that everybody would be employed, insured, and unionized (Erbakan 1991, 29, 65–66).

The contradictory nature of the model disturbed many other intellectuals and religious businessmen, who put pressure on the party to clarify the content of the Just Order or remove it from the agenda. In 1994, the party issued another pamphlet that answered some of the criticisms. The pamphlet opened by proclaiming that "the Just Order is the real pro-private-sector order" (Refah Partisi 1994, 1). The tasks of the state were restricted when compared to the first manual issued in 1991. The 1994 manual even claimed that there would be no strikes and lockouts in the Just Order, since there would be no need for them (Refah Partisi 1994, 23).

During the 1990s, the Islamist party received a crushing majority of poor and working-class votes thanks to its agitation for the abolition of "capitalist exploitation" and the interest system. The RP's one year in government, which occurred during 1996 and 1997, was a serious blow to the neoliberalization of the Turkish economy. However, Islamist activists and the pious intelligentsia never took the economic model they had developed seriously, and no one worked thoroughly on its internal contradictions. They assumed that the state controlled Turkish economy would find the right path when pious functionaries steered it. This lightheartedness about building an alternative economic program resembles Mohandas Gandhi's moralistic and inchoate attack against capitalism (Chatterjee [1986] 2001). What is more, before the Islamist program could be fully implemented, the military intervention of 1997 (which the secularist Association of Industrialists and Businessmen of Turkey [TÜSİAD] vehemently supported) obstructed the further politicization of the poor. The religious bourgeoisie used this opportunity to marginalize moral populism within the movement.

This synopsis of Islamism's economic challenge against secularist hegemony demonstrates that this was the least developed link in its chain of counterhegemonic articulation. There were more solidly anticapitalist challenges from within the ranks of Islamism (see Chapter 4), but these were not reflected in the national program of the party.

THE ABSORPTION OF ISLAMISM

A new political leadership emerged out of Islamism's military defeat in 1997. The new leadership set the scene for the absorption of Islamism into secular neoliberalism more or less successfully at all levels of the hegemonic formation.

Tamed Leadership

The increasingly neoliberal, prodemocratic, and pro-U.S. youth of the FP (Virtue Party) first tried to take over the existing party structure. Since they lost the ballot during a major party congress, they established a new organization in 2001: the Justice and Development Party (AKP or AK Party). The leaders of the AKP promised the secularist media and the military that they would not use religion for political purposes. They also visited the United States at intervals, where they held meetings—the contents of which never became public.

The AKP was but a variation on the center right theme discussed above. It desired to expand the power bloc through the inclusion of provincial merchants and businessmen along with religious intellectuals and professionals, while at the same time strengthening the hand of the neoliberal and internationally oriented sectors who once constituted the subordinate sectors of the bloc. In the absence of another promising center right heir, a vast number of center rightist politicians, intellectuals, and voters soon joined its ranks. This granted the AKP a resounding electoral victory in November 2002, after which it established a one-party government.

Professionalization and Charisma

The main authority figures showcasing the absorption of Islamism differentiated themselves from the old Islamist leaders by their professionalism, dialogue with the secularist media, and integration with global capitalism. The crucial characteristic of AKP leaders was that they retained their personal piety while frequently emphasizing how they were different from the Islamists. Tayyip Erdoğan, prime minister since 2003, metaphorically captured this difference by saying "we have taken off the Milli Outlook shirt," which implied that the AKP's leaders no longer shared anything with the Welfare Party–Virtue Party–Felicity Party's Islamists.

However, while this new emphasis satisfied some people in the base of the party who both desired to see pious rulers and wanted to avoid confrontation with the military, it alienated some who thought that the new leaders were no longer "one of us." So, in order to appeal to the alienated, the leaders had to demonstrate that they had not changed drastically. For example, the same Erdoğan who proclaimed they no longer had anything to do with the Milli Outlook also said "I did not change" as the 2007 general elections approached. The rigid secularists used this as proof that the AKP was a "fundamentalist" party and called for more military involvement in the regime. Such back-and-forth AKP maneuvers persisted after the party's electoral victory in 2007, too, preventing full reconciliation between the old elites and the Islamists.

Despite these swings and ambivalences characteristic of a passive revolution, Erdoğan had ultimately answered the popular research for a new charismatic hero. His youthfulness, paternal authoritarianism, popular roots, and piety have garnered consent for the policies his party implemented, as Chapters 5 and 6 will show.

Combining Globalism and Nationalism

Whereas the Welfare Party's vision for unity consisted of a creative combination of Islamism and nationalism, the AKP further added a pro-Western element to this hybridization. The change of heart in the West was central to this transformation. The United States, which had seen in Islam a viable weapon against communism during the Cold War, had started to shift its international policy to redefine oppositional forms of Islam as "terrorism." Both the increasing number of Muslims in Europe and this redefinition of the global hegemon led western European elites to ignore authoritarianism and repression as long as it targeted Islamists. Therefore, the turn of Turkish Islamists to Europe did not bear any fruit initially.

The AKP became one of the major players in the Muslim world by interpreting these changes constructively and cooperating with the United States. The AKP's relation with the United States went beyond a pragmatic alliance, as the party cadres (and gradually the followers) transformed Islamic politics based on the U.S. conservative model.[17]

The AKP combined this pro-U.S. turn with a rethinking of the Kurdish issue. Like its predecessor RP (Welfare Party), the AKP emphasized the need for unity between the Kurds and the Turks. However, unlike the RP, the AKP tried to establish unity on "global" (U.S.- and EU-defined) democratic norms. Erdoğan did mention Islam as a uniting characteristic between the two peoples, but he was careful not to imply that their Islamic unity would create a more Islamic state.

However, in the last years of its first governmental term, the AKP intensified nationalist rhetoric and policy (Cizre 2008; Duran 2008) so as not to lose support from the ethnic Turks. Its vision and practice of building unity, although creative, was ever fluctuating and unstable. The passive revolution in the sphere of building a unitary vision therefore remained the weakest chain in the emergent bourgeois hegemony (see Chapter 5).

In Between Conservative Religion and Islamization

The AKP mostly remained silent regarding religion in its first years, despite the intense religiosity of its top leaders and cadres. While AKP policies were more or less in line with the center rightist political tradition in Turkey until 2004, several moves in this year raised doubts about whether the party could bend in an Islamist direction. For example, the AKP government attempted to pass a law that could break the isolation of the İHLs (High Schools for Imams and Preachers). The military intervention in 1997 had restricted the ability of the graduates of these schools to enter regular universities and had channeled them to theology schools. The eight-year education bill that the military enforced also meant that students could start these schools only after eight years of basic education. This reduced their exposure to intense religious education at İHLs to three years before college. Even though the religious population had responded to this decision by a wave of protests in 1997 (see Chapter 3), the İHLs lost many students and less and less enrolled in the following years.

The AKP did not attempt to annul the eight-year education bill but drafted a bill to abolish the restrictions on the access of İHL students to universities. Rigid secularists interpreted this as the manifestation of its hidden Islamist agenda. The president vetoed the bill and the military insinuated that it perceived this bill to be a serious threat.

The secularist reaction was, to say the least, exaggerated. As opposed to the Islamists, the AKP had no agenda of Islamizing the whole education system. It was only striving to retain a very important resource: The restriction of İHLs was a blow not only to Islamism but to any religiously oriented project. In other words, fighting for the İHLs did not contradict the new party's project of religiously inspired center rightism, for its U.S.-style conservatism did not negate all things Islamic. After all, aren't schools with religious curricula a part of the U.S. education system as well? Other religious changes, like a further decrease in emphasis on evolutionary theory in textbooks and frequent broadcast of religious programs on TV, were not signs of a thorough Islamization either, but of Islamic politics' new boundaries in Turkey. These boundaries were more and more defined based on the framework of U.S. conservatism rather than the previous demands of the religious populations in Turkey.

Another significant trend under AKP rule was a partial Islamization of conduct among the dominant, secularist sectors. National surveys showed that while Islamists themselves gave up claims of the absolute purity of Islam, secularists started to think about God more than before and see the world through more spiritual lenses. Chapter 6 will give further details about how the absorption of religion into secular hegemony resulted in a passive revolution. The growing impact of religion on public life strengthened secular capitalist hegemony rather than undermining it.

Restoring Modern Space in an Islamic Way

The Islamists had won provincial and urban poor regions over not only by glorifying provincialism (the way the center right has always done in Turkey) but actually by integrating provincial masses with the cities and transforming the cities in the process of this integration. The AKP's ex-Islamists appropriated the strategies by which the Islamists approached the rural immigrants, while dropping belligerent metaphors such as *conquest*. Consequently, the rural-to-urban immigrants saw the AKP as their natural leaders against the elitism in Turkey, yet their combined movement did not entail a full spatial Islamization.

The AKP partially de-Islamized the urban space that the RP (Welfare Party) had Islamized (see Chapter 6). As the business wing of the Islamist movement now dominated the party, the emphasis further shifted to creating the proper urban infrastructure and culture that would attract investment. The overall appearance of cities was secularized, but cities also became more Islamic through the integration of Islamic businesses, consumers, and lifestyles. Finally, instead of attempting to ban alcohol everywhere (the Islamist utopia), the AKP imposed restrictions on alcohol sale and use, after the U.S. conservative model. The passive revolution crystallized in space through molecular Islamization in an overall consumerist, secular, and capitalist urban world—under guidance from political society and with the active involvement of civil society.

Sanctified Neoliberalization

Starting with its establishment in 2001, the AKP's ideologues presented it as the expression of an economic shift, but they did so using a quite spiritual language. Nazif Gürdoğan, a conservative ideologue and a member of a predominantly elite religious order (İskenderpaşa cemaati), interpreted this party (in Sufi language) as the representative of the "forces of light" against the "forces of darkness." He further defined the latter as proponents of centralized, hierarchical, and rigid organizations; and he defined the former as proponents of organizations based on trust, transparency, and distribution of authority.[18] In political economic language, he saw the party as the agent of flexible capitalism against organized capitalism represented by the nationalist sectors of the bourgeoisie. Yet, just like U.S. neoconservatives, he expressed this opposition in religious terms ("darkness" vs. "light"). Religious civil society (formerly Islamist newspapers, communities, orders, associations, etc.) combined its forces to sacralize the AKP's economic program. Without this spiritualization, neoliberalism could not be sustained. The molecular Islamization of economic discourse and dispositions were an inseparable part of the new capitalist hegemony.

Along the lines of this transformation, the AKP worked closely with the International Monetary Fund to cut public spending, control wages, roll back agricultural support, and privatize enterprises as well as natural resources

(Patton 2006). However, not all the economic results of the party's neoliberal policies were this straightforward: While real wages kept shrinking and unemployment increasing, the Gini coefficient (an orthodox measure of inequality) decreased, mostly due to some amelioration in the informal labor sector. These mixed results, which especially favored informal laborers, were among the reasons the popularity of the party was sustained among some sectors.[19]

.   .   .

This overall account of the rise and absorption of Islamism is insufficient by itself, as its carriers constantly constructed Islamic politics in the margins.[20] Activists conceived the Islamic movement as the conquest of the "alienated" metropolitan center by the allegedly more authentic periphery. Therefore, most of Islamist hegemonic work focused on day-to-day activity within peripheral populations. This requires us to complement a general history of Islamism with a detailed account of the way it worked on an everyday basis.

**POLITICAL SOCIETY AND CIVIL
SOCIETY UNCOUPLED**

Part 2

3 VICISSITUDES OF INTEGRAL POLITICAL SOCIETY

IN THE 1980S AND 1990S, the Turkish state faced a challenge to which it was not accustomed. The Cold War had prepared local authorities and pro-establishment political leaders to fight against the "red scare." Practicing Muslims could only be allies in this fight. But at the end of the 1970s, Islamists turned their ideological and political weapons against their benefactors. Moreover, they appropriated from their erstwhile enemies (the Left) the strategy of building dual power in (what the Turks called) "liberated zones" in peripheral neighborhoods. Yet, unlike the leftists, the Islamists tightly integrated the transformation of everyday life and social space with the construction of alternative authority patterns and political leadership.

One of the largest experiments to build an Islamic political society was carried out in Sultanbeyli, a region at the eastern border of Istanbul's Asian half. Sultanbeyli is located to the east of the former inland squatter district Ümraniye and to the north of two coastal working-class districts (Kartal and Pendik).[1] Sultanbeyli was only a village of 3,700 people before 1985. By the early 1990s, it had become a district of 80,000. In 2001, the district had a population of 175,000 and was the poorest district of Istanbul. It was also the locality with the highest Islamist party votes. Urban development had been informal ever since the mid-1980s and most of the buildings were still unregistered in 2002. They were also incomplete and poorly built, creating a brick scene of several miles on the main highway that connects Istanbul to Anatolia.

During its years of expansion, Sultanbeyli received immigrants mostly from the Black Sea region and the Kurdish areas of Turkey, respectively situated in the north/northeast and in the east and southeast of Anatolia. It also received immigrants from the same regions who had first tried out the central districts of Istanbul and had been disillusioned with their experiences there. Before these decades of expansion, the *muhacır* (Turkish immigrants from Bulgaria) used to constitute a significant population in Sultanbeyli.

I first studied Sultanbeyli between 2000 and 2002, when Islamic political society was in a deep crisis. In this chapter, I tell the story of my first visit, as well as the history of the transformation of political society in the district from the 1970s onward.

THE MAINSTREAMING OF THE ISLAMIST MOVEMENT

As will become clear in the next chapter, political society was crucial to the Islamization of the district. This chapter is dedicated to deciphering the multiple dimensions of Islamic political society in Sultanbeyli before 2002, since only such an analysis can set the context for the Islamization of civil society. In turn, the strength of both the dual power and the political unity that Islamists were trying to build ultimately depended on the organization and strategies of parties and political groups. An analysis of those parties and groups is necessary to understand why dual power and an alternative vision of political unity ultimately failed.

The Welfare Party, Islamization, and Mass Mobilization

The Welfare Party (RP) organized in every venue of society. Its youth foundation's (the Milli Youth Foundation, or MGV) work was crucial in this organization. In the Kur'an schools, the MGV targeted the hard-working students and invited them to the foundation. It gave them lunch and provided school supplies. The MGV was also organized hierarchically and popularly throughout the secular education system. It had representatives in almost every class, "hallway" (a collection of classes on one floor), and school. Each of these classes, hallways, and schools had their own chiefs. Each representative also had the duty to bring one person from school to the foundation every semester. The MGV organized approximately thirty-five thousand students between 1991 and 1996. The foundation provided health services, lodging, training in combat sports, and English and math lessons. It also organized races and conferences featuring revered religious scholars, as well as trips to holy sites on religious holidays. Most MGV members later became RP activists.

The RP had representatives in almost every apartment building. Its activists reached everybody and asked for support. But its victory also had a charismatic-ideological basis. "The Erbakan wind," as the party activists called it, attracted people to the party by promising the abolition of economic hardship, the demolition of the established order, and "people's power" (*halkın kendi iktidarı*).

The women's commissions worked especially diligently. While male activists could not enter every home because of Sultanbeyli's gender segregated structure, women could. Therefore, it was mostly the women's commissions that determined which families needed how much help, and the municipality's funds were channeled accordingly. When giving coal, food, and clothing to the families, the party activists made sure that they also organized *sohbets* (informal meetings where people gather and listen to a religiously learned person, pray communally, and eat snacks) at their homes. Or at the very least, they read chapters from the Kur'an and prayed for their dead, children, and the sick. Each Ramazan (the fasting month of the Muslim calendar), the commissions organized trips to the major mosques, where the party's leaders enlightened the residents about religious duties and religious history as related to the mosques. In this process, the less pious among the residents became more pious, bolstering the party activists' belief in the sacredness of their political mission.

The party ideology also defined helping the poor as a religious duty. This sacralization of service both bolstered the party's recruitment efforts and enabled it to organize rigorously. Elif,[2] born in 1967 in a Mediterranean city, was a high school graduate. She dressed colorfully, with pink shirts and colorful headscarves, but plain skirts. She was modest, unassuming, quiet, and unwilling to talk. She emphasized that under normal circumstances she would probably not give an interview, alluding to my status as an outside researcher and also a man, but she trusted her former coactivist who put me in contact with her. She hoped the interview would be good for the cause. Despite her reservations and caution, she became quite excited and her voice trembled when she talked about her days of activism. She was the organizer of the RP women's commission and remained active in the Virtue Party. She had gone to a Kur'an school for four years. She was also an instructor in one Kur'an school in the district for a year. After her parents' deaths, she lived with her uncle who used to closely follow *Milli Gazete*. In the late 1980s, this newspaper was inciting its readers to work for the party and help the poor:

> Both the feelings I got from *Milli Gazete* and my family members taught me that people should help each other. The paper also told us that this was a *hadis*:

"the most auspicious among human beings is the one who is beneficial to others." ["*insanların en hayırlısı insanlara en çok faydalı olandır.*"]

Due to her intense dedication, Elif was appointed as the head of the women's commission as soon as one was established in the district. She was proud because they saved many people from dire poverty. She told me that she could not forget one of them:

> Her whole body was covered with wounds. She only had a *çarşaf* [black overgarment that resembles the Iranian chador] on her and it had stuck to her skin. We had difficulty entering her home because of the smell. Back then we did not have washing machines. May God be content with her [*Allah razı olsun*], one of our friends gathered all her clothes and linens, and it took the whole women's commission to wash them all. Even after we washed everything with boiling water, the worms in her clothes did not die. God willing, those worms will be witnesses of our sincere work on the Day of Judgment.

Elif and others, as well as the RP's rivals in the district, underlined that it was this self-sacrificing work that granted the RP its electoral victories. Such work was enabled by unquestioning ideological dedication to the party, nurtured through newspapers, conferences, sohbets, the MGV, holy trips, and love for the leader. Civil society and political society were interwoven in winning the poor.

Radical Islamic Groups

Second to the Islamist party and municipality, radical groups constituted crucial nodes of Islamic political society in the district. In the 1980s and 1990s, there were a lot of local, unstructured, and radical groups in Sultanbeyli. They came together with the aim of training the right cadres for an Islamic revolutionary movement and an Islamic state. Most of them completely rejected the mainstream Islamist party, while others aimed to train their cadres in such a way that they could in the future constitute the nucleus of a group that would take over the party. These groups started as circles of friends and became more structured in time under would-be charismatic leaders. They rhetorically rejected hierarchy and authority and recognized no superior other than God. A small group of fifteen people active in the 1990s expressed some of the tendencies of such groups. This group declared everybody (but its own members) infidels. They even saw Sayyid Qutb (the model for radicals around the globe) as an infidel because he had "reinterpreted" the main texts. Their leader was a high school graduate who did not know Arabic. They specialized in reading *meal* (translations of the Kur'an). The group developed unusual interpretations regarding daily practice. For example, they did not turn their hands upward while praying (common in Islam) and declared that it was un-Islamic to do so because it implied that God is up in the sky, whereas God is actually everywhere. The group fell apart after the leader died in a traffic accident.

During my first visit to the district, there were still several radical groups like this one. In the case of more typical groups, the members first came together in a determined manner and started to read, but after a few months they disbanded. They usually started with reading Qutb's theological-political treatise, *Milestones*, and sometimes Mawlana Mawdudi's *The Four Key Concepts of the Qur'an*.[3] In most cases, nobody understood these texts fully, the group members lost their motivation, and they broke up. The most persistent ones went on to reading parts of *Fi Zilal al-Qur'an* and *The Meaning of the Qur'an* (the exegeses of Qutb and Mawdudi). Participants asked critical questions regarding the texts, and everybody criticized the readings. There was no leader whose interpretation was authoritative. Some groups had also started to read hermeneutic, historicist, structuralist, and post-structuralist interpretations of the basic religious sources, but these were the ones that abandoned their grandiose political dreams and tended to become civil society groups. The most persistent of these unstructured radical groups lasted a couple of years. They tended to be isolated from (and aggressive toward) ordinary Sultanbeyli residents.

The groups developed everyday practices that differentiated their members from other Islamic activists. They spoke a refined language. They walked around with erect postures. They did not bow their heads in front of secular or religious authorities. Unlike *medrese* (theological seminary) students, they did not kiss the hands of their religious instructors. And in contrast to the practice of the main Islamist party, kissing the hand of the political leader was also out of the question.

Then there were more structured radical groups, mostly connected to revolutionary Islamic movements at the national level. Most of these had a handful of members in Sultanbeyli. The X group was an exception. While the group was engaged in military training all over Turkey since the 1960s, its mass organizing activities started with a book club in the center of the district in the early 1990s. In a short period of time, they recruited around a hundred members. But they had a larger web of influence than that. The main out-reach activity was home sohbets. They differentiated themselves from what they called "traditional Islam" and, like many other radical groups, called their interpretation of religion integral (*tevhidi*) Islam. They did not go to mosques, even for the Friday prayers, as they saw Turkey as a part of *dar-ul harp*, that is, non-Islamic lands waiting to be conquered (where different codes of morality applied).[4] They also criticized "traditional Muslims" for so-cializing in gender-mixed environments, even though "traditional" women were covered. But *tesettür* (Islamic covering) also meant "sitting separate" for the X group. The people who became recruited to the community started to socialize in a segregated way ("sit separately"). One activist said: "We weren't able to tell our own mothers, sisters, and wives apart from other women," as clothing was standardized and even within the family men and women spent minimal time with each other. Instead they spent their time working for the cause.

The group members labeled the state "infidel" because it did not apply Is-lamic law. The recruits started to treat soldiers, policemen, and gendarmes coldly in their everyday life. In traditional circles, the more pious people turned toward more *zikir* (a form of collective Sufi worship where God's names are mentioned repeatedly and rhythmically). In their "integral" circle, the pious turned to knowledge, reading, and recruitment. The books they focused on were the writings of Sayyid Qutb, Mawlana Mawdudi, Ali Shariati, Fethi Yeken, and İhsan S. Sırma. Differing from nonradical groups, they were not inter-ested in the Ottoman Empire's contribution to Islamic civilization, which they perceived as Islam's deformation rather than its improvement.

In these early years of activity in Sultanbeyli, the group mostly consisted of construction workers, students, and teachers. An activist reported: "We were never like the Gülen community. We never had a target like building a web of corporations. Only one of us once tried to establish a *dershane* [private teach-ing institution preparing students for nationwide exams, a specialty of the Gülen community], but it failed, as we do not understand business. We used to say: 'stay away from money. Capitalism is infidelity.' We didn't say anything except that. And this is still the same." Isolating itself from mainstream Is-lamic institutions, the group had thus established what one Turkish journalist has called a "proletarian Islam." Yet, its members had a very shallow under-standing and criticism of capitalism, which was based on a straightforward rejection rather than thorough analysis.

Demir told me the story of his recruitment to the X group, which was typical of the recruitment of other university graduates into other radical groups. He was born in 1979 and raised in a southern town. He went to the High School for Imams and Preachers (İHL) in the same city and then graduated from a history department in a school in Central Anatolia. He became an instructor of history. His maternal grandfather was an imam. His father was, in contrast to his mother's side, a leftist and a construction worker. Demir himself was a construction worker until he graduated from college. He started to hang out with the circle when he was twelve. But until he was fifteen, he did not realize that they were a group. He was mostly coming and going to sohbets in this earlier phase.

> There wasn't anybody at my İHL who did not go to sohbets. These high schools are the best recruiting grounds for communities. After a while, they told me that they were a circle and that I would have to become a member if I wanted to continue to come to their sohbets. I had started to feel that something was going on, but I wasn't able to tell who they were until that point. Since I had seen nothing wrong from them, I agreed to become a member. . . . Nobody makes a real conscious decision about becoming a part of these circles. If you go to people and tell them that you're a community, they will be reminded of organizations. When they are reminded of organizations, they are reminded of being an enemy of the state. They hold you equivalent to the PKK [the Kurdish guerrilla group].

In order to prevent these worries, radical groups approached people quietly. Only Sufi communities and mainstream Islamist parties introduced themselves openly. Sohbets were recruiting grounds for the radical groups, just like they were for the Islamist party and for Sufi communities, but they used this resource differently. Unlike other radical circles, the X group had strong connections in the provinces and recruited working-class men too, mostly thanks to the influence of its İHL teachers. Following the 1997 military intervention, the group lost its military infrastructure after raids on its training camps, which demoralized its members and pushed the group into retreat for awhile.

Except for the X group case, there tended to be a seemingly impassable distance between the radicals and the poor in 2000–2002. This distance between the educated sectors and the poor in the district impeded the formation of new popular oppositional political options or the transformation of Islamist politics along more oppositional lines. A factor that fed into this problem was the reaction of ex-radicals against poor people. There were alternative urbanized and elite positionings in the district, especially among university graduates who had engaged in radical or conservative religious movements during their university lives and had moved away from these in the process of establishing themselves as teachers or shopkeepers. These ex-radicals or conservatives distinguished themselves from the people by emphasizing reason, education, cultural level, mobility, and individual freedom—values that they believed to be lacking in Sultanbeyli. When Islamism was on the rise, some of these values (such as reason) had served to mobilize the people, but now they tended to serve more as tokens of "distinction" (Bourdieu [1979] 1984). The primary social circle of these ex-radicals consisted of other university graduates, with whom they shared aesthetic tastes such as movie-going and poetry.

This was the case with one of the most well-read teachers in the district. Born in 1970 in a Kurdish village, Numan was a cleanly shaven, tall, thin, and energetic man who had participated in radical Islamic circles and Friday protests when he was a theology student at one of the major universities. When I attended his classes at the İHL in 2000, he worked on converting his students from traditional Islam to radical Islamism through deep theological discussions on fate, the meaning of existence, and so on. His activities attracted strong reaction from pious families, some of which declared him an "infidel." Dedicated to and certain of his beliefs, he laughingly dismissed the allegations. But as a result of this struggle, he had built a wall between himself and the district's residents. For example, he did not go to the teahouses, hotbeds of religious activism. I frequently met and chatted with Numan at his home during my first months in the district. As I did not want to disturb his family life, after a while I asked Numan to meet at teahouses. He was very reluctant, but at first he did not fully explain why. I finally convinced him. We met at the door of the central teahouse. As he entered, he wrinkled his face in revulsion and said:

> I hate these people. How can you stand them?
> R:[5] Why would you hate them?
> Numan: Don't you see those unpleasant, long beards? They sit here all day and do nothing. They are all followers of tarikats.

I was surprised at first, as I did not expect these reactions from an Islamist teacher. The attributes Numan singled out—long beards, membership in tarikats, and idleness—are actually components of the Turkish secularist perception of religious people. But in time I learned that the radical Islamists' perception of the "common man" was deeply shaped by modernist and rationalist influences. Generally a joyous and jocular man, Numan did not laugh and make jokes when we met at teahouses in the following months.

The radicals' and ex-radicals' individualization and the bread-and-butter concerns of the poor also hampered any meaningful communication. Ragıp, a small shopkeeper from an eastern Anatolian city who had engaged in Islamist politics in his university years, expressed his frustration with attempts at forming political relations with the inhabitants of Sultanbeyli:

> You cannot talk about ideas to a hungry person. You cannot incite him to think. First you have to feed him, heat his house, and dress his children. You cannot instill any ideology in poor people's heads. They demand bread from you when you try to do that. And I should ask this too: Are these really my troubles? Everybody lives his/her own life. Susan Tamaro puts this very well in *Follow Your Heart*: everybody lives his/her own fate. Maybe this is very egotistical, but I only help a good person when I see one.

Ragıp and others like him came across a barrier of economic destitution when they tried to spread their ideas in the district. Yet, it was exactly such bread-and-butter issues that had made the Islamist party—which was increasingly unable to mobilize some educated ex-radicals due to its pragmatism and submission to the state—successful. Moreover, the (Islamist) Virtue Party was more able to relate to and empathize with the common person and instill its approach to Islam in her or him. The educated and the oppositional did not see much value in the religion of the common person, which prevented them from developing meaningful relations with the poor. Their cultural capital increasingly resembled that of dominant sectors (as exemplified by Ragıp's reference to Susan Tamaro, a self-help author widely read among the Turkish secular elite), leading them to build their networks in a way that excluded the poor.

As a culmination of the opposition between real Islam and hearsay Islam that the Islamist movement itself popularized,[6] some educated people no longer had a sense of shared fate with fellow Muslims, especially with poor and uneducated ones. Even though the activists of the Islamist party also deployed a distinction between real Islam and hearsay Islam, they had a sense of shared fate with poor Muslims and did not usually display individualist traits. However, the growing middle class had started to perceive the lifestyles and political styles of these activists as relics of the past. The counterhegemonic project of Islamism had thus dynamited the broad and tight class coalition on which it stood. Individualization and practices of distinction thereby created the conditions for a major split in the Islamist movement and the creation of a more bourgeois-oriented party. Some ex-radicals (including Ragıp) were going to become the leaders of a new party and forge a new, even broader, but looser class coalition.

Street Action Without Party Leadership

Street action is crucial to the making and unmaking of hegemony, as it gives a chance to political society to link or unlink civil society and state. While social movement scholars have mostly focused on street action as an object in itself (studying its likelihood based on independent variables such as opportunity structures, resources, and framing), in our hegemonic frame of analysis, street action is understood as a link in a chain of articulation and disarticulation. It is important insofar as it allows hegemonic projects to naturalize an existing set of relations, or counterhegemonic projects to denaturalize them. Whether a project can make use of street action in this way ultimately depends on its political leadership. Tracing the changes in the relation between street action and political society in a specific locality will be crucial to the argument of this book.

Despite its leading role in the "conquest" of metropolitan municipalities, Sultanbeyli did not assume a leadership position in the Islamic street action of the late 1990s. Yet, it was still one of the major sites of mobilization. The major protests occurred in August and September of 1997 as a reaction against the parliament's decision to extend compulsory secular education to eight years, thereby closing down the middle sections of the İHLs, which the generals of the 1997 coup had singled out as one of the greatest threats against secularism. Islamists in several cities and districts of Istanbul took to the streets in response.

Massive protests also shook Sultanbeyli. For several weeks, after each Friday prayer, men, women, and children gathered in front of the central mosque, walked to the highway, and blocked it. While the most common slogans were against the government led by the Motherland Party (ANAP), Prime Minister Mesut Yılmaz, and the closing of the İHLs, smaller groups chanted in favor of Islamic law and booed the Atatürk statue that was on their way to the highway.[7] There were several skirmishes with the police and attacks against journalists from mainstream newspapers.[8] Second to the protests in the leading Beyazıt mosque, police interventions were most organized in Sultanbeyli.[9]

Media coverage of the events did not indicate any leadership. When I inquired about the protests in Sultanbeyli four years after they occurred, most people used the adjective "spontaneous" to characterize them. However, there were leaders, even though they were not in total control of the events. Those who initiated the events were young Welfare Party members, acting independently of their superiors. Nothing was well planned or thought-out. It was mostly protests in Beyazıt (a central neighborhood of historic Istanbul) that inspired the young activists and incited them to action. The two leading figures in the protests, Bekir (an engineer) and Nazmi, shared their experiences with me. A week after the first protest in Beyazıt, Bekir convened his friends:

> After the Friday prayer was over, twenty friends remained in the mosque yard. We wanted to protest the ANAP, but didn't know exactly what to do. We had been raised in a legal party and movement. This was our first experience with illegality. While we were waiting, Nazmi put his hand in his pocket and pulled out the Kur'an, raised it, said *Allah-u Ekber* [God is great], and started to walk. So we walked behind him. More people started to follow us. After walking a few steps on the main street, the police blocked our way. We turned upward, we took the side streets, but we couldn't make it to the ANAP, as they blocked us once again. We only shouted a few times and we disbanded.

Nazmi, the leading figure who initiated the protests, was from an eastern city and was a twenty-eight-year-old petty municipal clerk at the time. His family had come to the district in the beginning of the 1980s "because it was a place where the Muslims could live with comfort, just like [their] village." In their hometown, the whole family followed a certain *şeyh* (Sufi master):

> I'm a little calm and quiet, but when there is an attack against faith I cannot bear it. I could not stop myself. At home, I took the Kur'an-ı Kerim [the Holy Kur'an] with rage, and came to the central mosque to cry out that we weren't dead, that we wanted our children to be raised as Muslims. After the prayer, I waited, but nothing was happening. That's why I started the protest with *tekbir*.[10]

Bekir felt he needed to intervene to give further explanation of their motivations: "We did not do this because we were against education. We did it because we wanted to be both religious and become, say, doctors. Why shouldn't we be able to do both?" Bekir was still insulted by the secularist media that had framed the street action as "protest against eight years continuous education," and he pointed out that defending the İHLs had a quite different meaning for them.

The following week, there was much more participation. Since there was no police violence in the first week, people were relaxed. They blocked the highway during the protests of the second week. This time around, the police followed the protesters from the sky with helicopters and on the ground started to use pepper gas. While there were around two hundred protesters in the first week, during the third and fourth weeks there were more than five hundred according to secularist newspapers and more than two thousand according to Sultanbeyli residents.

The gradual increase in police violence decreased the popularity of protests. The neighboring military unit also came into the district after the week of the most crowded protest. Soldiers patrolled the municipal building. They also formed a convoy on the highway and marched, in the words of the activists, "as if there had been a coup." Starting with the third week, Koçak (the first elected mayor of the district,[11] 1989–1999) also banned municipal employees from participating and threatened those who had participated before, though he was seen as the Islamist archenemy by the secularists. The top Islamist leaders of the district not only refrained from organizing and leading the protests, but after a point they became impediments. After the fourth week, there was less and less participation. In the final week, there were only around ten protesters.

After Beyazıt, Sultanbeyli had become the biggest center of the protests in Istanbul. The participation in Sultanbeyli was in at least one sense more remarkable because activists from all over Turkey had flown into Beyazıt, whereas in Sultanbeyli the participants were residents. Despite protests all over Turkey, street action did not lead to any victory. The new laws regarding education did not change, the government was not replaced, and (as outlined in Chapter 2) the military sustained the repression of the movement for the coming two years. Actually, if anything, the memory of the protests deradicalized the activists. During my fieldwork, the ex-activists repeatedly referred to the days of street action and emphasized that they were in the wrong and that illegal protests did not accomplish anything. One activist told me, "We were fortunate that some fanatic did not attack shop windows. Events like this are prone to such fanaticism." Nazmi, the initiator of the first protest, said that years after the protests he became more interested in education, even if this meant he had to send his children to "the other" (secular) schools. Then they would climb to the top and make changes from up there.

Due to this recent deradicalization, combined with the shutting down of the Welfare Party and the much more moderate platform of the Virtue Party, Islamists were no longer in a position to lead mass protests by 2001. Islamic political society was mainly inactive as the street exploded yet once again that year as a response to a severe economic crisis.

Throughout the 1990s, big capital had turned to lending due to high interest rates (provided also by public banks). This created a vicious circle where the state undertook more and more loans to pay the interest. The economy collapsed under this heavy debt burden in February 2001. A severe recession and the depreciation of the currency followed (Yeldan 2006). All this added to the casualties of neoliberalism, which had been accumulating since the early 1980s.

In April 2001, the popular sectors of Turkey were to give their most violent massive reaction to impoverishment ever since the depoliticization of the 1980s. Paradoxically, the wave of protests that lasted for ten days and involved numerous clashes with the police were led by tradesmen and artisans who are known in Turkey for their conservatism and extreme right-wing nationalism. Indeed, most people in these walks of life are either center rightist, Islamist, or right-wing nationalist.

The protests were a reaction to the International Monetary Fund (IMF) plan that had totally unregulated the rates of foreign currency as a response to the economic crisis that had erupted in February 2001. This deregulation rendered more than half the population of Turkey much poorer overnight. Hence, the militancy of the protests was a part of the global peripheral pattern that had come into being in the 1980s: More IMF intervention in the economy created more militant popular action (Walton and Ragin 1990). The IMF plan in Turkey was ironically implemented by a coalition government made up of the nationalist Left (the Democratic Left Party), the right-wing nationalists (the Nationalist Action Party), and an ineffective center right party (the ANAP). Although the wave of protests was covered in the media as "tradesman protests," the majority of protesters were composed of unskilled, unorganized, informal workers and the unemployed. The formal working class and legal leftist organizations and parties did not join these protests, the participants of which (tradesmen, urban poor, and artisans) they usually perceive as essentially reactionary. Only a handful of illegal and small leftist organizations were active in the uprising.

Like everywhere else, there were demonstrations in Sultanbeyli after the Friday prayer on April 6th. The central mosque was totally surrounded by police forces before the prayer started. After the prayer was over, the construction workers, youth, and shopkeepers who exited the mosque did not go to work or coffeehouses as they usually did but stayed in front of the front wall that marks the boundary of the mosque and faces the Virtue Party (FP) headquarters. People with wide kin networks especially populated the two sides of the boulevard and stood shoulder to shoulder with their close relatives. Several minutes after the end of the prayer, police officers started to walk around, waving their clubs and saying "do not stay here, go away." Nobody took them on, and most people stared at the sky and blankly looked around in order to imply that they had nothing to do with whatever was going on. All of a sudden, a dozen middle-aged men standing in front of the FP building across the street raised their hands and gestured to the people in front of the mosque to descend down to the boulevard that separated the mosque and the party building. People on both sides started to chant "government resign" and "damn [Prime Minister] Ecevit." Groups of various sizes slowly left the pavements on each side of the boulevard and joined the people who had started to flow into the boulevard. It was mostly the case that the decision to march forward or retreat was taken by packs of kin. As research has shown, the availability of kin or other informal networks can become a factor conducive to revolt in certain situations. Whether solidarity networks stymie radicalization or bolster it ultimately depends on their interaction with other forces (Arjomand 1988; Denoeux 1993). Kin groups, which usually kept the residents of Sultanbeyli from engaging in direct action (see Chapter 4), had become a means of mobilization as soon as taking the street was deemed legitimate all over Turkey. The men who initiated the action were affiliated with several parties ranging from the Great Unity Party (BBP) and FP to the People's Democracy Party (HADEP), but they were not the top administrators of their parties. Hence, there was a semblance of political leadership in the protests, but it was fragmented. Civil society and political society were poorly articulated.

The two streams of protesters combined to block the boulevard traffic. All this had happened so swiftly that the police were not able to stop it. The chief officer climbed onto a police vehicle and started to shout something into a megaphone, yet his voice was totally drowned by loud boos. The driver of the municipal bus that happened to be at the forefront of the traffic started to honk his horn, driving his bus toward the crowd. As the police around the bus started pushing the crowd with their shields and lightly hitting some people with their clubs, the crowd was again split in two amidst boos directed against the police and the bus driver. Taking advantage of this opportunity, two bands of police officers lined up on both sides of the boulevard, opening up enough space for cars and buses to pass. The police went on to disperse the masses on the sides of the boulevard with their shields and clubs. However, about a hundred people were able to gather again in the middle of the street at the point where the two bands of police officers terminated. Even though parts of the dispersed crowd gave up resisting, several packs ran down side streets and reached the main group by taking detours, resulting in a crowd of several hundred. This mass had marched one hundred meters when tanks blocked their path.

Boos against the police multiplied in volume, eventually cut off by the same two chants: "government resign" and "damn Ecevit." Like other demonstrations all over Turkey, there were a few people who raised up their index fingers, an Islamic gesture witnessing the existence, singularity, and supremacy of God. The gesture was accompanied by *tekbir*s, to which some responded with the chant *"Allah-u ekber."* The same police officer made another announcement and was again suppressed by boos. Since it became obvious that marching farther was impossible without clashing with the police, the crowd started to disband. Only a very small group of people tried to remain where they were and fiercely protested the police with the slogan "sell-out state" (*satılmış devlet*).

However, in the blink of an eye, several bands of people started to shout "To the highway! To the highway!" and started to run in the direction of the highway that cuts across the district. Whereas there were people of all age groups in the crowd that blocked the boulevard, only people between twelve and forty heeded this call and started to walk quickly in the direction pointed. The multiclass coalition also crumbled, as it was mostly informal workers and the unemployed who marched forward.

Having relaxed after dispersing the crowd, the police did not perceive what was going on at first, but they came running after most people had progressed about two hundred meters. There was still about one kilometer to go until the highway. Since several groups of people were heading toward the highway without leadership and in a scattered manner, the police did not have much difficulty in stopping them. Only unrelated individuals were able to escape the police and run toward the highway. Officers used more extensive force in stopping them. The symbolic, as much as strategic, destination was not to be reached. Sultanbeyli residents were not able to block the highway as they had a few times in 1997 under a more persistent Islamist leadership.

After all this was over, packs of people began to gather along the main boulevard. The police took half an hour to disperse these packs without using much force. Subsequently, tanks, buses, and police automobiles left the main boulevard, to return fifteen minutes later as people had again started coming together in front of the central mosque. After dealing with this last potential event and shutting down the agitative music that was broadcast from the FP building throughout the protests, they did not again take the risk of leaving the district but stayed around for several hours.

This amazing series of incidents during which the residents of Sultanbeyli gathered together five times—and were dispelled by force or the threat of force five times—testified to the resolution of the people to protest against poverty, the government, the prime minister, the police—in a word, against the state—at certain conjunctures. Yet, it also showed that such protests were bound to be ineffective in the absence of political leadership. Moreover, the failure to reach the highway demonstrated that the lack of political leadership was likely to result in avoidance of militant confrontation, even when the crowd gave the police a hard time by mostly foot-dragging.

Though the most active people in the protests had given a clear message to the Islamist party and to other people by starting the event in front of the FP building, the top leaders of the FP had restricted themselves to watching the events from their windows and making their sympathies clear by playing loud and agitative music. Some of the supporters of the party told me that the reason the Islamist party could not organize and lead the protests in Sultanbeyli was its timorousness: "Every time it moves, it gets a slap on the face. This causes timidity in the party." Partially as a result of this timidity, the FP was far from organizing and channeling a radicalizing artisan and poor population that saw the Islamist party as its natural leader. Another major reason for the semipassive role of the party during the protests was the increasing lack of belief among the FP leaders that any good could result from the actions of poor populations.[12] Despite their residence in Istanbul's poorest region, the party's organizers in Sultanbeyli were under the influence of the nationwide shift from an ideological line that emphasized the salvation and liberation of the poor to a position that glorified the accumulation of capital by religious entrepreneurs. Even though the conjuncture had led the informal networks of the poor and tradesmen to take on militant action, the lack of a counterhegemonic intervention made it impossible for their community-based strategies to transform the way the state related to the poor and to the market.

There was less expansive police presence in Sultanbeyli on April 13th, the last day of the protests at the national level. Only two police cars, one minibus, and several police officers with guns and clubs were waiting in front of the central mosque. Forty people gathered in front of the central mosque after the Friday prayer. After waiting for ten minutes, they realized that nobody else was leaning toward another protest like last week's, and they dispersed. Following them, the police also left the main boulevard.

It was right after this that I saw Hüsnü, a religious and conservative construction worker, wandering around in front of the central teahouse. Hüsnü was a mild-tempered man who was thoroughly interested in science. He spent the days when he did not have to go to work by following earthquake-related Web sites. He was working on building an instrument that could predict earthquakes in Turkey and abroad. He complained that he couldn't get any scientists to look at and evaluate his instrument, which (he held) had successfully predicted several minor earthquakes. He wanted his two daughters, who were in primary school, to be educated people and avoid the economic and social difficulties he had experienced. For the moment, they seemed to be doing well. Hüsnü was respected as a construction worker, but the educated people of the district mocked him because of his amateurish interest in science. He took both his job and his engagement with science very seriously, and he distinguished himself from the others in the central teahouse who "did not read enough."

Hüsnü and I entered the teahouse together and started talking about the recent protests. He had consistently avoided any involvement. I asked him why he thought the demonstrations in Sultanbeyli were not as massive as those in central Ankara. His response was rather informative about the reasons why he did not join the protests:

> The people here are poor. Poor people do not get involved in things like this. When they do, it is very different. Nobody can hold them. They make a lot of damage. If the economy continues like this I don't know what I will be doing in three months. I might get involved in any kind of rebellion.

Hüsnü perceived the austerity protests as totally destructive. He thought that involvement of people like him might make them even more destructive. He reckoned he might join a protest only if he lost himself. In this sense, joining a protest was a sign of lost honor for him. He imagined demonstrations as events where all reason and good understanding are discarded and where people are no longer themselves. Of course, this vision had a lot to do with Hüsnü's previous involvement with the right-wing Nationalist Action Party (MHP), which he quit to join a rather pro-state, nationalist religious community (Menzil Cemaati of the Nakşibendi order).

Yet, Hüsnü was not alone in thinking of the April protests in this way. Indeed, another construction worker—with no ties to the nationalist party or to Hüsnü's community—who joined us in our conversation interpreted the protests as a sign of the approaching doomsday. In sum, a lot of destitute yet cautious people had avoided the ten days of protest due to worries about honor, control, and safety. Yet others like Veysel, the Kurdish construction worker whose marginalization is narrated in Chapter 4, avoided the protests because they had become convinced during their prior involvement that mobilization did not lead to any positive results for them. Likewise, the leaders of the High Schools for Imams and Preachers (İHL) had also avoided the protests in 2001. When political society did not intervene street action actually became a depoliticizing venue amenable to the reproduction of hegemony.

Among the most common slogans of the April protests were "damn the IMF" and "police without honor" (şerefsiz polis). Whereas the first slogan was an affirmation of the common sense belief that foreign institutions are one of the root causes of poverty (see the subsection "Nationalist Critique of Exploitation" below), the second one was a significant break with the statist common sense of popular sectors (see the subsection "Islamist Populism and Dual Power" below for statism). The crisis had given an opportunity for the popular sectors to repeat, assert, and reproduce the anti-imperialism already present in common sense. However, both the urban poor and the tradesmen are quite sensitive about the Turkish state and its key institutions, such as the security forces. It was especially astonishing to hear tradesmen chant against the police, as nationalist and pro-police sentiments reign supreme among this sector. Slogans such as "state without honor" and "sell-out state" were expressions of a clearer and more formidable break with common sense, even though they were voiced less often during the protests. Yet, Islamists could not make use of this weakening of statism to unlink civil society and state.

There was a wide ideological mix in the fragmented leadership as well as among the followers of the April protests, and Islamists constituted one of the significant ingredients. This was the last time the Islamists rose up against the unregulated market. After the closing of the FP and the establishment of the Justice and Development Party, there was going to be less and less Islamic street action, and definitely not any Islamic street action against the free market, as I will further demonstrate and analyze in Chapter 5.

Absorption of the Radicals into the Welfare Party

In the 1980s, radical Islamists rejected any government post and any institution or political party that worked within the system. However, they started to appreciate the Welfare Party (RP), which used to be seen as a part of *küfür* (the infidel world), after its modest electoral success in 1991. In the general elections of that year, the right-wing Nationalist Work Party (MÇP) and the (Ottomanist) Reformist Democracy Party joined the RP list to thwart the 10 percent election barrier, as a result of which the RP got 16 percent of the vote. This was a rightist show of power. Yet in 2000, some radicals remembered these elections as the first steps in the Islamists' return to nationalism and away from their emergent Islamic internationalism of the 1980s.

Many radicals in Sultanbeyli were also in the process of reaching the conclusion that their small groups would not be able to expand much more than the X group, which itself had around one hundred members compared to the RP's thousands of members in the district. After this point, radicals started to join the party. Yet, the party's leaders did not have total control over these radicals. Some of these people became the leaders of street action in the late 1990s, which as we saw above contradicted the directives of the RP's top leaders.

While the party opened its doors to repentant radicals, it also fought decisively against the remaining radical groups. The party was as inimical toward groups such as the Islamic Great East Raiders Front (İBDA-C), Hizbullah, and so on as it was to secularists. An activist coming from the Milli Outlook tradition approved of this open antiradicalism. Necmi was one of the young municipal functionaries who had an Islamist past but now leaned more toward a liberalized, modernist version of Islam.[13] He came from one of the established families of the district that actively supported Islamist parties ever since the Milli Salvation Party. He had spent most of his youth as an activist in the RP and tried to live up to its social requirements. He jokingly told how he took *extra* ablutions (more than five times a day) to satisfy other members of the party. Yet, in time, he started to find these rituals too formalistic (*şekilci*) and decided to redefine his relation with religion. In this process, he shaved off his rounded beard. His group of friends, constituting a radical flank in the party, had disobeyed the RP authorities in the district and led the major street protests in Sultanbeyli. Despite this short-lived rebellion, they had not quit the party, and in time they moved in a more centrist rather than more radical direction.

A tall and charismatic man, Necmi strongly believed that he had political potential and slowly worked his way up with the aim of running in future elections. Whereas in the past he used to organize street protests, he now organized conferences in the district and fought against what he perceived to be "ignorance." He and his friends—grouped around the "Furkan Center," which provided weekend education, film showings, computers with Internet access, and hosted a canteen—periodically discussed the latest theological and political books in the Muslim world as well as the Islamist classics. In 2002, he believed that the Justice and Development Party was going to be the vehicle to spread his understanding of Islam. He joined this party with the hope of having a major voice. Nevertheless, he still spoke of the RP in positive terms:

> This country owes a lot to Erbakan Hoca. He has carried out many services. But nobody could understand this. He appeased the radicals. If it were not for him, there would be radicalization in this country. Actually, the real conflict in the 1990s was not between Islamism and secularism, but between the RP and the radicals who denied the legitimacy of a party. Hoca protected people from these radical groups.

The party carried out this "service" by marginalizing members suspected of being linked to radical groups and by controlling the youth who tended to go in a radical direction. In 2001, the Virtue Party (FP)—which was about to be closed down by the regime—still went on operating similarly. For example, at one party rally I attended in central Istanbul, the party activists forcefully removed a small group of youth linked to an armed circle (İBDA-C) who chanted a couple of radical slogans.

Yet, the more decisive process proved to be the moderation of radicals (rather than their full exclusion or the radicalization of the party apparatus), along with the integration of loyal party activists to the system. Once Islamists took hold of the metropolitan municipality in 1994, many previously dedicated activists started to use their posts for personal gain. The willingness to give to the poor and to the cause decreased. After the military intervention in 1997, the last opponents of such corruption gave up, as they also became convinced that an Islamic transformation was not likely, and they lost their eagerness to oppose (what they saw as) immoral enrichment. The bourgeoisification in the RP thus coupled with the ramifications of the military intervention to decrease dedication to the cause. Even many FP members argued that at the end of the 1990s RP activists had started to lose sincerity and no longer trusted each other.

As a result, at the time when the FP was established concomitant to the closing of the RP, not only those with radical pasts or links to radical organizations, but even loyal activists who strove to keep up a mainstream Islamist line, were marginalized in the organization. Pragmatic conservatives, who were by no means ready to sacrifice much, now controlled the party. Therefore, the FP was already socially weak when it received a decisive legal blow only four years after it was established. I was sitting in the furniture store of Mahsun, one of the former prominent Islamists of the district, on the day when the Islamist party was shut down for the fourth time in its short history of little more than a quarter of a century (July 22, 2001). Mahsun, a corpulent, dark-skinned, fifty-five-year-old İHL (High School for Imams and Preachers) graduate with a long beard, claimed that he stopped going to the party after corruption took its toll and the party became politically inactive. His opponents, however, argued that he also partook in corruption; that the real reason he stopped his activism in the party was because he was marginalized due to his Islamism. As the legal decision regarding the FP neared, his son Fevzi (a tall, nervous, rowdy teenager) turned on their small, old radio. He started manually tuning in to various channels and waiting.

We took our chairs, which were by the window during our earlier conversation, and brought them close to the radio. When the court decision was being announced, Fevzi leaned tensely against the column next to the radio. Mahsun was moving his fingers nervously. After the decision, they stared at each other unbelievingly. They were frozen for a moment. Finally, Fevzi stood up hitting his hands harshly against each other and saying, "They *did* shut it down!" After him Mahsun also stood up and started shouting: "The generals are making the decisions. Everybody else is a figurehead. We should rebel against this decision. We should raid the police station." Fevzi said that they would shoot people in response. Mahsun replied, "Nothing can happen without paying the price." Despite this heated rhetoric, Mahsun knew such mobilization was not a possibility. He then criticized the FP, which was not ready to pay any price:

The leaders of the FP are also to blame. This closing is the punishment of God: after the party overtook the municipalities, everybody started to pursue material gain [*kemik davasına düştü*]. The people who were poor before we had the municipalities now have cars!

Fevzi added to his father's comments that there used to be seminars and lessons in the headquarters of the party for the youth. Now all those had come to an end and everybody was minding their own business. Together with pointing to the loss of legitimacy of the Islamist party as an organization, such complaints also showed that those who wanted to radicalize the party were more and more marginalized within the movement. Corruption and deradicalization fed each other in a vicious circle, pushing people away from the Islamist party.

With some Islamists marginalized and others corrupted, nobody was left in 2001 to protect the FP against court decisions. Worse, with the committed pushed to the side and the rent-seekers in positions of control, no active popular will could put pressure on the party to make sure that it remained unified. After the FP was shut down, the organized attempts to establish an Islamist political society came to an end.

As there was no sign of a deeply organic articulation between the party and its followers in the aftermath of its closure, pragmatists and liberals within the party sensed that they would not lose much by splitting off. Hence, the lack of popular action in favor of the FP interacted with corruption, bourgeoisification, and deradicalization to encourage some to establish a new political party (indeed, a new movement with a new ideology). The establishment of the Justice and Development Party set the ground for thorough changes in Sultanbeyli's civil and political societies, discussed in Chapters 5 and 6.

ISLAMIC AND SECULAR AUTHORITY IN THE DISTRICT

Second in importance to the political party, sociopolitical groups, and street protests, struggles between authority figures were crucial to the making and unmaking of Islamic political society in Sultanbeyli. Before 2002, authority in the district was founded under the auspices of Islamic political leadership. While hegemonic secular authority in Turkey is generally based on the routinization of Atatürk's charisma, combined with some bureaucratization and a modicum of traditional authority, the importance of the elements in this combination reveals much local variation. In conservative regions like Sultanbeyli, official authority is based more on the marriage of bureaucratic authority with traditional authority. The Islamist movement needed to mobilize religious charisma against this combination in order to institute dual power. But first, a leftist or secularist alternative to the usual conservative combination needed to be pushed out of the way so that Islamist authority could become the main challenger.

The Defeat of the Left Alternative

Since the Turkish Left had rejected traditional bases of authority, it either needed to build a solid organizational structure or depend on national or local charismatic figures to establish any authority in Sultanbeyli. Partially due to the timing of the district's founding, neither of these was possible. Radical socialist organizations such as the Revolutionary Left (Dev-Sol) were active in the region at the end of the 1970s. Leftist activists walked from door to door trying to organize the youth and the workers. There was some initial success, and the youth especially started to join these organizations. However, the military intervention in 1980 cut this experience short before it could become rooted.

This left only the establishment Kemalist parties as representatives of the Left. While in many other parts of Turkey Kemalists were partially associated with the left populist Republican People's Party (CHP) of the 1970s, Sultanbeyli's newly urbanizing residents had one-to-one relations with the CHP and other Kemalist parties when these were moving away from social justice platforms. In the 1980s and 1990s, parties such as the Social Democracy Party (SODEP), the Social Democratic Populist Party (SHP), the Democratic Left Party (DSP), and the CHP no longer provided trustworthy leadership and no longer promised welfare in a convincing way. They based their platforms mostly on being against conservative religion, which did not resonate well with pious Sultanbeyli residents. They were not well organized, while the Islamic parties had women's and youth commissions, ballot box observers (müşahits), and neighborhood units everywhere. They no longer opposed the system but only centered on opposing the Islamists. During the governmental and metropolitan rule of the SHP, there were crises, hunger, drought, corruption, and unemployment in the district, which all left bitter memories among the residents. Finally, Sultanbeyli residents (like most other people, including social democrats) disliked the CHP leader Baykal. When Bülent Ecevit—the charismatic center leftist leader of the 1970s—led the Left at the national level, a

center left party was able to get an important portion of the vote in Sultanbeyli. In the 1999 general elections, the DSP got 10.41 percent of Sultanbeyli's
votes.[14]

Apart from the situation in the district, the dismal state of the Left nationwide resulted in many conversions. Especially among the workers who had
come to Sultanbeyli not from the countryside but from other Istanbul districts, I encountered many converts from the Left. Korhan, a fifty-two-year-
old retired public worker and a union organizer, summarized his change of
heart in these words:

> In the past, we expected social justice, redistribution, and sharing from the
> CHP. We used to say: "Labor is the most elevated [*en yüce*] value. But we could
> not see these in the CHP. We saw only corruption and favoritism. I made up my
> mind after a district congress in Şişli, where I was among the founders of the
> SODEP's district branch. Even though I was a prominent member, they kept
> me along with other union organizers out of the room in order to have their
> non-union delegate elected. I quit the party and remained nonaffiliated for a
> while. I was searching for something. Once I saw how the RP [Welfare Party]
> municipalities worked, how the RP raised the wages of workers and officials
> when it was in government, and how it distributed clothing, food, and educa-
> tional funds, I became an RP member. They honestly applied social justice.

Korhan's narrative exemplifies how workers with a social justice concern
abandoned the leftists and joined the RP in the 1980s and 1990s. While many
like him who were leftists in the 1970s lost their reasons to remain so, most
Sultanbeyli residents who had direct experiences with the Left only after 1980
never had any reasons to become leftists in the first place. With only corrupt
and exclusive bureaucratic organization and no local charismatic figures, the
center left wing of Turkish political society had no chance of offering the people of Sultanbeyli material and emotional connections to authority figures.
Ecevit, the final card of the center left as a charismatic figure at the national
level, had become the prime minister in 1999 of an ineffective, impotent, and
corrupt nationalist coalition government, which put an end to any remaining
identification with leftist authority figures.

Islamist Populism and Dual Power

Due to the defeat of the leftist alternative, the struggle regarding authority
figures in Sultanbeyli was shaped around a conflict between the conservative

(center right) tradition and Islamism. For the conservatives of the district, Adem Ülker—the headman[15] of Sultanbeyli between 1984 and 1988—was the ideal authority figure. Ülker had a long beard and usually wore a skullcap, baggy pants (*şalvar*), a plain shirt, and a cardigan. He was a physical engineering graduate and had worked as a teacher before going to college. After college, he went into distributing and marketing liquefied petroleum gas (LPG). After that, he became a manager in car firms. Before Ülker went into the LPG business, he wanted to sell "white goods" (household appliances). But his customers would need to pay in installments, as most people would not be able to afford paying up front. He wanted to get a *fetva* (religious decree) for such a payment plan (which would require involvement in *faiz*), but his *şeyh* (who was one of the prominent Sufi leaders of Turkey) did not decree the needed fetva. He gave up. So, even the pro-establishment founders of the district were deeply pious and were actually more religiously correct when compared to the Islamist authority figures who were to replace them.

Ülker was the Motherland Party's (ANAP) candidate in the 1989 elections, and he lost to the Islamists. He was proud of his influence in the district and argued that he lost the elections because of electoral manipulation. "Everybody respected me. As the headman, I got everything done. This was possible because I had an engineering degree, and officials listened to what I said." Ülker differentiated himself from other past and current authority figures in the district by emphasizing his technical education. His understanding of Islam was mostly based on making the community more moral and beneficial to the country (in terms of education, economy, etc.). He did not emphasize Islamization. In short, rather than a charismatic figure who focused on mobilization and his ties to the masses, Ülker was a conservative whose legitimacy was based on traditional Sufi ties, professional identity, and bureaucratic capability. In line with the conservative tradition in Turkey, he integrated his Sufi identity with the market and the state. Traditional Sufi communities and merchants of the district supported Ülker in the 1989 elections, and even those who shifted away from the ANAP later remained sympathetic to him, as he was both an Islamic conservative *and* had good relations with the state.

With Ali Nabi Koçak, Sultanbeyli's mayor between 1989 and 1999, the bases of legitimacy shifted. The Islamist party used to receive around 60 percent of the votes when he was the leading figure, and this ratio dropped almost to 40 percent after he was replaced. Most construction workers and unemployed or semi-employed people in the district still venerated Koçak in 2001 and

frequently referred to his long, Islamic beard and unending charitable activities. The background of the old mayor suggested there was much more to his
popularity. Koçak went through years of official religious education under the
aegis of the Republic to finally become a *müftü* (religious jurisconsult).[16] After
years of official service as a müftü in a provincial town, Koçak settled in Sultanbeyli and quickly became popular due to his religious arbitrating power.
His identity as the müftü did not only attract religious populations; it also instituted a religious legitimacy structure competing with the state's legitimacy.
Below, he narrates a turning point in his career as a political figure:

> Before I was elected, people did not go to the court, but invited me as a müftü,
> and we solved the problems with fetva. . . . After my first election, the people
> from the Black Sea and the Easterners got into a fight. The men from the Black
> Sea had their women shoot a man from Erzurum[17] because he seemed to be
> from the Republican People's Party, but supported the Welfare Party in the
> elections. That day the gendarme was expecting fifty dead. But we intervened.
> They objected and said they would demand more soldiers from İzmit. "Don't
> do that, leave it to me, the people trust in me," I said. "Just give me the people
> inside as a trust, and I will deliver them in the morning." They could not be-
> lieve it. But I took the injured one and the women who had fired the rifle, I
> collected the young and the old, and that night we reached peace. Let alone any
> deaths, there was not one person wounded. . . . It then continued like this. Even
> when a man was going to divorce a woman, he came to the municipality.

In line with the Turkish-Islamic ideology of the 1980 coup, local state authorities such as the gendarme left some bargaining space to religious authorities
when they could not resolve issues. Yet, since religious authorities were more
successful in arbitrating at the popular level, this broadened their space of action. People, especially those from conservative regions, tended to shift to
working with religious authorities whenever this was possible, since secular
law still lacked the aura of normality that religious law had for them, and (in
the case of Sultanbeyli) also because the nearest court was still two hours
away at this time.

In Sultanbeyli, however, it was particularly to the former müftü with his
officially sanctioned religious authority, and not the other religious authorities in the district, that the majority of the people turned for intervention in
times of crisis. Even though there were plenty of men with a fuller grasp of
Arabic and a history of more intense religious education in the district, not

that many people made use of them. Being a product of the secularist state elevated Koçak above these competing agents. Another major reason why Koçak was so widely supported was his position in the land market. He was a real estate dealer as well as the municipal mayor, which allowed him to sell and distribute land in the way he wanted.

When combined with the political currents in the 1980s, the interaction of these forces had the unintended consequence of turning the local municipality into an institution of dual power: The municipality acted as a court and welfare state and also organized wedding ceremonies and other traditional celebrations. It distributed coal, clothing, and food to poor residents. Due to the informality analyzed in Chapter 4 and Koçak's special position in the land market, it was also able to distribute cheap land to poor residents. Since the residents saw Koçak, as well as the local municipality as an institution, as the main actor behind these deeds, they nicknamed him "Robin Hood."

Nevertheless, a certain move interrupted Koçak's rise and attracted a severe reaction from official circles. In 1996, a military unit in the neighboring region Samandıra erected a statue of Kemal Atatürk in the middle of the main boulevard, which immensely disturbed the Islamist shopkeepers and residents of the area. Koçak relocated the statue to a remote neighborhood park of the district. This was perhaps a premature move, a too-early attack on the institutionalized charisma of the founder. Doğu Silahçıoğlu, the commander of the unit, responded by storming the district with tanks, and re-erected the statue. Koçak could have become a charismatic hero if he were to prevent the re-erection, but (due to the way the RP had developed as a nonviolent party) he had no armed forces to oppose those of the military. Following the event, even the local headquarters of the Virtue Party (FP) turned its back on Koçak. When he ran for member of parliament in the national elections of 1999, the FP first listed him in the fourth rank in the first region of Istanbul. But then it dropped him to the eighth rank, where he had no chance of winning. Most people in the district thought this happened because the party wanted to give a message of peace to the state. Koçak reacted fiercely to this interpretation when I brought it up during our interview in 2001:

R: When I asked around why you were hindered, people said this happened because you were on bad terms with the state.

Koçak: I was not on bad terms with the state! Is Doğu Silahçıoğlu the same thing as the state? . . . I am statist, I am in favor of the state. The state has to develop so that the nation can be freed. The state has to make the nation develop. It has to be a guide. If the nation leads and the state follows, nothing can be done.

In 2001, even when talking about his opposition to the state (his attack on one of its central symbols—the body of the founder), Koçak translated his action by arguing that he was only attacking a person, a peripheral commander, not the state itself. He tried to make sure that his resistance did not endanger his nationalist and statist credentials. Here I use "statist" in the sense of one who emphasizes the security and existence of the state over the welfare and rights of citizens. Statism in Turkey goes hand in hand with nationalism, as most people see a strong state as a prerequisite for a strong nation. Used in this sense, rather than in the narrower sense of Kemalist etatism (which also encompasses the idea of a dirigiste economy), statism is a common ideology in Turkey and cuts across ideological differences like Kemalism and Islamism, and Left and Right. Statism in political society thus constitutes one of the strong links between civil society and state in Turkey. Whereas the liberal attack on this ideology gained some ground among professionals and businessmen in the 1980s and 1990s, tradesmen and the working class mostly remained statist.[18] Therefore, Islamists, Kemalists, and right-wing nationalists in Sultanbeyli all battled over who was really statist and whose statism was bogus. Koçak also tactfully balanced his Islamism and attack against the system with a strong dose of statism. Despite that, the political downfall of Koçak started after the statue incident, never to stop. The FP finally replaced him with a mild figure (Yahya Karakaya) during municipal elections.

Yet, the amalgam of conservatism and opposition, religiosity and nationalism, statism and resistance against the state embodied by Koçak—his seemingly inconsistent but ultimately imaginative articulating power—allowed him to retain his status as one of the most popular political and religious men of the district by 2001. This mix especially appealed to the supporters of the FP, a party that was moving more and more toward blending Islamism and nationalism, and opposition and loyalty. The secularists still saw Koçak as the supreme threat. But he had his Islamic detractors too. According to many Islamists and conservatives, Koçak was very authoritarian. He could not stand opposition. He did not even allow people he did not like at the party headquarters. Conservative merchants supported Yahya Karakaya, believing that even though he did not have much ability, he could work with a team. Even some of those who had come to the district to build an Islamic state supported Karakaya at this point, as they started to believe that Koçak was a "capitalist" hiding behind religion but really working for money.

Karakaya (1999–2004) of the FP turned out to be a failure. A longtime Islamist activist and a top leader in the district RP, he replaced Koçak as the mayor after the Islamist party shifted to the center. However, Karakaya was mostly ineffective as an administrator. During his municipal rule, no major problem of Sultanbeyli was resolved and there were more allegations of corruption. Worse, there were rumors about the mayor's personal life. Ultimately, the national (secularist) press disclosed a videotape displaying the mayor with prostitutes. Karakaya argued that the tape was a farce. Whatever the truth, the scandal reinforced the emergent belief that Islamists could engage in corruption just like the secularists and partially dispelled the aura of sacredness around the movement. Also, unlike Koçak before him, Karakaya was a publicly silent figure who neither propagated the Islamic cause nor defended his policies as the mayor. He was the only Sultanbeyli mayor who declined to do an interview with me.

From 1989 onward, Koçak's bearded pictures had become the symbols of Sultanbeyli at the national level. Yet, even at the local level, Erbakan's charisma mattered more than Koçak's, and it was the charismas of both figures combined that integrated people to the municipality. FP supporters had a deep commitment to Erbakan and almost deified him. For example, a middle-aged librarian who was one of the top organizers of the FP's youth branch said:

> Erbakan did not need fame, because he was noticed as early as when he was an engineering student in Germany. He was so successful that he was one in a million. He is the most important person after Sultan Abdülhamid [the Second]. If they were to demolish the whole world and give him the chance, he could rebuild it with God's permission. He is the person who started all Islamist organization in the world. He is both a man of science and a man of state.

This deep love for Erbakan reinforced commitment to Sultanbeyli, as Erbakan's family had land in the region.

Erbakan was also revered because he was connected to the deceased *şeyh* of the İskenderpaşa community, Mehmed Zahid Kotku. Some believed that Erbakan established the Milli Order Party upon his order. Some even held that before dying, Kotku had convened all Sufi leaders and ordered them to obey Erbakan. As the story went, the şeyh was crying, but it was "as if blood were coming out of his eyes rather than tears." Despite this alleged Sufi support, the RP's relations with the Sufi communities in Sultanbeyli were muddled throughout the 1980s and 1990s, and Sufis frequently complained that Erbakan had replaced party for community. In short, from 1989 onward, the conservative authority structure instituted by the regime and symbolized by Ülker (bureaucratic authority bolstered by traditional authority) was challenged by charismatic religious authority (itself supported by traditional authority and serving bureaucratic authority). Because of the ambivalence of the RP itself, it was unclear whether Koçak's and Erbakan's authority acted as a link between society and dual power (an emergent Islamic state) or a link between society and the existing secular state. The Justice and Development Party (AKP) would later resolve this ambivalence.

As already stated, not all pious sectors were happy with this challenge to conservative patterns of authority. While some merchants wanted to revert to old patterns of conservative authority and replace figures like Ülker for Islamist authority figures, other religious people foreshadowed what was to come in a few years and battled for the full rationalization of authority. The confrontation at a teachers' meeting demonstrates how some residents fought for this. During a meeting of teachers at my school, secularist and religious teachers were discussing who was to blame for the current condition of the schools. Hulusi, a secularist teacher, said that everybody in Sultanbeyli, especially the administrators, were hypocritical. Teoman, a young, religious teacher with a carefully trimmed mustache and neatly combed hair—a native of the district and a quite ambitious man—objected to Sultanbeyli's identification with its administrators:

> The administrators and the people have no relationship. The former are
>   appointed by central authorities.
> Hulusi: The administrators of the municipality *are* elected and native.
>   *They* are the most hypocritical ones. They appear to be [pious]
>   Muslims, but do not fulfill the requirements of being one.
> Teoman: You are a teacher. Why does their Muslimness concern you?
>   Let's not bring up our sub-identities.

An Islamist teacher intervened at this point and said, "When you come here, you think that these men are Islamists, and therefore they should be honest, but then you see that it's not like that." Teoman criticized this approach too and said, "You should not think like that. You should not make decisions about your job based on those criteria." Teoman, usually a smiling and mild-tempered man, angrily asserted here the autonomy of administrative and religious realms. He reduced religion to a secondary identity that should not disturb the efficiency of administration. He emphasized that nobody should base his or her career choices on religious and ideological grounds.

This intervention was in line with Teoman's political outlook. Teoman came from the Turkish and conservative part of a mixed eastern Anatolian city where Kurds and Turks, Sunnis and Alevis, Islamists and nationalists live side by side, quite often in tension with each other. The Sunni Turks of this city, which constituted a significant community in Sultanbeyli, mostly upheld the Turkish state and nationalism in their struggle with the minorities. Even when they sympathized with Islamism, they tended to interpret it in a nationalistic and statist way. Islamists coming from this city were in the forefront of de-Islamization at the end of the 1990s, even though most of them had fought for Islamization a decade ago. They thought that Islamism had started to threaten security, order, and stability, thereby harming the state. Hence, religious identity had to be subsumed under national identity in order to block this trend. Teoman and his circle of friends (though they sided with the Islamists some years ago) propagated this understanding of Islam in the district and also tried to transform Sultanbeyli along these lines.

Teoman and his friends were not alone in the district in battling against the charges of corruption (which had started to weigh heavily on the shoulder of religious Muslims) through "rationalization" and "secularization." Especially professionally oriented pious Muslims of Sultanbeyli had started to think that technical, economic, and administrative issues should become independent of religion and function according to their own rules. This neutrality, they argued, would benefit everybody in the district. This rationalization in the authority structure would seem to confirm the classical insights of Weber ([1904–1905] 1992) regarding world-historical rationalization in the case of Islam too. However, I point out that we need to interpret changes in the authority structure in the overall context of hegemonic struggles. Rationalization in Sultanbeyli was not a spontaneous process but one possible result of the secular state's dismantling of dual power. This rationalization took hold decisively only after the AKP systematically organized it (see Chapter 5). In other words, political society is the key to determining which type of authority is going to reign at the end of the day.

The State Between Civilizing Mission and Legitimacy

The legitimacy of Sultanbeyli's official authority figures depended on bureaucratization combined with tradition (e.g., male authority). The routinized charisma of Atatürk was mostly in the background (as pictures in each office, a controversial statue, sculptures in the yard of every official building, etc.). Pious residents were mostly silent about Atatürk except when asked explicitly, and then they only reproduced memorized official discourse unbelievingly. Aside from the previous mayor's attack, Atatürk symbols all over the district were in harm's way. For example, one early morning, some unknown residents dumped a pile of feces over the Atatürk sculpture in a schoolyard minutes before the teachers arrived.

As the normalization of the regime could hardly be carried out through identification with the Atatürk cult under these circumstances, official authorities emphasized integration of squatters into bureaucratic structures through civilizing them. The crux of the difficulty of this civilizing project was that there was no determinate unit upon which the state could enact assimilation. As I will also demonstrate while discussing the urban-rural opposition and the differentiations between communities (in Chapter 4), the residents changed self-definitions according to who was listening. For example, when speaking to a "civilizer" (a public official or a secularist activist), immigrants behaved "civilly," and hence like an *Istanbullu*—a word that literally means "from Istanbul" but connotes an urbanite who has thrown off the yoke of rural tradition. When among his fellows, the immigrant criticized the urbanites relentlessly.

Public education was one of the sites where the difficulties of hegemonic interventions could be observed. Teachers frequently contrasted Sultanbeyli to the villages they had taught in and complained about the lack of consistency in the former's "culture" when compared to the latter's. Fehmi, a young, blond, tall primary school teacher who had taught in a village of Kars (a small eastern province) for several years, talked to me about this contrast during the annual registration process of public schools, with the expression on his face turning slowly from nostalgia to disgust:

> The education in Kars was much better. The classes were smaller. The teachers were more respected, and their demands were realized. Even [Kurdish] chil-

dren who came to school without knowing how to speak Turkish learned how to read and write in a short period of time. Besides, there was culture in Kars. This district, by contrast, is cosmopolitan.[19] A culture will be established here too, but maybe in fifty years. The students who come to school are neither, say, *Karslı* [from Kars], nor *Istanbullu*. Say one was born here ten years ago. When he goes to his village they call him Istanbullu, but when he comes here he isn't Istanbullu.

Just after Fehmi completed these words, one of the middle-aged shopkeepers of the neighborhood who had several children at the school entered the administrator's office. Fehmi told him that there had been an earthquake in Erzurum that morning. The man told Fehmi that he had not heard about it and did not seem to care much. Fehmi picked on him in a joking tone:

An earthquake has occurred in your hometown, and you don't know about it!
The shopkeeper (smiling): No, *this* [pointing his index finger toward the ground] is my hometown. I have severed all my ties with Erzurum. I don't even go there. I am now Istanbullu.

Most residents of the district were aware of the stakes involved in being pigeonholed into places of origin and resisted such classification by claiming Istanbul, even though they identified themselves primarily by their places of origin in other circumstances. Teachers and other officials were not content with such an embracement of Istanbul, since they thought that being Istanbullu comprised a set of manners that these residents lacked. They sought maximization of control through instituting their definitions of being an urbanite and withholding legitimization from hybrid ways of attaining Istanbullu status.

How, then, did official authorities have any basis of legitimacy, if indeed they did? The urban and civilizing policies of states are, more often than not, far from being monolithic (Evans 2001). The Turkish state also displayed fluidity, in that it did not always operate as an external civilizer. It had contained a lot of conservative and religious people in its low- and middle-level civil bureaucracy, especially during the rule of center right governments. These officials acted with a more refined understanding of Turkish society, even though they also were the carriers of the civilizing mission. During the national census of 2000, for which I worked as a surveyor, I encountered an official from the district branch of the Department of National Education who exhibited this in-between position while lecturing to the surveyors (who were charged with collecting information at people's homes) about the details of their duties. He told the surveyors how to avoid alienating the people during this already unpopular activity:

> Rules are important. Don't behave as if they don't exist. The people will beat you up on the spot. . . . In Anatolia, daughters-in-law and children are not permitted to talk. In this case, get the information from their elders. Don't force them to talk. . . . You may see retarded children chained and tied up. . . . These are normal things.

Here, an old, conservative man of rural origin with personal knowledge about popular practices "enlightened" educated, young people of urban origin about proper comportment in the houses of Sultanbeyli. He introduced to them a different understanding of normality, which was alien to their modern imaginary. His aim was making the census more efficient and useful to the state, as conveyed by one of the first sentences that introduced his lecture to the young surveyors: "The state relies on you [*devlet size itimat ediyor*]." If the state was not experienced as a totally alien and hostile entity at the popular level, it was mainly through this normalization of the civilizing process by upwardly mobile actors of popular origin. Conservative officials were better at linking society and state. Secularist hegemony owed a lot to them.

Education was another factor that built a bridge between the state and the squatters and helped the secularist project become partially hegemonic. In spite of all the negative values attributed to the present education system among religious people, which even kept some families from sending their children to school, most inhabitants of the district believed that a strong public education would solve problems of districts like theirs. It would make people qualified for high-income jobs, educate students who would eventually build hospitals and roads, and raise responsible people who would pay their taxes and abide by the rules. In 2001, education, which the people of Sultanbeyli perceived to be the precondition of "modernization," was expected from the state. In the eyes of the residents, education was indispensable not only for development but also for the making of masculine subjectivity. Kerim, a construction worker, evaluated his father's and his own fatherhood with reference to education:

> One of our neighbors in the village had only one child, he was well-to-do, but he gave his child away as a shepherd. We were six brothers, my father was

poor, but he didn't give any of us away as servants. He said: "you are going to read." . . . I am poor too. But what would become of my fatherhood if I couldn't ensure that my children are educated? If his children are bright and willing to read, a father has to sell his jacket if need be, and make them read.

According to Kerim, one of the most certain ways of proving adequate father-hood was making sure that one's children are educated, even if this took the whole fortune of the family. In such ways, the residents of the district combined some communally upheld expectations (strong male identity) with opportunities and meanings that the state provided. The Turkish state, after all, had partially gone beyond acting as a solely external agent by naturalizing the value of mass education.[20]

Despite these meaningful relations established between the people and the state, the feeling of alienation from the latter was more immediate in Sultanbeyli. The corruption of state officials had as much a role in this alienation as the partial externality of its civilizing project. Inhabitants especially complained about corruption in public education. They thought that a considerable portion of any kind of payment they made for the education of their children went to the pocket of greedy and dishonest school directors. Neglecting the larger picture, where neoliberalization had removed immense funds from public education, they put all the blame concerning the worsening of education on the representatives of state. Whatever the root causes, the observable decline in the quality of public schools was a final blow to the legitimacy of the state in poor neighborhoods.

In such a condition of weakened legitimacy, the existence of dual power could indeed lead to a revolutionary transformation. Official authority, therefore, ultimately had to sweep away the remnants of dual power by force. The local government started to be more effective after the military intervention of 1997, when Ankara appointed a rigid secularist governor, Hüseyin Eren, to replace the old governor, who had more or less good relations with religious people. The new governor aimed at reducing the number of women roaming the boulevards of the district in *çarşaf*. In Turkey, the secularists perceive the çarşaf that some conservative women wear as one of the primary signs of religious reaction against secularist reforms. This type of dressing, though generally much less popular than other conventional and contemporary forms of covering,[21] was relatively normalized in Sultanbeyli. The çarşaf had come to symbolize the district in the mainstream secularist media and was one of the new secularist governor's main targets.

In his public speeches that I attended, Eren targeted religion in general and Islam in particular as impediments to national development. He served alcohol at receptions during national holidays to which officials working in the district were invited. Religious teachers and other observant public and municipal employees stopped attending these receptions, where they thought their behaviors (such as not drinking alcohol) were surveilled and noted. Eren assured that secularist dress and appearance codes, such as shaving the beard, were strictly applied also at the local municipality. During his time in office, the police started to control the mosques more vigilantly. One secularist center right newspaper named him "the super governor" and praised him for closing down seven Kur'an schools that provided education to 3,300 children.[22] Whereas religious people complained about the official pressure in the district, some nonreligious residents spoke approvingly of the local governor for having lifted the communal pressure that they felt especially during times like Ramazan, the fasting month of the Muslim calendar.

It was in this environment that Teoman and others like him could carry out the rationalization of authority, laying the foundations of alternative patterns of authority that were only going to be decisively established with the emergence of the Justice and Development Party. It should again be emphasized here that political society is this interlocking of political leadership with authority figures—only their interaction and joint activity can link citizens to the state. While in the 1990s the Islamists were on their way to constituting an alternative political society and preparing the citizens for an Islamic state, by 2000 this political society was partially tamed and partially demolished, intensifying the organic crisis (a severing of civil society from political society) already in place since the late 1970s.

ÜMMET OR NATION?

Turkish nationalism was a strong link between society and state, a mainstay of political society in Sultanbeyli. Islamism needed to break or redefine this link in order to denaturalize the Turkish secularist system. While internationalist Islam found only ephemeral adherence in the district, ethnic differences proved mightier challenges to national integration. To many, internationalist Islam mixed with some nationalism seemed to be the best response to these divisions.

In Between Islamic Internationalism (Ümmetçilik)
and Nationalism

In the 1980s, university youth especially were exposed to transnational sources. They ardently read Pakistani, Egyptian, and Iranian authors such as Mawlana Mawdudi, Sayyid Qutb, Ali Shariati, and Murtaza Mutahhari. Their radical ideas created an Islamist youth that defined itself as "unbending" and "unrelenting," and this masculinity also attracted right-wing nationalists to Islamism. The references and the historical examples these young people used to define themselves started to be transnational (e.g., the massacre against the Muslim Brotherhood in Hama became a part of collective memory). Qutb and Hasan al-Banna were revered and followed because they sacrificed their lives. A former radical Islamist said: "Actually, we did not understand much, but we were convinced by their rhetoric that their message should be spread immediately."

In the 1960s and 1970s, Islamists used to condone Americans because they were "pious Christians" fighting against the "atheist Russians." The most common Islamic phrase they used to refer to Americans was "people of the book," which meant that they were among the followers of one of the textual, monotheistic religions confirmed by the Kur'an (Christianity, Judaism, and Zoroastrianism). In the 1980s, however, the anticommunist sympathy for the United States was replaced by an Islamist critique of imperialism.

The youths started to see local religious leaders as outside of Islam, as they were a part of the "system." They defined Turkey (as well as all existing Muslim countries) as *dar-ul harp*. Turkey's role in the Middle East as a U.S. ally played an important role here. The university youth also condemned the local, national, and sectarian references of traditional religious leaders. They saw themselves as above national and sectarian belonging. An ex-radical pharmacist described those days in the following words: "Sunni and Shia, we did not distinguish between the two. That Shariati was Shiite was not at all important for us. What was important was his perspective on the struggle." Some radicals believed that people who died fighting in the Turkish military were not martyrs, as they did not die for God. So they rejected military service along with government posts. This discursive attack and passive resistance against the most revered institution in Turkey was the apex of *ümmetçilik* (Islamic internationalism).

These radical ideas found adherents for a time, but groups that went as far as giving *beyat* (an oath of loyalty) to Khomeini were marginalized. Moreover, it was mostly college graduates who propagated this nonsectarian, non-nationalist line in the district. Especially (but not exclusively), Kurdish and young college graduates emphasized Islamic internationalism. Yet, among people without university diplomas only certain tenets of this radicalism were accepted. The ordinary Islamist never stopped holding the interests of Turkey above the interests of other Muslim countries. The only exception to this pattern was primary school and high school graduates who had worked in Arab countries and had been influenced by Arab Islamic movements.

Kutsi's story demonstrates the persisting influence of Islamic internationalism and the sympathetic doubts it raised. Kutsi was a pensive man who weighed his words and talked calmly. He used to be the disciple of a religion teacher at a public school in his Black Sea hometown. Sometimes the teacher came to Sultanbeyli to spread his ideas and renew his networks. His followers praised him for converting many Marxist-Leninists to Islam, being the person who knows Shariati the best in Turkey, and raising "true scholars" out of simple village imams. He was imprisoned for six months because he established an Islamist association in his hometown. Now he had 250 followers. Kutsi quit being a formal member because of his reservations: "There is one point on which I don't agree with him: he has *beyat* to Khamanei. He receives a lot of support from them." Iran kept on spreading its revolution through such networks. Teachers like this one were primary sources for the reproduction of Islamic internationalism. However, their influence was more and more marginalized in the district.

Organizational marginalization was not the only process that sidelined Islamic internationalism. Along with the absorption of radicals into legal parties, Islamic internationalism was also absorbed into Turkish nationalism. Milli Outlook parties had always been nationalist parties, but, with the absorption of radicals, they indecisively zigzagged between emphasizing their nationalism and integrating more internationalist demands. At several turning points, more nationalist-oriented Milli Salvation Party (MSP), Welfare Party (RP), and Virtue Party (FP) members in Sultanbeyli strayed away from these Islamist parties. On the other hand, radical groups failed to attract a lot of people precisely because of their internationalism, and even residents under the influence of Islamization opted for mainstream Islamist parties. Veli was an example. He never joined any radical Islamist groups "because of the love [he] felt for [his] country." Radicals were distributing pro-Kurdish and pro-Iranian journals for free in the 1980s and early 1990s. He read these for a while, but as they encouraged "non-national" feelings, he stopped reading them. Despite the fact that his whole family was nationalist, Veli joined the RP because it was more Islamic. While his family members missed some regular prayers, he started not to miss prayers after this change. Nevertheless, he remained a nationalist and resisted *ümmetçi* (Islamic internationalist) currents in the party.

Nationalist Critique of Exploitation

Even criticisms of the system were based on nationalist ideological elements, such as the expectation of an independent and developmentalist state. Though (corporatist) developmentalism was gradually dismantled in the 1980s, expectations based on it had become part and parcel of common sense. A lot of the criticism of informal workers focused on aberrations from an independent and developmentalist state, as if this were a universal norm. The integration of hopes regarding social justice into nationalism also strengthened this ideology in Sultanbeyli, channeling potentially antisystem desires to the banks of official discourse. I encountered such hopes in countless conversations in teahouses, coffeehouses, the municipality, and party headquarters.

The absorption of potentially anticapitalist demands into nationalism went hand in hand with the search for charismatic leaders and integration into mainstream Islamist parties. Gökhan was a young man who had been active in the Welfare Party (RP) throughout his youth. He was a janitor in the municipality at the time of my research, though he frequently changed jobs. He had become involved in the party after he watched the propaganda tapes of an RP leader of the 1990s, Şevki Yılmaz. His beatification of some prominent figures within the Islamist party exemplifies how nationalist, antiimperalist, antipoverty, and procharismatic codes were deployed within the context of the Islamist movement:

> We Turks are all very productive people, but they always block us. Let me give you some examples. Before Erdoğan was the municipal mayor of Istanbul, the Social Democratic Populist Party had done everything to get precipitation. They had even imported rain bombs from Europe. After he became the mayor, Erdoğan went where he had to—he went to his creator and prayed for strength, rain, and prosperity, and God [*Rabbim*] did not let him down. . . .
>
> There are no limits to the underground wealth of Turkey. In my hometown [the Black Sea region], there are lots of forests, but the wood is taken from us and

used elsewhere. If they had processed it there, if they had invested in humans there, built factories for them, the abundant water of the region wouldn't be wasted. The Southeast [Turkey's Kurdish populated region] is like that too, with all its oil and other resources. If they had provided food, employment, and bread to the people there, there wouldn't be any problems. They say that a lot of factories suffered losses. No enterprise will suffer losses as long as you place faithful and honest people and managers there. . . .

When [the observant administrator] Veysel Eroğlu became the general director of İSKİ,[23] this institution was next to nothing, but today it is one of the select institutions of the world. . . . Another reality is this: In Turkey, they don't like those who do business. The foreign forces or someone doesn't like them. They want you to receive orders from the United States or Israel and they don't want you to move forward. If we can get rid of this disease, there won't be any problems. All of them will be solved. If someone had given trust to this country, the people of this country could pay these debts. . . . They would sell the bracelets of their wives if needed, but definitely pay the debts. It is sufficient that the ones who are ruling us be real men.

Gökhan believed that the abundance of underground resources and productive people and a few honest and faithful leaders, which he contended were already in abundance in the country, were enough to overcome all the difficulties Turkey was facing. If it were not for their blockage by imperialists, faithful people could pay all debts through self-sacrifice and save the country from poverty.

This emphasis on national resources and leaders kept under control by foreign powers reduces every kind of conflict *within* Turkey to the problem of imperialism. In this way, Gökhan (like activists of various colors using the same codes) was able to implicitly dismiss the Kurdish issue and guerilla warfare as artificial problems that would disappear once imperialism had gone away. Gökhan's emphasis on believing and God-fearing leaders was the primary characteristic that differentiated the Islamist discourse from other authoritarian discourses in Turkey (Kemalism and right-wing nationalism), which were all united by an emphasis on unused resources and certain types of leaders ready to process them. Rival discourses also reproduced the popular belief that the real reason Turkey could not develop was dependency. Finally, these discourses resonated with popular culture by assigning the struggle against dependency to charismatic leaders. Through all these combinations, the common sense criticism of poverty and anti-imperialism reproduced the desire for national unity and ruled out alternative discourses such as ümmetçilik. At this level, a resolutely nationalist political society seemed to be the best armor for the state. Ümmetçilik had weakened existing political society by consistent attacks, but it had not instituted an alternative vision and an alternative political society to successfully relink society and state. However, there was a more serious challenge to national unity than ümmetçilik.

The Turkish-Kurdish Divide

In spite of strong nationalist rhetoric, Sultanbeyli was not a united district. Divisions based on Turkishness and Kurdishness proved impenetrable. Kurds and Turks of Sultanbeyli generally shared in the visions propagated by the nationalist republic and its Kurdish nationalist opponents—Kurds as "separatists," Turks as ruthless oppressors—though religious feelings mitigated the harshness of these depictions. These visions were reproduced in the locality through recourse to everyday "evidence," such as the reluctance of Kurds to learn fluent Turkish, their tendency to speak Kurdish even in the presence of Turks, and their aversion to education (which was thoroughly Turkish nationalist). This division affected the formation of neighborhood networks and identities, to the degree that Kurds and Turks established their own coffeehouses and shopped at different stores.

At the school where I taught, Kurdish students sat in the back of the classroom. They usually did not participate in class and did not take the lessons too seriously. Most of them did not have the resources to. They came from poor families and did not have any expectations for a diploma. Some of them did not have a full grasp of Turkish (those who could speak could not properly write), which made it nearly impossible for them to get something meaningful from the math, history, or English classes, which were all instructed in Turkish. Teachers of Turkish origin (a majority of the staff) tended to neglect such problems. When I tried to bring up the subject, they usually changed the topic rather than arguing with me. Kurdish students especially had already started to organize into gangs, which were not common in public schools before the 1990s. The gangs were, at this point, not involved in large-scale crime, but there was already some prostitution, drug dealing, and fistfights. Among Turkish students too, these all spread with the strengthening of the Nationalist Action Party (a party enmeshed in gangs and the mafia).

The nonintegration of Kurdish students occasionally led to explosive situations. I was caught in the middle of one of these while performing monitor duty. As violence increased and quality of education decreased in public schools, policing violence has become one of the teachers' informal tasks. As a part of these tasks, teachers took turns to prevent trouble in the courtyard during the breaks. On one of my watches, a fifteen-year-old Kurdish boy came to the gate of the courtyard but could not enter as the gate was locked. He shouted out to the students angrily: "Bring the vice principal to me!" I went in to fetch the vice principal. As we came out of the building together, the boy took out a gun from his pocket and directed it at the vice principal, who was beside me and about one hundred yards from the boy. We were petrified. The boy then smiled viciously, slowly tilted his forearm upward, and fired in the sky. We then spent some time calming down the students who were screaming and wildly running around in panic. I later learned that the vice principal had caused this boy to quit school the year before I came to Sultanbeyli. I observed and heard similar situations involving Kurdish students especially during my first visit, but, unlike my second visit, none of these ended up in serious casualties.

However, tensions did not coalesce into a racializing conflict yet. This had to do with the way in which the conflict unfolded at the national level. Since the macropolitical strategies of both parties were more flexible than racist ones (e.g., the Turkish state mobilized feudal Kurdish networks in fighting against the Kurdish guerrillas, and the Kurdish national movement established various types of coalitions and links with the Turkish Left), local actors had the possibility of adapting multiple tactics with regard to their others. As elsewhere in Turkey, the Turkish majority in Sultanbeyli embraced Kurds who denied that Kurds were a separate nation and who did not think that they should have rights based on ethnic status. They would be spared this "tolerance" after 2003.

In the early 1990s, the Welfare Party was able to speak across ethnic divisions and convince some Turks and Kurds that ethnic identity was not relevant, mostly relying on the *ümmetçi* discourse it had partially integrated. However, state pressure and Turkish nationalist reactions from within its own ranks pushed the party to water down this cross-ethnic emphasis. Even though the Virtue Party was still able to moderate the friction between the Turks and the Kurds in 2001, inhabitants of Sultanbeyli no longer saw it as an organization that could bridge these differences. The Turks reacted against the employment of Kurds in the municipality, while the Kurds now saw the party as too Turkish nationalist. There was a glimmer of hope in the 1980s, but by 2000 Islamists had missed the opportunity to establish a new political society that could smoothly integrate Turks and Kurds and mobilize this integration for building an alternative state. By 2006, the ethnic polarization *within* Islamic parties would be much starker.

Based on Gershon Shafir's (1995) distinction between different forms of nationalism, one could argue that there was a recent (though yet incoherent and indecisive) shift in Turkey from "hegemonic nationalism," which seeks to assimilate minorities, to "corporate nationalism," which seeks to lock them in disadvantaged urban locations, restrictive cultural identities, and low-paying jobs.[24] This shift was a response to Kurdish nationalism, which was very effective in the 1980s and 1990s; the emergence of a Kurdish business elite; and the migration of millions of Kurdish peasants escaping from the civil war between the Turkish military and the Kurdish guerrillas (1984–1999), who now constituted competitors in urban markets. Islamism perhaps resisted this shift when compared to other popular ideologies but could not escape from its influence. This weakness constituted the underbelly of Islamism. Only successful organizational strategies and thorough institutionalization mitigated this weakness.

•   •   •

In conclusion, hegemonic political society in Sultanbeyli was no longer able to link society and state, but Islamic political society had also failed in this task by the end of the millennium. As the next chapter will demonstrate more fully, state, political society, and civil society were unlinked (partially as a result of Islamic activities), but existing Islamism had not found a way to relink them.

4 THE MAKING AND UNMAKING
OF INTEGRAL CIVIL SOCIETY

POLITICAL SOCIETY IS NOT SUSPENDED in midair. It is defined by its relations to civil society and the state. To refashion the whole political and social structure, political society has to re-create civil society. This is what Islamic political society concentrated on until 2002. An Islamized civil society, in conjunction with and under the guidance of Islamic political society, thoroughly reformed everyday life, social uses of space, and relations to the economy in these years. Yet, especially after 1997, it became clear that the refashioning of civil society in an Islamic direction was far from complete.

ISLAMIZATION OF EVERYDAY LIFE

Early on, an emergent religious civil society (networks of immigrants, kin, and merchants, as well as foundations, schools, conferences, Sufi communities, etc.) thoroughly Islamized the district. The Welfare Party was central to this process.

Life Before and After Islamization

Before the mid-1980s, Sultanbeyli (back then only a village) did not have a distinctly Islamic color. Hasan, a prominent merchant of the district, narrates a slice of life in the 1970s:

> In the wedding and engagement ceremonies of the *muhacır*, people drank *rakı* and danced. *Çengis* [traditional male dancers] were brought; they dressed up like belly dancers and danced, in the muhacır tradition. Nobody intervened. Actually, for the [non-muhacır] youth of the district, this type of wedding was more attractive. In the coffeehouses, until alcohol was banned,

people drank beer. People gambled. Everybody respected this, and nobody intervened.

Islamization would push all these practices to the margins in the 1980s. A forty-five-year-old university graduate with thick, dark hair and a rounded beard, Hasan saw what was to come later as an aberration from true Islam. Even though he was a deeply devout man, he did not approve of the zeal of the late 1980s and 1990s. Remaining in contact with but keeping a distance from all religiously conservative parties, he consistently preached moderation.

Until the first Kur'an school was built, the political division in Sultanbeyli was between the center left and the center right. This changed as a result of the interaction between rural immigrants from Erzurum and Muş (conservative eastern provinces) and the merchants, booksellers, and publishers from Tahtakale (a neighborhood on the European side of Istanbul) who migrated to the district at the end of the 1970s. These sectors started to become a decisive force with the building of the first Kur'an school, and they shifted from the center right to voting for the Islamists. The Kur'an school's foundation was laid around 1983 and its construction finished in the mid-1980s. This was the height of the Islamic politicization, and the key families of the district all sent their children to become *hafız* (one who has memorized the Kur'an) at this school. Kids from the surrounding regions (as far as Bartın, three hundred miles to the east) also came to this school for education. This institution was at the forefront of increasing religiosity. Informal, home-based Kur'an schools also spread around the same time. For most families of the district, their children growing up in the 1980s were the first generation to have any textual Islamic education. Textual knowledge was not a part of rural tradition, except for families like Vanlıoğlu, coming from a past of *medreses* (theological seminaries), who built the first Kur'an school. Kur'an schools, therefore, started to replace textual piety for folk piety, but only partially partook of more radical patterns of Islamization.

Along with the Kur'an schools, Tahtakale booksellers and publishers were quite influential in Islamizing the district. Whereas the Kur'an schools worked more on the ritual practices and textual religious knowledge of the rural immigrants, the Tahtakale booksellers and publishers combined this new religiosity with Islamic political consciousness. They attracted the new residents of Sultanbeyli, and especially their children, to the Islamist party. By 2000, many of the booksellers and publishers had left the district. Cevat, an old, tall man with a long, white beard, was one of the exceptions. Cevat had learned his Islam from a mystic scholar of the Black Sea region. He ran a bookstore in Beyazsaray (a courtyard of secondhand booksellers, the hub of the Islamic intelligentsia) for thirty-five years. He had joined many discussion circles in Beyazıt, Tahtakale, and Tophane, where the Islamist ideology in Turkey was forged during the 1960s and 1970s. He was one of the founders of the Milli Salvation Party (MSP). He came to Sultanbeyli in 1969 and purchased a plot of land with Erbakan. He left the MSP along with a contingent of nationalist-oriented Islamists at the end of the 1970s but kept on supporting the party from outside. He was one of the founders of the first Kur'an school. He had established a bookstore in Sultanbeyli too, but since there were no sales, he had to close it down. Even though he did not leave the district like the other booksellers and publishers, this experience resulted in disillusionment with Sultanbeyli: "If I had sold books of some other [secular] kind, I would not have to close it down. But then, what account was I going to give on the other side?"

Cevat then focused on giving lessons to men between the ages of twenty-five and fifty. The lessons were based on İlmihals (manuals for doctrine and ritual) and Hadis books. He did not know Arabic. Other than giving basic instruction about rituals and dogma, he also regulated social activities of the students. Together they found the poor, the widows, and the orphans of the surrounding neighborhood and helped them. Cevat explained why they did this based on the traditions of the Prophet: "According to the hadis, we are responsible for forty houses around us. So, we are taking care of those forty houses." He also found marriage partners for and arranged the wedding ceremonies of his students. When talking about his activities, Cevat did not tightly differentiate between religious and nonreligious activities:

> The community here is very ignorant. They really need a thorough education. None of them have ever followed an İlmihal. They do not know where to put their feet while praying. They pull up their trousers in the middle of the prayer. They itch. If they knew *fıkıh* [Islamic jurisprudence], they wouldn't behave like this. The hadis we teach also touches on daily issues. For example, I distribute candy to children. Then they go home, and they say "a grandfather with a long white beard has given me candy." I also love animals, and teach my students how to love animals. I always smile and teach my students to smile.

Cevat's activities exemplified the mainstream, nonradical Islamic activism in the district. Like the radical Islamists, mainstream Islamists emphasized learning based on written sources and integrated seemingly nonreligious aspects of life (loving animals, giving candy to children, wedding ceremonies, etc.) with religion. But, as opposed to the radicals, their understanding of textuality was based on İlmihal and jurisprudence and was fixated on the minute details of ritual performance. Again in contrast to the radicals, they had very close relations with the surrounding community

The Islamizing influences in the mid-1980s were not restricted to Tahtakale booksellers and publishers, the local schools, and the Islamist party. Prominent preachers came from the city center and gave sermons. Conversely, youth of the district convened together and drove to more central districts to attend Islamic conferences. Some of these youths radicalized and were no longer convinced that a political party was the way to go. Around the same time period, translated sources circulated heavily in the district and spread the radical ideas of Sayyid Qutb and Ali Shariati, among others. These ideas included a rejection of medieval Islamic tradition in the name of pristine Islam, as practiced by Muslims before the ("counterrevolutionary") Umayyad Empire; *tekfir* (excommunication) of all existing Muslim regimes, even of those that apply Islamic law; return to the Kur'an and the Hadis, at the expense of traditional theology and jurisprudence; rejection of obedience to anybody but God (combined contradictorily with revolutionary vanguardism); criticism of Sufism, which the radicals found obedient, impure, supernaturalistic, obscurantist, and inegalitarian; and a strong rhetoric of social justice and equality.[1] Starting in the 1980s, many young people were exposed especially to Qutb's extensive exegesis, *Fi Zilal al-Qur'an,* and his *Milestones.*

At the end of the 1980s, *tarikat*s (Sufi orders and communities) also started to organize. The more organized ones were the Adıyaman community, the Mahmud Efendi community, and the Süleymancıs. The İskenderpaşa community, the Rufais, and the Kadiris came second to these. The relations among these various Islamizing factions were not always peaceful. For example, there were tensions, even physical fights, between the Süleymancıs and the Islamist political party.[2]

In the general elections of 1987, the Islamists could not overcome the election barrier, as they received only 7 percent of the votes nationally. By contrast, in the 1989 municipal elections, the conservative rural immigrants, the booksellers and publishers, and the Islamic communities (with exceptions such as the Süleymancıs) all mobilized under the leadership of the party. Along with other election maneuvers,[3] this emergent bloc of Islamist votes gave the Welfare Party (RP) its first metropolitan victory.

By the late 1990s, radical youth mobilization had lost some of its force, and the major Islamizing agents were the political party, the schools, and the Sufi communities. Before the military intervention in 1997, four Kur'an schools were especially influential and populous: the central school, two schools belonging to the Mahmud Efendi community, and the other to the Süleymancıs. When I studied the district between 2000 and 2002, the more engaged residents learned religion primarily from these schools, the Sufi communities, and the RP, secondarily from the radical Islamist circles, and less so from officially approved sources such as the Directorate of Religious Affairs.

So, how did these Islamic institutions change an ordinary person's life? Nazife, an instructor at a Kur'an school, gave an example:

> People who did not even know how to pray came to Sultanbeyli. They learned how to pray after they joined our community. My sister-in-law, for example, was a woman who dressed revealingly [çok açık]. Then, she came here and saw the MGV's [Milli Youth Foundation] activities. She was especially interested in seminars about the education of mothers and children. She joined my *sohbet*s. After a while, she said that she wanted to learn the Kur'an and cover her head. I told her not to cover right away, and added that she has to understand why she should cover first. She reacted because I always talked about the virtues of covering in my sohbets. I gave her a translation [*meal*] of the Kur'an anyway and said, "first read this and then cover. You should at least know which verse tells you to cover." She eventually became a very good Muslim. I know a lot of people who have changed like this.

The seminars of the MGV (the semi-official youth foundation of the RP) were quite influential in the 1990s. These led many people to be practicing and veiled Muslims. However, these seminars did not only push people to practice religion and dress religiously. They also taught people to combine their rituals and dressing with textual knowledge and with motherhood duties. Sohbets played a similar role.

In 2000, Islamist activists still carried out similar practices through sohbets and seminars. The resultant religiosity was different from what conservative rural people practiced in their hometowns. In Sultanbeyli, ex-peasants (along with formerly secular inhabitants coming from other parts of Istanbul) learned how these practices were based on classical texts and how the totality of life had to be reshaped based on these texts. Ex-peasants also neglected many details about the movements, gestures, and rules of recitation during the prayer. They learned these from Islamic activists as much as from formal sermons and preachings in mosques.

Below is the account of Samet, who became more religious after he moved to Sultanbeyli, partially due to the religious and political inclinations of his wife's kin networks, which included the family of an Islamist neighborhood headman:

> I learned everything here. When I lived in Levent [in downtown Istanbul], I used to drink every night, or every other night. I saw a very different environment here. For example, there are no Tekel shops [government-controlled shops where alcohol is sold], beer houses, or taverns in Sultanbeyli. Also, family structure is very important here. My wife was not against alcohol formerly, but now she is. And she is against it for good reason. Maybe if she weren't, I would end up as an alcoholic, and I would die.

The positive evaluation of religious control was also linked to the imagination of the self as a weak being: most men thought that they were naturally inclined to lose control of themselves and therefore believed that some form of external limitation was warranted. Samet, for instance, thought he would not be able to withstand temptations of alcohol on his own. In sum, as people moved to Sultanbeyli, they became more observant, more knowledgeable about Islam, and more diligent about the sinful practices in their lives, while the district itself became more Islamic.

This collective (and contested) work on everyday life is similar to what Europe experienced during the Calvinist insurgency. Philip Gorski (2003) has shown that Calvinism's contribution to modernity was not restricted to a work ethic but involved self-discipline in general. In this disciplining process (the cornerstones of which included regular Bible readings and control over the individual's time), each controlled each, as the community believed it should eradicate even the appearance of sin in order to be a model. Similar to Islamists, Calvinists zealously advocated reform programs, popular education, and relief for the poor in order to build the ideal Christian society. They punished drunkenness, fighting, calumny, and social offenses. They also reunited couples, reformed abusive husbands, located missing fathers, rechanneled social offenders and orphans to work, and mediated disputes between employers and workers (19–22, 57–58, 63–67). However, the degree of disciplining prevalent in early modern Europe simply could not hold sway in secular Turkey, as religious institutions did not have the same exclusive domain over the bodies of their members. This lack of thorough control allowed ordinary people to resist religious transformation.

Everyday Resistance Against Islamist Interventions

Between 2000 and 2002, the resistance against Islamism worked on several levels. Mostly, it was in the form of not complying with the religious criteria Islamists put forth. Islamists of various orientations tried to convince the people that their version of Islam (including belief in the correct dogmas, intricacies about ritual, etc.) was the only sound one. Some went as far as arguing that those who did not support them or avoided attending their activities might become unbelievers. In particular, the members and leaders of the Virtue Party (FP) always told people around them to come and pray with them when the call to prayer was read. This happened in teahouses, the municipal building, workplaces, and party headquarters but not in government-controlled sites like schools.

The people resisted this type of enforcement simply by going on with their lives, beliefs, and practices as they imagined they had always done. Samet (see previous subsection) was someone who formerly led a moderately religious life but who also engaged in non-Islamic activities like drinking. In Sultanbeyli he faced many pressures to lead a more religious and political life, but he did not submit to these totally:

> If I pray, fast, give my alms, [the FP activists] can't force me to attend their meetings. I will go if I please. If someone is praying, and the other is not, he can't say "come on, you pray too," he shouldn't say it. *Her koyun kendi bacağından asılır.*[4] On occasion, an FP activist comes and says "let's go pray." My friend is next to me; maybe I am ashamed [of being forced to pray]. I perform my prayers, I fast, and I also perform my Friday prayer. . . . Well, actually, I don't perform my regular prayers [*vakit namazı*]. Would I not? I would. I can't because of material distress. If I didn't have material distress, I would perform my regular prayers too. I have nothing in my pocket, I don't have a job. What can I do?

Popular materialism, which scholars have shown to be one of the basic dimensions of traditional popular religion,[5] allowed people to give this commonsense message to the Islamists: first fix the economy, then we can pray. Workers thus used poverty as a shield against total Islamization. Samet was Islamized enough to quit drinking, fast, and perform the Friday prayer, but he still did not pray regularly.

Other residents coming from more conservative backgrounds adapted more easily to the cultural environment dominated by Islamism. Praying regularly had indeed become the norm in the district, and many people behaved accordingly between 2000 and 2002. However, the majority of even these people were more reluctant to abide by the dictates of radical Islamism. In the 1980s and early 1990s, radical circles were more influential. Their understanding of religion was based on total submission to Islam and the rejection of any authority but God. They demanded that people become well-versed in the Islamist literature. They wanted the community to mobilize its resources to fulfill the understanding of religion that radical publications propagated. Remzi, a young, calm, and strongly built technician from eastern Anatolia had participated in the *sohbet*s of these circles when he was young, but by 2000 he had given up the attempt to become the Muslim they demanded. A high school graduate, he found radical texts incomprehensible:

> Understanding Qutb is very hard. For example, *Milestones* is an incredibly hard book, not everybody can understand it. One has to have a good Kur'anic education. . . . *Fi zilal al-Qur'an* influenced me especially in its emphasis on staying away from *riya* [hypocrisy], and giving all your life to the cause. I actually forced myself a lot. Maybe this is not good, because not everybody can be like Qutb. I then tried to keep a distance from it, rather than totally engaging. After that, I was content with what I knew and tried to live accordingly, and stopped trying to learn everything and live the perfect Islamic life.

Many people eventually rejected radical Islam because it was too demanding on their lives.

The secularist resistance to Islamist interventions crystallized as rejecting the hierarchy based on religious knowledge altogether. One winter evening in 2001, we were sitting in a coffeehouse with Zafer, a maintenance worker at a public university who was also an active member of the secularist Republican People's Party. After Mükremin—a construction worker who was previously on the center left but who became religious and started to attend adult education courses provided by imams—came, he slipped a rosary into Zafer's hand and asked him to hang this in his house. Zafer tested him by asking, in a half-joking tone, what the ninety-nine beads of the rosary meant. Mükremin told him that these expressed the *esma-ül hüsna,* which denotes the ninety-nine beautiful names of God. "If I asked you to count these now, you would not be able to," said Zafer. "I would count them, but you would not understand. Come in your spare time and I will tell you," was Mükremin's answer to this challenge. In this conversation, which the participants carried out in a half-joking manner, there was in fact an invitation and a competition. Zafer subtly belittled Mükremin's born-again religious knowledge and implicitly rejected his invitation. During the following months, each time we met, Zafer complained about how his ex–fellow activist Mükremin was spending his life acquiring futile knowledge. Secularist activists like Zafer, secularist officials, and ordinary people influenced by secularism avoided invitations to religious knowledge by arguing that secular education is much more important than religious intellectual formation. Even though a minority, many people in the district remained unconverted to a religious lifestyle.

Hybridization of Islamism

The hybridization of everyday life, rather than the outright victory of any single party, was the result of these interventions and resistances. What I was able to observe between 2000 and 2002 was this hybrid outcome rather than a purely radical Islamic, purely mystic, or purely secular district.

This hybridization was observable at individual, group, and institutional levels. As previously mentioned, Remzi (the technician who found Qutb difficult to understand) had engaged in radical circles but ultimately distanced himself from their most radical preachings. In his interview with me, he summarized the thinking that eventually prevented him from embracing the antimystic teachings of the radicals:

> I heard the discussions about mysticism, but I did not believe the criticisms. For if mysticism was wrong, it would disappear. It would not persist this long. It couldn't have so many followers. The mystic leaders are great people—they are revered and they are remembered with compassion. So I reasoned that mysticism is right.

However, Remzi also told a story about his suspicion-ridden engagement with a mystic community after he quit radicalism. During one of his visits to the *dergah* (community center), people were eating from a cauldron. It was a really big cauldron and created the impression that the food inside did not decrease. One person said, "This cauldron never gets empty." Allegedly, this was because of the mystic leader's *keramet* (miracle worked by God through a person). But Remzi had seen the back entrance of the *dergah*, where bread and meat were delivered in trucks. He told this to the other followers. They got very angry and criticized him. What he wanted was to "enlighten" these people so that they could stay with the community after the *şeyh* passed away. He once joked about this "plan" and said "I am educating myself so that there will be qualified people who can replace him." They again got very angry, as the *şeyh*'s death and his replacement are not things to be taken lightly. So, even though Remzi had joined a mystic community after his rupture with radicalism, aspects of the radical critique of mysticism had stuck, which made him work toward the rationalization of his new community. When that failed, Remzi eventually quit the mystic community, too. He ultimately joined a circle of ex-radicals who read the most current Islamic publications and discussed the latest ideas circulating in the Muslim world. The unintended consequences of radicalism were thus variegated: involvement in radical Islamic political society had not severed Remzi from participation in non-Islamist civil society, but it still thoroughly transformed his way of relating to such civil society.

Orhan, a neighborhood imam and an ex-radical, demonstrated another aspect of hybridization. He exemplified the balance-seeking attitude of many Islamists in Turkey who had become critical of the appeal to reject religious tradition in favor of the basic classical Islamic sources. He had flirted with these ideas when he was an undergraduate but finally became critical of them. He still respected radicals such as Qutb, but he thought that radicalism was not the way to go.

Although a young man in his thirties, Orhan was one of the most admired imams of the district. As an appointed imam, he officiated in one of Sultanbeyli's outer neighborhoods. He was at the same time pursuing graduate studies at a theology school. Every weekday, he took the bus to central Istanbul for class. He had worked as an imam in his own village too for a short time.

The residents of the area credited him with attracting more and more people to regular and Friday prayers thanks to his flexible approach. Mükremin (mentioned above) started to frequent the mosque after listening to his sermons and then ended up taking religion lessons from him. The imam before Orhan used to openly encourage people to vote for the Welfare Party in his sermons. People said Orhan's superiority was in avoiding such divisive remarks. However, this did not mean that he was apolitical: rather, he was "nonpartisan" (avoided affiliation with any specific party) yet quite political. I witnessed that in many of his sermons he attacked the rulers of the country who did not go by the holy book and held them responsible for the social and natural calamities Turkey experienced (e.g., the financial meltdown in 2001 and the earthquake in 1999). While decidedly calm and appeasing in his one-to-one interactions, he could get quite excited and angry in his sermons.

Orhan's home, which was a few blocks away from the mosque, was frequently visited by residents who sought religious advice. They usually came after the regular prayers, sat in groups in his living room, and listened to him patiently while he answered their questions. His guests, most of whom were primary school graduates, also borrowed books about religion from his wall-to-wall library after getting advice on specific issues. In one of these conversations, Orhan responded to a question about radical Islamists' protests against the veiling ban in universities, during which radicals held up the Kur'an and chanted Islamist slogans:

> The return to the sources was thought of as a solution but it itself became a problem. Certain things started to be ignored. We should return to the book and to the sources, but also to the real and to the objective. We have cultural realities peculiar to us. However, I do not mean that our national culture should shape religion. . . . Today many Muslims recognize the veiling problem as a religious problem, but from days of old it is our cultural heritage. . . . Our mothers and sisters are veiled. How are you going to solve the veiling problem? Some are going to say this is a religious problem, and this is correct. But we shouldn't forget that this is also our cultural reality. If you make the veiled girl's mother cry while you are trying to make her continue education, you cannot solve the problem. Most people have seen veiling from their mothers, and they don't do it in a strictly religious way. But the mother will defend the headscarf in such a way that she won't uncover her head even if you chop her head off. When we are trying to solve the issue by returning to the book, or when we are in the position of solving it as a state, we have to act in accordance with our own realities.

Whereas radicals proposed a defense of strict religious principles, some former radicals like Orhan found this impractical. They preferred a defense of traditional culture, which they defined as a composite of religious and cultural (ethnic, civilizational, etc.) elements. They found this more practical: for example, it was easier to defend and spread the veil as a national-religious tradition and characteristic rather than as a solely religious dictum.

At this juncture, the main ideologues of the Virtue Party (FP) had shifted to this position and were defending the veil in this way on television and in their newspapers, but their messages were not always this clear. These Islamists were walking a tightrope, since their position could easily be assimilated into the nationalist, conservative line of action that codes religion as an aspect of national identity. Therefore, Orhan was very careful to not espouse a nationalist line of argumentation ("I do not mean that our national culture should shape religion"). Nevertheless, as the slippage at the end of the quotation (framing the state as "we") suggests, he could not avoid sliding to conservatism, as he depoliticized religious issues and made them a matter of cultural "essence" and invited the state to intervene for the resolution of such problems. On the one hand, this strategy was more flexible, since it articulated ethnic and civilizational as well as religious discursive elements. On the other hand, it tended to merge Islamism with the nationalist state and invigorate the hegemonic structure instead of strengthening an Islamic counterhegemony. The shift from radical Islamism to mainstream and hybrid Islamism was a defense mechanism in a political environment where debate and struggle had become impossible because of the military intervention in 1997. In sum, in 2001, many former radicals sought the solution to the problems of Islamism by hybridizing it with traditionalism and Turkish nationalism. Islamic political society changed unevenly and had difficulty in keeping up with the pace of such changes in civil society.

Another trend in the district was hybridization with consumerism. After the military intervention in 1997, many of the radical networks did not evaporate but became less influential and less committed religiously. Some of these went into business together. Others remained as circles of friends. Ali, for example, did less religious readings, even though he retained many of the friends he had made in the previous decade. He was a short, brunette, jocular, energetic, thirty-five-year-old hardware dealer married with two children. His circle included construction workers and shopkeepers of his age. They still hung out together, but instead of reading religious books they were more likely to play games, watch films, or surf the Internet—an activity that did not always end up in religious Web sites. I spent a lot of time with Ali and his friends during my stay in Sultanbeyli. While they enjoyed political and religious discussions, they did not invest a lot of time in them. They prayed together only occasionally (though they did not miss Friday prayers). Some of my informants did their best to learn social scientific perspectives and tools from me, so that they could broaden their cultural spectrum and strengthen their religious and political positions. Others like Ali and his friends, however, were more interested in sharing my lifestyle: most of the time, we would watch television, surf the Internet (where my language skills proved helpful), or listen to (folk or popular) music. Whereas the former circles of informants were characterized by higher education and/or closer connections with religious parties and communities, those like Ali and his friends were less engaged in politics. Nevertheless, they still voted for parties such as the Virtue Party (FP) or the Great Unity Party and defined themselves as devout Muslims. They also regularly followed religious and conservative newspapers but rarely read books about religion. They did not see any conflict between this political position and their less religious everyday practices. For example, when I asked them about how they reconciled piety and flirting with women in virtual chat rooms, they were surprised and offended and refused to give any answer. Their hybrid religiosity defied any categorical thinking. The lack of penetration of such networks by political society added to the persistent organic crisis.

In short, by this time, the link between Islamic political society and civil society, quite tight at first in the 1980s and 1990s, had slackened. Islamism had lost its revolutionary fervor and its claim to transform the totality of everyday life. Yet, it had also become a naturalized part of many residents' identity and life, though it was merged and reconciled with nationalism, traditional religion, and modernity.

THE ISLAMIC PRODUCTION OF URBAN SPACE

In addition to the transformation of everyday routine, a hegemonic project also transfigures social space. In the early decades of the Sultanbeyli district, associational activities interacted with political society to create an alternative space. But this transformation of space by the joint activity of Islamic political and civil society reached its limits by the turn of the century.

The explosion of immigration to Sultanbeyli in the early 1980s was preceded by a period of legal ambivalence concerning the ownership of land, which set the context for the transformation of social uses of space. Several legal cases that remained unresolved for more than twenty years attested to the lack of clarity concerning what proportion of the village was public land and how much of it was private. The ownership of the private parts of the village was also dubious. Even before the huge wave of immigration during the 1980s, several plaintiffs and defendants had started to parcel their land and sell it for relatively cheap prices, as they were unsure about the future of their holdings. Such parceling gained pace after the construction of the new highway that cut through the district began in the early 1980s. The construction of this highway, which created expectations regarding an economic boom, was also one of the decisive factors that caused the huge flow of immigrants to this particular region of Istanbul. While one fourth of the resulting district was constructed as a result of occupation of public lands (forests, treasury lands, and lake basins), the rest was built through the buying and selling of land the legal status of which was, and still is, suspect or blurred.[6]

The Making of the District: An Islamic Fortress

Why did all the religious communities, booksellers, publishers, and radical activists discussed in the previous section choose to operate in Sultanbeyli? Among other things, this had to do with Erbakan's charisma. In 1974, the MSP (Milli Salvation Party) had come to power as part of a coalition government. Emboldened by the new political configuration, Erbakan's brother and mother, who had been coming to Sultanbeyli during the summers, started to tell the people that this region was going to be a developing area, a highway was going to pass through it, and so on. Under the influence of this propaganda, religious publishers and merchants from Tahtakale started to settle in the district between 1974 and 1980. There was some leftist activism in the region at this time. After 1978, religious people also started to be active. They formed a teahouse. The youths built a library in this teahouse and read together. They gathered money among themselves and bought books from Beyazsaray. They did not play cards or gamble but instead discussed religious and political issues.

All Islamic circles, from the Sufi communities to radical groups, invited their comrades to purchase land in the district. These ties had an influence in the selling of land, too. Women were especially active in attracting relatives and co-locals to reside in the district by telling them that Sultanbeyli was the primary place of religious awakening. The word was spread as far as Erzurum in the east and Germany in the west, and many families bought land in the district without ever having seen it.

Erbakan invited more and more people to settle in the district by saying, "Sultanbeyli is today's Anadolu Hisarı," comparing the region to the fortress that the Ottoman state used to control traffic on the Bosphorus. During elections, politicians from the city center came and told people that the "system" was against Muslims and by just settling in this district people were resisting the system; the residents were "the heirs of the companions of the Prophet." Appeals to the impoverished were wedded to Islamic imagery. Koçak propagated that he was the friend of all the poor, everybody would have their own land and home, and he would not respect the law until this promise was fulfilled. He reportedly said, "I am going to give construction permission on every square meter on the earth." Koçak thus promised to liquidate hierarchy in social space while also distributing the land unequally: reportedly, bigger plots were given out to party associates and more powerful families.

However, some residents of the district were unhappy about the way Sultanbeyli was built as an Islamic fortress. Even the members of some Sufi communities argued that Koçak had done a lot of damage to the district by semi-legally opening it up to construction. Everybody bought cheap plots and so did the religious communities. This was one of the reasons for the Islamic concentration here. Another reason was the mayor's identity as *müftü*. Because of this, everybody grew Islamic beards. They gave Islamic names to their businesses such as Sünnet (traditions of the Prophet) Kiosk or Community Kiosk. The real estate dealers grew beards so that the mayor would do business with them. After the Welfare Party was shut down many shaved their beards. In other words, the Islamic color of the district, according to some, was partially based on stealth economic motives. More secular residents complained that (especially before the 1997 military intervention) Islamists tried to push those who did not live pious lives out of the district. The marginalization and subordination of pious people in secular parts of Istanbul was thus reversed in Sultanbeyli, at least until 1997—signaling that an Islamist hegemony was replacing the extant secularist hegemony. While those with party and Sufi community connections (and at least seemingly more religious lives) gained the upper hand in the district, Islamists at the same time naturalized the new hierarchy through the language of spirituality and faith-driven equality.

There were also radical Islamists who did not find Sultanbeyli Islamic enough. Among them was Yasin, the middle-aged Islamist shopkeeper whose transformation introduced this book. Yasin came from one of the established pro–Welfare Party families of the district. After graduating from an İHL (High School for Imams and Preachers), he worked in Saudi Arabia as a construction worker. He then found a job in the public sector in Turkey but decided to go into business after he had saved enough. His friends frequently visited his office in order to pray together and discuss the political issues of the day. They, like him, were all İHL graduates, but only some were businessmen. The others were teachers, hosts on Islamist radio channels, and local representatives of national Islamist dailies. All were critical of the district and of the Virtue Party that controlled it, which (they thought) was too submissive. Yasin criticized both the party and the district as follows:

> The Islam in Sultanbeyli has no peculiarity. That Islam is different here is only propaganda. There is nothing exceptional. Whatever you have in Anatolia, you also have here. People are not conscious. Everybody still obeys parties, religious orders [tarikat], and religious communities [cemaat]. They worship human beings. Nobody says, "Let's read the holy book and live according to it." You cannot come across anyone who knows the book [Kur'an] and the traditions of the Prophet. The Islam here has only one advantage: It holds people together in a place that has so many differences. If you take that away, everybody will be on each others' throats.

Living up to his own criteria, Yasin regularly read the basic religious sources (the holy book, books on the lives of the Prophet and his companions and on religious jurisprudence, etc.) and discussed these with his friends. They also collectively worked on improving their Arabic, in order to develop a more "conscious" understanding of Islam. Crucial in this associational endeavor were those who had pursued degrees in theological universities (in Turkey or abroad) after graduating from theological high schools. These latter mentored the others while refreshing their own knowledge of the language. Although he had been active in protests against the state in the 1990s, Yasin was now less interested in either mass outreach or party politics, as he was disillusioned by the people and the politicians of the district. As mentioned earlier, this detachment of Islamic political society from Islamic informal networks was becoming more and more typical of the district.

Islamists like Yasin were not fond of Sultanbeyli because it did not live up to their radical notion of Islamism in which Muslims follow nothing but the word of God and the Prophet—not even the parties, orders, and communities that speak in God's name, since they allegedly distort the holy message by mixing it with local and national "customs." Radicals like Yasin constructed their position through differentiating themselves from the "ignorant," "unconscious," and "Anatolian" believer. This type of Islamism was common among people like Yasin, who were İHL graduates, had worked abroad in Muslim countries, and were middle-class rather than proletarian or subproletarian.[7] While the overall Islamist rhetoric was based on abolishing social distance, a new intellectual Islamist elite thus distanced itself from the common folk.

Nevertheless, Yasin also praised religious life in Sultanbeyli since it had reduced the importance of the Turkish-Kurdish division. Islamists of Sultanbeyli argued that if it were not for Islam and the Islamist party, Kurds and Turks in the district and all over Turkey would engage in serious clashes. He had lately started to appreciate this aspect of Sufi communities in particular. For many radicals, Sultanbeyli was not the Islamic fortress it claimed to be, but it was still better than secular districts.

Body Politics and Spatial Symbolism

Islamist strategies manifested themselves in the articulation of bodily comportment with space. After the 1980s, Islamists both wore ties and took their shoes off in public places. In Turkey, the tie is one of the strongest symbols of modernity and Westernization. Before 1980, most Islamists did not wear a tie, which enabled hegemonic secularist sectors to portray them as backward-looking reactionaries, as they had associated Western dress codes with technological development and modernity. Appropriating the tie after the 1980s signified that Islamism now appropriated (what had come to be) symbols of Western modernity.

Yet, Islamists also continued to take off their shoes in public places under their control, which secularists interpreted as a sign of their persisting backwardness. In a well-distributed bulletin of the Sultanbeyli municipality published in 1995, the mayor Koçak was pictured in a photograph with four male visitors. In this photograph taken from an unusual angle, the feet of the men, which were deliberately included, catch the eye: The visitors do not have on shoes. Koçak, along with many other municipal functionaries, shopkeepers, and headmen of the district, always had his visitors take off their shoes. In Turkey, most people do not wear shoes at home. However, hegemonic sectors regard replicating this behavior in the public sphere as uncivilized, provincial, and reactionary. By taking shoes off in formal offices, Islamists signaled that their offices were not just offices, they were like home. Islamists argued that common people, who were usually treated degradingly in public offices because of their perception as ignorant and rural, could feel at ease in their offices—another discursive-spatial move to abolish social distance. They legitimated this practice further by emphasizing that they prayed regularly in their offices and therefore the floors had to be kept clean. What secularists saw as uncivilized and filthy, they reinterpreted as a sign of cleanliness and civility.

Another Islamist spatial strategy in the realm of leisure was a differentiation between teahouses and coffeehouses. The latter are places where men play cards and board games and drink tea. Teahouses, coffeehouses where men do not play games, exist also in conservative provincial towns. However, they are not very common in urban centers of Turkey. Small-scale pious entrepreneurs or religious institutions founded innumerable teahouses in the very center of Sultanbeyli, enabling Muslim men to associate without committing any perceived sins. Men drank tea all the time at these sites, just like in coffeehouses, but they also read conservative and Islamist newspapers, went to their prayers on time, spent the fasting month (Ramazan) together, and discussed political issues. Illiterate people also benefited from the collective reading of newspapers, and the less literate developed their reading skills by going through the pages of several newspapers every day. Activists from religious orders and the Islamist party frequently came to these teahouses to organize or agitate. In short, Islamism instituted a particular urban spatial structure that fed back into the movement and facilitated mobilization by providing new resources. These resources included informal groups that carried out collective reading of ideological newspapers, collective fasting, and political debates. Yet, perhaps more crucial was the production of new sites for agitation and organization (teahouses) in addition to mosques, which are usually the spatial focus of mobilizing activities all over the Islamic world. Islamic political society thus partially created its own civil society.

The production of spatial symbolism had both bottom-up and top-down sources. On one hand, restaurants, homes, workplaces, and other places built by ordinary residents, as well as wedding ceremonies and other rituals, were gender segregated. On the other hand, political leaders structured political meetings, rallies, and party headquarters around gender segregation to set a model for the residents—the refashioning of civil society by political society. Friday sermons frequently warned men about the irreligious sexual behavior in other districts. Below is a typical sermon given in an unregistered radical mosque in 2001:

Muslims forgot *shariah*. In Ümraniye, Muslims are employing women with miniskirts and sleeveless blouses in order to attract customers. But, there is no need to do business with unbeliever customers who would be attracted by these women. . . . Muslims should Islamize their surroundings. Islam is not a religion that can be restricted within the conscience; it has to organize life— in the workplace, in the apartment building, and in employing people.

Sermons such as this one were very influential during my first visit. One of the central goals of religious institutions was restructuring urban space based on the separation of the sexes.

The town square was home to a mosque, Islamic cultural centers, teahouses, headquarters of Islamic parties, and stores where Islamic paraphernalia were sold, along with gender-segregated restaurants. Nearby was the municipal building. The building's windows resembled mosque windows, and its roof resembled a mosque dome. Its color was green, a color predominant in the district. As in other workplaces in the district, workers and clerks at the municipality regularly prayed in the rooms where they worked. The employees of the municipality could see Sultanbeyli's main graveyard through their windows, which was intentionally placed there to remind them of death so that they would not engage in corruption.

The military intervention of 1997, which repressed Islamic organizations and parties nationwide, also decreased their activities in this particular district and closed down some of their sites of agitation, such as religious teahouses and youth organization centers. Especially important was the shutting down of the teahouse adjacent to the central mosque, which was the main organizing ground for Islamic communities. This military unlinking of Islamic political and civil society, however, had no positive counterpart, that is, the relinking of civil society and secularist state. This incapacity contributed to the persistent organic crisis in Turkey.

Land, Property, and Community

While the political party and Islamic communities were central in the migration to the district, so were co-local and kin communities. The interactions between these groups gave their color to Sultanbeyli. Residents of Sultanbeyli visited the municipal building to talk about problems they, their kin, or their co-locals faced. A few months before the general elections of 2002, an angry, poor-looking, retired construction worker with white hair, a thin, white mustache, and a villager cap came to the office of a municipal official in order to complain about the new development plan of the Islamist local municipality (the aim of which was formalizing the informal land structure in Sultanbeyli). His building was on Y Street, which the municipality had decided to broaden from five to ten meters. This new regulation necessitated that his garden wall and trellis be destroyed. He was very angry and tried to look determined, but he talked in a crying tone. He started shedding tears when talking about the places in his garden that were going to be destroyed:

> They are taking three meters of my garden. I am doomed!
> Official: Uncle, I can listen to your problems, but I am only an official. I can only give information. I cannot do anything.

The retired construction worker was getting ready to leave when the official interjected a final remark:

> The municipality should have given plots of land of equal size to everybody years ago. Yet we could not get accurate information from everybody about what they were doing with the land. But you are also at fault. Why did you construct buildings without title deeds? That was a risk. And you knew it was a risk when you were doing it. You either become rich or go bankrupt when you take such risks. Now you're paying the price. So tell me, who is to blame?
> Man: It's again the municipality. Why did it let us construct those buildings? Didn't it see us doing it?
> Official: The municipality was aware of everything, but they were firing officials who intervened. Once a man told the president that he had two hundred votes, nobody was able to touch his building.

After this, the tone of the retired man changed entirely. He was no longer crying. To the contrary, he started smiling and talking in a jovial tone:

> Now *I* have twenty votes. In fact, I have voted for every party, including the CHP [Republican People's Party] and the Nationalist Action Party. Then I stuck with a certain [Islamist] line. But because of this development plan, my line is going to change.
> Official (mockingly): Uncle, how could you vote for so many different parties? Who are you going to vote for after this?
> Man: Who I'm going to vote for now is evident and certain!
> Official: For the AKP [Justice and Development Party]?
> Man (with pride): Yes, that party!

The retired construction worker left the office with an air of victory, ultimately able to assert his political strength. This interaction raises a number of questions: What did having twenty votes mean? How could it transform a crying face into a smiling one? What did mentioning the AKP do for this performance? Why did these assertions add up to a perceived victory on the part of an ordinary resident?

Starting with the 1980s, the decreasing central (national and metropolitan) control on land allowed families, kin networks, and co-local communities to occupy land and build homes collectively without much meddling. While this was also true for most urban regions of Turkey, it was more so for Sultanbeyli, which became an urban region exactly when central control was decreasing. Such collective occupation and construction strengthened existing kin and communal ties. For example, family members who lived in different parts of the country gathered in Sultanbeyli in order to help each other occupy land and build residence. Protecting the newly built homes under the legal confusion summarized above also required the cohesion of community. In this context, phrases such as "I have twenty votes" became the cornerstone of everyday political discourse in the district. These phrases indicated the largeness of the occupying community, which was typically represented by a male elder, and asserted its strength. In the 1980s and 1990s, the Welfare Party (RP) controlled squatting during occupation, construction, and protection. This patronage system both secured the housing of the immigrants and the stable local power of the RP.

The interaction between the retired construction worker and the municipal official indicates that politics in Sultanbeyli depended on patronage, family, and land structure as much as on ideology and religion. Having a big family meant voting and bargaining power and therefore larger plots of land and larger buildings. Differences in the size of kin networks and patronage ties in time created hierarchies (based on real estate) among ex-peasants who had started out relatively equally. Men of the district also derived honor from this political and familial power. Masculinity was constructed not only through securing land and lodging with the help of big families but also through enforcing masculine honor in daily situations, as when the retired construction worker said, "I have twenty votes." When they could not protect their land, which amounted to failing to protect their family honor and masculinity, men felt that they were "doomed."[8]

Nevertheless, the trouble that informality created pushed the local municipality to formalize the land structure in the district. For this very reason, the officials in the municipality started telling the inhabitants that they had certain tasks and duties and could do nothing beyond them. "I am only an official. I can only give information. I cannot do anything," the response of the municipal official to the retired worker above, became a standard line.

Due to the informality of land markets and housing regulations, squatters tended to vote for the potentially most effective patron—that is, whoever was most likely to come to power in the next elections. This was one of the primary reasons why they shifted their votes so often and why toward the end of the first phase of my fieldwork they tended to vote for the AKP (which they correctly guessed would come to power in the 2002 elections). However, most squatters remained loyal to the Islamist party throughout the 1990s. In the words of the retired construction worker, they "stuck with a certain line" during that decade. The AKP's success, as we shall see in later chapters, consisted of severing the squatters from this line by using religion, patronage, and community ties: co-local associational activity was essential both to the making and unmaking of counterhegemony.[9]

This land, communal, and municipal structure also structured other aspects of urban space. Kin and co-local communities settled together in certain parts of the district. They preferred shopping from the businesses of their own co-locals. In teahouses and coffeehouses, they tended to chat with each other. During my first visit, the FP publicly approved these practices as long as the co-local communities were linked to each other through religious and political networks. The Kemalist parties (the Republican People's Party and the Democratic Left Party), by contrast, saw the salience of hometown communities as one of the major problems of the district and the most significant impediment to the urbanization of its residents, while they also covertly tapped into co-local communities for support. In sum, while the Islamists glorified rural and provincial belongings, the secularists wanted to keep urban identity hegemonic.

However, there were also people who warned me against taking the prominence of co-local identities as an unchanging characteristic of the district. An active member of the RP's women's commission argued that things were quite different before 1997:

Back then, co-local and kinship ties were not that important. I am from [the southern city] Adana and I traveled all around Turkey. When I saw people from my hometown, I was happy. But when I encountered people from the RP,

I embraced them with warmth and without reservation. Wherever I went in Turkey and visited an RP headquarters, they greeted me like their kin.

Some Islamist activists thus argued that party and ideological identity used to be more important than co-local identity. However, most people did not agree with this reconstruction of the past. This prioritization of party and ideology was either an idealization of the past, a phenomenon restricted to a handful of "true believers," or by 2001 most residents of the district sought to forget this sweeping ideological commitment. In any case, between 2000 and 2002, Islamic politics worked by articulating co-local networks to its project, rather than by excluding them.

BETWEEN RADICALISM AND THE MARKET

Unlike everyday life and social uses of space, activities of Islamic political and civil society regarding relations to the economy were never tightly integrated in the district's history. In its initial two decades, Sultanbeyli's Islamist activists were divided between an anti–private property radicalism and the market. The economic liberalization of the 1980s and the inflationary economy granted merchants and tradesmen the opportunity to make a lot of money quickly. The exploding land market in the district provided additional opportunities. Most of them adapted to this environment immediately and started to get rich. Others reacted to their appetite but also made use of some opportunities. The radicals of these two decades were in the purgatory between abundance and commitment.

Yaman's story demonstrates that, the peculiarity of Sultanbeyli notwithstanding, the "purgatory" experience was a national one. Yaman was born in a Kurdish province in 1960, though he came from a Turkish family. He attended an İHL (High School for Imams and Preachers) in another Kurdish province. Yaman became a Milli Turkish Student Association (MTTB)[10] member when he was fifteen and then an Akıncı (a pro-MSP youth activist) after he became a theology student. He had a network of friends during these years and their activities included going to theaters and writing Islamist slogans on walls. They gradually drifted away from the MSP. After the 1980 coup, they stopped writing slogans and focused more on reading Islamist books. These readings increased their sympathy for Iran. But they also started to visit Iran, which eventually dampened the sympathy. However, the radicalism thus introduced persisted for a while. He summarized the things they believed in back then, which he now called "utopian Islam," as follows:

A shariah state was going to be built. Everything was going to be like a rose garden [*güllük gülistanlık*]. Everyone was going to be like the companions of the Prophet. We longed for a simple life. Since we were coming from villages, we longed for that kind of life. We thought like communists. We believed that the properties of Muslims should be held in common. We used to say, "My money is your money, and your money is my money." Our motto was, "Property belongs to God." Of course, sharing was easy when none of us had any property. When we started to be involved in trade, all of this changed. Actually, had the state given money earlier, nothing would have happened. When we graduated in 1985 and became public employees, all this was forgotten. After I became settled, I went back to my friends one day. I had to help them financially. But this was very hard for me, as I had already attained a higher standard of living. I had to pay electricity, water, and telephone bills, and take care of my children and family. . . . We had developed [utopian] fantasies because of the Iranian Revolution. We were mesmerized ["*insan öyle bir cazibeye kapılıyor*"]. At that moment, we could even die for [an Islamic revolution]. But this enthusiasm lasted at most fifteen years.

At the end of the 1980s, Yaman taught religion at middle schools. He then became a shopkeeper. Before Yaman came to Sultanbeyli in the beginning of the 1990s, he had already moved away from redistributive radicalism. He attributed this radicalism to simplemindedness, peasant origin, and an irresponsible, unrealistic attitude emanating from youth. As in the case of Yaman, critical response to the market either took the form of bonding and sharing in evanescent informal networks (of friends, kin, or co-locals) or fighting for a complete transformation of the state. Formal and long-lasting associational responses to marketization were quite rare.

Fikret—a short, thin, fair-haired barber—was another ex-radical. He was born in the eastern Black Sea region in 1962. He graduated from an accounting program in the beginning of the 1980s. He then came to Sultanbeyli and started to propagate radical ideas. The Kur'anic terms for autocrats (*tağut*s), clergy (*belam*s), and the rich (*karun*s), which had entered the language of Islamists through the books of Ruhollah Khomeini and Ali Shariati, were central in his narrative. He now spoke of these in a detached tone:

Shariah for us was different from what people going to the Friday prayers understood. We wanted to get rid of *tağut*s, *belam*s, pharaohs, and, especially economically, *karun*s. We had no money back then. We were all floating in the air. We saw getting anything from the state, from the system, and from the other side as our right. We included all these in *harp fıkhı* [the jurisprudence regarding *dar-ul harp*]. Once you invoke *harp fıkhı*, everything is religiously licit [*helal*]. The property, wives, children, and life of anyone on the side of the system were seen as appropriatable. The traditional circles emphasized *çarşaf*, but the radicals wanted to enforce only the long coat [*pardösü*] and the veil. No women would be allowed to wander on the streets uncovered. The religious state, which would be built on the precepts of shariah, would expropriate the *karun*s. In its place, a free market based on principles of mutual help and common holdings would be established. We were influenced by socialism, but actually we denied everything. We didn't want to be communists either. We wanted to redistribute property, but we had no systematic program.

Shariati (who saw modern states, traditional Islam, and class differences as the main impediments in the way of an authentic Islamic life) was especially influential on Sultanbeyli's radical youth in the 1980s. Breaking away from traditional religion, they differentiated themselves from ordinary believers and mosque-goers. While imposing the veil on women, they reacted to some of the Sufi communities that upheld the *çarşaf*, which they thought unduly restricted their female comrades. However, the radicals were as vague, if not more, as the Welfare Party (RP) in their economic model. Unlike the RP, they combined the ideal of the free market, not only with a redistributive state, but with outright common property. Like the RP, they did not know how to reconcile their apparently contradictory principles. Again in contrast to the RP, the radicals had no overarching national organization or charismatic leader, which fueled their confusion and indecisiveness further. Fikret himself was prosperous in the end, became one of the prominent shopkeepers of the district, and started to respect the property of others. In 2001, he owned several apartments inside and outside of the district.

The discourse and longings of RP activists in the same decades were more modest. Yet, the RP also emphasized redistribution. Osman was a retired worker, exemplifying the concentration of the working classes among RP (and then the Virtue Party [FP]) activists (as opposed to students, professionals, merchants, and tradesmen among radicals). Born in 1950 in a Black Sea province, he was a primary school graduate. He had lost some of his hair, had a long brown beard, and usually wore baggy trousers. Despite his age, he was the most brisk and foolhardy activist I encountered in the district. He climbed up and down the stairs of the FP building at an incredible pace and worked for the party day and night. After he converted from the Nationalist Action Party to the RP in the mid-1980s, he devoted his life to the cause. In 1989, he came to Sultanbeyli to help his party organize. In 2001, he was one of the top administrators of the FP. He enthusiastically described the activities of the RP between 1989 and 1997 as follows:

> The rich of this district were all [pious] Muslims. We as the party asked them to help us so that our beliefs and cause would be predominant in Sultanbeyli. They gave their alms to us. That is how we could have these broad and paved streets. Our activities were all done in order to serve our faith. Around the idea of the Just Order, Kur'an schools and İHLs spread everywhere. During Koçak's era, there wasn't even one restaurant or shop that sold alcoholic beverages. Efes Pilsen [one of the main beer companies in Turkey] came up with a project of three billion [Turkish liras], but the mayor rejected it. In essence, the Just Order was taking from the rich and giving to the poor.

Workers with primary school diplomas constituted an important contingent among RP and FP activists, even though the top positions in the local party were typically held by merchants, real estate dealers, tradesmen, and shopkeepers, who were more educated. Most of these workers accepted the party's program of taking from the willing Muslim rich to give to the poor and to build infrastructure and schools. (Alms, they held, were to be taken from the nonwilling as well.) Unlike the radicals, a radical redistribution of property by force was not a part of their visions.

As the radicals moderated, they also started to join the RP. Their relations with the top administration were initially fraught with tensions. Around 1993–1994, the radicals organized to replace Ali Nabi Koçak and the RP's administrators. There were different accounts as to why. According to sympathetic accounts, they criticized Koçak for being "capitalist." This man "fed" (i.e., bribed) those around him in order to preserve his "kingdom." Moreover, there was a lot of money circulating in the municipality, and even people within the party were questioning what was happening. The administration was telling them that they were building Sultanbeyli's infrastructure with that money. But, according to the critical account, they were using only a small portion of that money for legitimate purposes. The rest of it was "going into people's pockets" (i.e., being used for personal enrichment). Since this money had no formal status (due to the informal status of land in the district), it was impossible to control where it was going. Even though the radicals were no longer completely anticapitalist, they were still somewhat critical of capitalism and were trying to prevent an unjust accumulation of wealth. According to the detractors, however, the radicals disliked Koçak because he did not help them financially. Their real aim was to get bigger plots of land. A man called Dumangöz became a candidate with the support of these radicals, but he lost in the party primaries.

Despite the abortive attempt, this political competition had significant consequences. In the process of participating in legal politics, the radicals became politically disillusioned and got engaged in construction, real estate, and other businesses. Consequently, they started to move away from their radicalism. But their initial participation also democratized the party: this was the first time a candidate was nominated from the ranks against the directives of the party hierarchy. Koçak's authority was no longer unassailable. There were thus two unintended consequences of the radicals' adventure with legal politics. Their participation paved the way for the liberalization of the party. It also further integrated radicals to the market and resolved some of their contradictions.

By 2000, there were still rhetorically anticapitalist radicals in Sultanbeyli, but none of them were politically active. During my first visit to the district, a deepening engagement with the market showed itself not only in the realms of trade and production but also in consumption. The desire for urbanite leisure time, apart from worship time and teahouse (or coffeehouse) time, was slowly emerging in Sultanbeyli. Though it was mostly university graduates who expressed this need in a self-conscious manner, high school graduates (or those among them who were materially secure enough to think about these issues) also wanted to have the opportunity to engage in activities such as eating and drinking in chic restaurants and cafes.

However, workers looked with astonishment at the recent attempts (by the municipality and by local and extra-local entrepreneurs) at building a district populated with luxurious cafes, restaurants, and stores. They silently protested the flowering of such places when they themselves were grappling with hard work and having difficulty in procuring the basic necessities of life. Veysel, a construction worker in his late thirties, complained thus about the construction of a fountain in the center of the district: "Look at what the municipality is dealing with when men like me are hungry." Though he was an active member of the FP, Veysel did not take this issue to the local leaders, as he had already been marginalized within the party due to his alleged sympathy for the Kurdish guerrilla group (the Kurdistan Worker's Party, or PKK). He was now cautious enough not to take any "disruptive" steps. There was no visible, public protest in the district against further marketization, despite discontent among workers. Why didn't the workers voice their dissatisfaction with marketization in Sultanbeyli and with capitalism more generally?

Lack of Popular Organization

The workers of Sultanbeyli were organized informally in kin and co-local networks, as well as in parties. Yet, as opposed to the tradesmen of the district, they had no unions or chambers of their own. They also had no organized impacts on the political parties of which they were members. Together with the informal structure of their sectors (mostly, construction and textiles), this disorganization emanated from various ideological and religious influences. Paradoxically, their informal organization in networks and teahouses reproduced their disorganization, through both providing resources and a meaning framework that rendered formal organization futile.

The canonical Islamic imagination of poverty, which is based on contentment (*kanaatkarlık*) and the rejection of the relevance of economic hierarchy, was widespread among the workers. Their interpretation of Islam, partially shaped by officially appointed preachers, exhibited both a criticism of lifestyles of the rich and an affirmation of the condition and lifestyles of the poor. The sermon of the imam of the central mosque during the days of the February 2001 financial crisis gives an idea about some central aspects of this imagination:

> What the poor and the rich have at their table is the same. Don't they eat the same cheese and the same olive? Their tables only have more ornamentation. And in reality that is not ornamentation but poison. Therefore, do not envy them in vain. Look, a very prominent scholar has said "I have been to so many graves of the rich and the poor. They wrap up the rich in shrouds, just like they do to the poor." I don't know if I could explain? The one who wants to understand will draw very beautiful lessons from this. I had once seen a gravestone on which was written, "He has taught in the Fatih Mosque [one of the largest mosques of historic Istanbul] for forty years." You see the gifts Allah grants to some of his subjects! If you are going to envy anything, envy this.

In this sermon, the imam both constructed a class position by treating the crowd in the mosque as a poor community in contradistinction from the wealthy and reproduced his own power by emphasizing that real status comes from religious knowledge, not from money and comfort. In short, religion in Sultanbeyli taught the poor to be content with their situation, despise the wealth and luxury of others, and spend their energies trying to gain religious status instead of wealth. This position contained the seeds of a critique of capitalism based on the lifestyles it produces, yet it also diverted the attention of the poor away from inequalities of wealth.

This interpretation of religion had a strong hold over the common sense of the workers, and it was quite frequently put to use in coping with inequality. For example, in a teahouse where old men occasionally glanced over newspapers, the conversation revolved around Cavit Çağlar (a Turkish politician who got rich through fraud), who preferred to stay abroad for some time in order to avoid imprisonment. Vahdet, a retired construction worker, commented thus concerning the news about the warrant of arrest for Çağlar:

> The man is rich, but he has no peace of mind. Now he won't be able to come here. He will die in Switzerland. Gaining *helal* [religiously licit] money is a different kind of thing. I would prefer the peace of mind and the happiness of the poorest man to such wealth.

The others at the table silently nodded. After a few minutes, Vahdet slowly but loudly read another piece of news about the possibility of Saddam Hussein having cancer. Then he added: "Look, the man is very powerful, but maybe he is going to die at this young age." The man near him contributed: "No one can remain in this world." These consolations worked as the reproduction both of a tradition that denied extreme wealth and power and of the acceptance of honest poverty. These men—who were not in a position to reap the benefits of the explosion in the informal land market in Sultanbeyli ten years ago, let alone have access to the opportunities for fraud enjoyed by Cavit Çağlar—made virtue out of necessity by denying what was already denied to them (corrupt wealth).

The most popular criticism of inequality among the residents of the district thus focused on financial corruption. Indeed, most workers thought that inequality in Turkey was mainly due to fraud and similar abuses. They had witnessed some people from among their own co-locals become rich in the big city through suspect methods. Stories about aged co-locals purchasing land illegitimately on the banks of the Bosphorus, constructing apartment buildings on the coast, becoming unbelievably rich, and marrying young women were widespread. Also influenced by the frequent media coverage of large-scale fraud, they thought that the other rich people in Turkey must have accumulated their lot through similar means. Quite often, while chatting in informal settings, workers judged that wealth in Turkey was totally ill-gotten and *haram* (religiously illicit).

Likewise, most construction workers thought that the wealth of the contractors (their bosses) came from suspect sources, not from the exploitation of their labor power. A sturdy, dark-haired, forty-year-old man with a thin mustache, Recep was among the hardware dealer Ali's friends (previously mentioned). As he worked day and night, he rarely participated in their Internet browsing and other activities. Although very critical of construction workers poorer than himself (whom he found lazy), he was also quite cynical about big business in his sector. He talked of them in his characteristically silent but tough tone:

> The man who comes from the construction sector cannot become a big contractor. He can at most do buildings of three to four stories, and he can do that because he has once worked as an apprentice [and is therefore experienced]. Those big contractors are politicians. They acquire their booty during the elections. The people of the construction sector can only feed themselves and those who work with them. . . . I don't work with contractors. You cannot find honest men among them. They employ people and do not pay them.

Instead of claiming a more just share of this profit, which was thought of as unjust, many construction workers chose to avoid working with big contractors to the degree this was possible. Consequently, they strove to run their own small businesses, in line with the petty entrepreneur ideology (widespread among the workers), which envisaged small capital as "cleaner" than big business. In other words, even when inequality was realized as illegitimate, construction workers tried to avoid it instead of organizing and challenging it.

Even though doing business was not a priority at this point as much as it would become in five years, this belief in the possibility of Islamic, just, clean business led some of the workers to dream about becoming small entrepreneurs. Halil was a middle-aged and rather pious construction worker. He spent most of his time in the central teahouse, where he pushed other people to observe religion more diligently so that Turkey could go painlessly through these troubled times. He believed that the 2001 economic crisis occurred because the leaders and the people of the country did not practice religion properly. He insisted that only about 5 percent of Turkey's population were true Muslims. The rest appeared to be Muslims but wandered around without ablution. Such uncleanliness invited disaster. The only way out was intensified religious practice.

Yet, this did not mean that Halil restricted himself to religious solutions. He worked as hard as he could and always tried to stay employed. He also had dreams of investing his small savings in clothing or shoemaking. He behaved as though he were not aware that his savings would not be enough for building a workshop (assuming that he gave me an accurate estimate). He constantly asked around about where to channel his funds, confident that one day he would get the right advice. He also believed that everything could be taken care of by working hard, that this could even terminate the crisis initiated in February 2001 if coupled with religious uprightness. If people had gathered together their "under pillow" savings, he reasoned, they would have both used their money wisely and created new working opportunities.

A restricted number of construction workers thus saw themselves as would-be "Anatolian tigers" (the popular label for religious, provincial entrepreneurs, who have gone into the market in the 1970s through combining the savings of religious people) instead of seeing themselves as laborers. They thought, in good Weberian spirit, that all the opportunities were out there, and all they had to do was work hard, have control over their *nefs* (desires of the flesh), be frugal, and think like an entrepreneur. As a result, they imagined conservative, religious capitalists as "one of us." There could not be a more thorough identification with actors of a different class. This imaginary identification, to the yet-restricted degree that it was successful, channeled the attention of the subproletarians to becoming more like those successful religious men and prevented them from engaging in organized activity against their poverty.

The lack of popular action had to do with the structure of the informal economy as much as with the religious and ideological influences analyzed above. One reason the dominant sectors were not challenged in Sultanbeyli, where informal methods of production prevailed, was the mutual empathy that existed between the employer and the employee. As boundaries between hierarchical positions were very fluid, especially in the informal construction sector, there was astonishing solidarity between employer and employee instead of conflict. Both parties experienced mutual empathy arising from insecure and ever-shifting positions in the process of production. In the following excerpt, Mirsat (a construction worker) narrated how the death of a relative (who was also a construction worker) as a result of a work accident was handled almost without friction and without appealing to a court:

> A lawyer told me to sue my brother's employer, as he had not insured my brother. But I said, "This is also a miserable man. He is a constructionist too. Did he do it consciously? No. Did he have something against my brother? No. Now, how can I sue him? If he has made my brother do his business, is this a crime? . . . Now, if I sue him, if I take three to five pennies, if I put him in jail, what will I have gained? I will have lost my humanity and personality! . . . I too employ others. The same thing could have happened to me.

In the construction sector, the "constructionist" label is used to refer to workers, petty subcontractors, and little "entrepreneur-workers" who do piecemeal work as freelancers and employ several people along the way. The common label reflects the fact that a lot of people shift quite often between these positions depending on the state of the economy and their market situation. Yet, in Sultanbeyli, the label "constructionist" also hid some inequalities endemic to mobility opportunities and created a semblance of commonality and equality in a sector where ethnic and sect minorities (Kurds and Alevis) were more often than not bound to remain as plain workers. In short, "constructionist" signified a contradictory class location, in the sense Erik Wright (1985) has used this concept, as well as membership in an imagined community.

Building on this code of commonality, Mirsat saw the employer of his brother as a fellow poor man and believed that he had good intentions, just like himself. Engaging in conflict under such circumstances was perceived as being inhuman and dishonorable. Mirsat's position in this situation was more conflict free than was usually the case, given his religio-ethnic majority status as Sunni Turkish and his ability to find work as a freelancer most of the time. Nevertheless, workers employed by people like Mirsat himself also frequently deployed the imagined commonality in a manner that rendered conflict and organization unlikely, if not utterly impossible.

Furthermore, since workers of Sultanbeyli hardly had access to the basic necessities of life, they could not reserve funds for activities other than subsistence. They were overworked and spent most of their time outside the district. They returned home extremely tired and unable to take any action in the district. The subordinate position of women in Sultanbeyli also prevented their wives from taking any action in the names of their families.[11]

We should add to the dearth of time and energy another factor that characterizes poor populations and distinguishes them from the formal working class: the higher costs associated with challenging employers. Ulvi, who was very vocal about the "oppressive" and "exploitative" nature of Turkish society, was also pessimistic about his power to change it. I had many long conversations with Ulvi, who was the uncle of my apartment-mate. Despite his demanding job, he was a rather skinny, forty-year-old man, but his gestures (and especially his darting eyes) glowed with energy. He frequently visited his nephew and during these visits told me at length about his experiences in his hometown, in Istanbul, and in the construction sector. In one of our long conversations about the plight of construction workers, he again voiced his resignation about any possible change in the construction business that would benefit workers. As I insistently kept asking whether nothing could be done, he replied:

> Ulvi: I could do nothing about it.
> R: You say your individual power will not be enough. But can't construction workers get together and do something?
> Ulvi: We live daily. [When my employer infringes on my rights,] I don't have the money to buy a ticket and go to court. . . . Just think, thousands of men wake up at six and rush to Bebek, Etiler, and other centers of Istanbul. Why? They are going to bring bread from there to the *varoş* [a poor suburb]. You go there, you do your slave business, and then you eat here. How can a slave do something against the big emperor? He won't even talk to you, he will say to the security guards, "Fire that man." The other man who works with you will also be worried. He will say: "Are you mad? Are you going to get me fired?" How can you resist? You don't have a chance.

These dire circumstances set off subproletarians from the formal working class, if not against it. My conversation with a twenty-four-year-old, right-wing nationalist welder demonstrates how the structural difference between these two constituents of the working population could easily be coded as a conflict of interest. Selami, a subdued man with a slight hunchback, had come to Sultanbeyli from an eastern city when he was sixteen. He summarized his experience in the district in one sentence: "I have suffered all the hardships of my life here." He had been very unhappy about the district throughout. When he learned that I was doing research about the district, he started counting all the bad qualities of Sultanbeyli. He further added:

> I was cheered up when I went to Polenezköy [a high-society region, for work]. I was depressed again when I returned. There is no hope here. All the celebrities are there. There's a lot of employment. There is no employment here.

He also complained about the typically highly skilled workers of the Confederation of Revolutionary Worker Unions (DİSK), whose strike banners he encountered on his way back to the district. Their wages of 700 million liras ($500) a month, and their dissatisfaction despite those wages, troubled him:

> I could do the same business for 250 million. Aren't we both human beings? Why are you taking so much money? Isn't this injustice? And they go on strike without shame! But now they are all working as gentle as lambs [because of the 2001 crisis]. All the strikes have stopped.

Selami's reaction to organized labor, though hardened by his right-wing nationalist ideological sympathies, was typical of the poor residents of the district. Instead of harboring hostility toward the bourgeoisie, many informal workers also shared Selami's wish that there were more bosses. (Yet, admiration for the luxurious life of celebrities was less rampant among other [Islamist] residents, due to the religious illegitimacy of consumerism.) Selami's appreciation of employment-creating entrepreneurs and his dislike of more well-off sectors of the working population made it rather unlikely for him, and for many other inhabitants of Sultanbeyli who shared his feelings, to unite with other workers in challenging (or even negotiating) any aspect of the system.

A final factor that prevented self-organization of the workers was the patronage mechanisms in Sultanbeyli. At least for better-connected workers, there was always someone in the neighborhood or the workplace to whom all complaints were addressed (in exchange for votes or other forms of support). They assumed that this person was responsible for solving the problems of the community. As seen in Veysel's case, this attitude precluded unmediated action against poverty. Veysel was a construction worker who had been deeply involved with the Islamist party in the past. He restricted his engagement in, but did not abandon, active politics after doubts about his sympathy for the Kurdish guerrillas marginalized him in the party. Whereas he had been someone who struggled for collective gains in the past, he was cynical about the influence of people like him on institutions. He still participated in Islamist rallies and political meetings but only irregularly. He was usually depressed, silent, moved slowly, and looked down when speaking. Veysel's lack of trust in any kind of self-organization or formal political venue was emblematic of the disbelief among the subproletarians in their capacity to challenge poverty.

The following exchange between Veysel, Hamdi (a center leftist worker in the formal public sector), and me demonstrates the depth of Veysel's indifference. The dialogue concerned the sharp and never-ending rise in school fees (a trend inaugurated after the liberalization of the economy in Turkey), about which there was a great deal of disquiet in the district. However, there was no popular attempt to organize this dissatisfaction and force the state to halt its project of getting more and more money from the citizenry for (constitutionally free) public education. Parents frequently cornered managers and teachers and complained about the price of education. This created a certain pressure on the schooling system, but authorities were aware that popular reaction would be restricted to such complaints. When I was sitting in one of the coffeehouses of the district with Hamdi and Veysel, the inevitable subject came up due to my position as a teacher of the district. Hamdi said, in an angry tone:

> If they are going to keep on getting money from us, they should change the constitution and write down "education is not free."
>
> R: This is not the solution. The state should put aside more money for education.
>
> Veysel: We cannot demand that from the state. I would not be able to explain [what my demand is]. Am I the same as a teacher or a director? You have read so much. Your demand would be more effective than ours.
>
> R: Individuals, whether educated or not, cannot succeed in doing such a thing by themselves. We can do this only if we come together.
>
> Veysel: Ah, you mean union? I participated in many strikes and protests. I never saw that do any good.

For a period of two years, this was the tone of our conversations with Veysel whenever I brought up the topic of self-organization or collective action. Among the workers of Sultanbeyli, there was almost a complete lack of trust in the potential for self-organization. Instead of dealing with problems through popular democratic methods, the general tendency was to find people of higher status and make them voice their claims. Such a strategy was both part of the personalistic structure of politics in the district and a mechanism that reproduced the powerlessness of the poor residents.

The RP had answered this need for mediating persons and institutions and promised to transform this personalistic mechanism into a political one. In other words, it had attracted people who expected patronage from the party to later transform them into political agents. Most workers, like Veysel himself, had first contacted the party through clientelistic connections and for purposes of procuring personal gain (most typically, employment and land). However, the party had taught them to fight for ideological and general political goals once they were engaged. The party had thereby converted patronage mechanisms into a means for ideological transformation and mobilization. After the coup in 1997, this politicizing path was closed down. Yet even before that, the Islamist party had itself left out some poor people from its struggle, due to its internalization of nationalist ideology and its marginalization of the Kurdish voice within the movement. Many ardent Islamist Kurds such as Veysel quit day-to-day activism and became less involved in the movement as a result of depoliticization. Under these circumstances, it was indeed more practical for Veysel and others like him to seek patrons rather than act as citizens or class-conscious workers.

"The Just Order": A Temporary Solution
Informal networks thus reproduced traditional Islam, the emphasis on corruption, an emergent work ethic, and informal working and political conditions, which put workers in an ambivalent position with respect to inequalities. Workers were mostly critical of these but did not have the capacity and willingness to organize against them in civil society. Under these conditions, the Just Order program seemed to offer a perfect solution. The RP claimed that it would both establish a morally sound market economy and protect people from poverty, while also abolishing major inequalities: there was no need for major associational activities regarding the economy (outside the party).

Islamists freely combined a leftist language of labor, equality and anti-exploitation with religious motives to attract workers' support. Rıdvan, a fifty-year-old man, was one of the RP's top administrators in the 1980s and 1990s, and he boasted of having enrolled many workers in the party. He was a High

School for Imams and Preachers (İHL) and theology school graduate, who had then become a teacher. In the 1970s he was a Milli Turkish Student Association (MTTB) and Akıncılar organizer, first in the southeast and then in the Black Sea region. His party activities caused him to quit teaching after the military regime of 1980, during which he was imprisoned for a short time. He then came to Sultanbeyli and consecutively opened and closed several shops, all of which went bankrupt because he was spending most of his time organizing and he ignored his shops. Rıdvan remembered the language they used to attract workers to the party:

> We were telling people that they could live without being exploited. We were going to put an end to unearned gain. We were going to recompensate labor justly. There would be no poor people under the Just Order, as Islam has a social solidarity component. . . . Sultanbeyli lit the spark for the Just Order. People came from Anatolia to this district without anything. The municipality did not ask to see title deeds. We provided financial and moral help so that they could build their houses. We created a social help fund to aid house construction, education, and wedding ceremonies. People living in Germany, the Black Sea region, etc. sent their alms to the district so that we could feed and provide heat for the poor, so that the service here would provide an example to other districts and cities.

Rıdvan eventually settled down after the military intervention in 1997, quit his official posts in the party, and got a government job. In 2000, he provided underground Kur'an education for the children of FP members and sympathizers. In the 1990s, Islamists also told Sultanbeyli's residents that under the Just Order the citizens would consume as much as they produced, education and health services would be free, the state would take care of the poor, alms would be taken by force if needed, garages of the rich would be turned into lodging for the poor, and extravagance and ostentation would be prevented. Rıdvan claimed that they implemented these social changes partially in this district in the 1990s, though not in the country as a whole.

Interestingly enough, it was the merchant, tradesman, and professional (librarian, teacher, etc.) leaders of the movement who had distinct recollections of the Just Order rather than the working classes, the primary addressees of the program. When I talked to workers about the program in 2001, they only had vague notions of what it was about. The workers did not have a full memory of what was going on and what they desired back then. The Just

Order basically expressed a desire for equality and justice for them, but they could not delineate what this exactly meant socioeconomically. Most of them emphasized that ruling based on the Kur'an would bring about justice, and the details were not that important. A forty-five-year-old construction worker from Gümüşhane said: "The Just Order is ruling with the statements of the Kur'an. Our forefathers have done this and they have spread throughout the world. They have always ruled with justice." Another construction worker born in Bayburt in 1962 interpreted the Just Order along the same lines:

> In the Just Order, people are really going to be equal. Cenab-ı Allah [God his Majesty] did not create humans as different from each other. Everybody is equal. In the Just Order, those who obey God the most and who perform their prayers will be valuable. Some trust their material opportunities to establish superiority, but this is not true superiority. If you are righteous, if you know God's orders, if you provide Islamic education to someone, then you are really superior. This is one of the things the Just Order will establish.

In other words, at least for some workers, the Just Order was a code word for an Islamic order where the more pious people would be primus inter pares.

For some other workers, it was Erbakan's charisma that constituted the backbone of the Just Order rather than either the programmatic details or a regime based on the Kur'an. In answering what the Just Order would look like and how the RP had attempted to implement it, Osman (the brisk FP administrator and retired worker previously quoted) mentioned that kurbans (animals sacrificed during a major Muslim holiday) were distributed in sixty countries by foundations that Erbakan had built. He had also built many factories throughout his life. After this point, he started to tell a lot of mythic stories about Erbakan:

> In 1974, King Faisal declared that he would take care of all the finances of heavy industrialization in Turkey. But the United States made his nephew stab him because it was worried about Erbakan's success. . . . Al-Qaradawi [one of the most prestigious conservative ulema in the Islamic world] was chosen to head the Islamic Council in Morocco and he declared that Erbakan was the head of Jihad. The heads of 142 Muslim nations who were present there kissed Erbakan's hand. . . . Bayram Meral [then president of the Confederation of Worker Unions of Turkey, or Türk-İş] took union representatives with him in order to topple Erbakan. Erbakan received him at his post. Meral said

they wanted a 30 percent raise. But Erbakan gave them 50 percent and said, "You cannot be the representatives of workers, the real workers' representatives are us." Meral was surprised and said, "You have surpassed even the father of workers [center-leftist] Ecevit, I congratulate you," and he kissed his hand.

So, Erbakan's charismatic personality would solve the problems of all workers, without the need for a workers' movement. After the interview, there were tears in Osman's eyes because of the passion he felt for his leader. He concluded by mentioning his wish that this book would be auspicious for the movement, which he labeled "Erbakan's movement."

Nevertheless, not all residents were this enthusiastic about the Just Order. Many argued that the Islamist party did not actually deliver its promises about social justice. When talking to FP activists, I asked them how they perceived such grievances. I also inquired why the FP no longer propagated the Just Order in the district or elsewhere. Some FP leaders (especially those who would eventually go over to the Justice and Development Party) commented that this program was empty propaganda and it was not realistic at all. Those who still sympathized with the program looked for the reasons in the corruption of the activists. For example, a teacher previously active in the youth commissions said: "As Muslims we were poor, we were not accustomed to wealth. Once wealth came, all the promises were quickly forgotten." One of the top administrators of the party underlined that there were still people working for the Just Order and added:

> Those who quit defending the Just Order have failed the test. They gave up the struggle in the name of the people. They are now in cahoots with the dominant forces. We are eventually going to establish the Just Order, where there will be no exploitation either in production or in distribution.

The emergent disbelief in such proclamations intensified the organic crisis rather than leading to a flowering of associational activities regarding the economy.

The Islamist Strategy of Capital Accumulation

After the Welfare Party reopened under a new name in 1997 (as the Virtue Party, or FP), it was less willing to emphasize social justice, and it preferred to combine Islam with a support of the rising conservative Anatolian bourgeoisie rather than with leftist ideological elements. Yet, it still assured the poor that this new combination would also bring about a system where there would be no poverty. Even as late as 2002, the poor supporters of the Islamist party in Sultanbeyli still referred to the utopia of the Just Order, and some claimed that the party was going to implement it one day.

The shift in the line of the Islamist party had brought the proliferation of Islamic businesses to the foreground even in poor regions like Sultanbeyli. Some Islamists posited religious firms controlled by religious scholars as the real cure to the ills of capitalism. Frequently agitating against capitalism, the discourse and method of organization in question recognized poverty and "exploitation" but used the discontents arising from these two as fuel for what I have called an "alternative capitalism" (Tuğal 2002). Lacking political or civil alternatives that could mobilize their restricted energies and funds, religious workers channeled their resources for the blossoming of an alternative profit-making project. In such efforts, capital did not present itself as capital but as Islamic civil society (a collection of foundations, cultural centers, etc.).

I came across the organizing and mobilizing efforts of alternative Islamist capitalism in the district through my connection with Gökhan (a janitor in the municipality; see Chapter 3). Gökhan invited me to a conference organized by the FP's newspaper (*Milli Gazete*), telling me that he had something important to discuss with me before the conference. When we met, he talked in an ardent tone about a project "like the Kombassan" that he and his friends were developing. Kombassan was the first major firm that established itself by combining the small savings of religious people. In time, this resulted in the establishment of a large holding company.[12] After Kombassan, this method of "interest-free" investment became popular among religious people. Several young people from Sultanbeyli who had studied theology and Islamic law in Pakistan had decided to establish a chain of educational and cultural centers after Kombassan's example. Gökhan asked me to become a member of this chain as a teacher and as a small investor in order not to enter "the system of contemporary slavery," so that I could "work for myself." He added: "People who share the same belief and the same longing are establishing the first center of this chain in Sultanbeyli. Maybe we could in this way become means for the *liberation* of some" (emphasis mine). I told him that I was there only as a researcher and therefore could not join such a group. He told me that I could join them as soon as my research was over. I answered that I would consider the issue again then. In his zeal, Gökhan kept telling me about the project even after I rejected his proposition. He was so passionate about this issue that he had invested all of his last paycheck in this organization even though he had no money and was in a lot of debt.

After the conference was over, Gökhan introduced me to the founder of the organization, who was a recent graduate from a theology school in Pakistan. The latter started the conversation by telling me that the teachers of the organization were going to have weekly meetings. After asking me whether I was married and getting a positive answer, he emphatically added that their wives were also going to have parallel meetings. He implied that these meetings would be in separate rooms. Through differentiating their lifestyles in this manner, pious entrepreneurs attempted to attract the financial resources of other pious people who could just as easily invest in nonpious organizations instead. The cofounder, seated next to the principal founder, was talking about their project in a more animated tone. "We are doing this with the love of worship," he said. The organization, which they were going to name "the Crescent Foundation," was going to get into the export and construction businesses after they settled in the education business, the latter told me.

After I told them that I had no time for such an engagement these days, I tried to communicate my doubts about such (Islamic) enterprises by saying that these started with good intentions but turned into firms that oppressed their own workers. Before I had a chance to expand on my thoughts, they started to defend the project, barely able to control their anger. The cofounder reported the following anecdote, apparently answering my question, but in effect shifting the emphasis of the conversation from social justice to entrepreneurial success: A "citizen," in his words, had gone to Erbakan and asked what they were going to do now when all Islamic firms were going bankrupt. Erbakan reportedly answered: "You are going to learn how to establish firms that are not going to go bankrupt." If they did not do this, they told me, Muslims were going to remain weak in the face of the present system and they were going to disperse, as all other opportunities for struggle had been blocked. The main organizer said the final word: they were going to have an inspection board composed of experts of Islamic jurisprudence and exegesis. In front of this board, everybody, including himself, was going to be equal. In this way, they would avoid the mistakes that other Islamic firms had made.

The presentation of Islamic capitalism as anticapitalist and antisystem shows how the religious population dealt with its internal contradictions. Though power differentials had become salient even before the inauguration of the chain, Gökhan, the janitor, thought that this project would provide a context in which he would be "working for himself." In this way, people with religious credentials mobilized workers who were resolved to fight their own subordination, only to support the accumulation of capital. Even though Gökhan displayed a will to fight the present system, religiously learned people rechanneled his energy to feed their potential money-making machines. Gökhan saw Islamic capital as the only path to his "liberation" from "slavery," whereas his future bosses saw it as the most practical way of becoming capitalists by differentiating their lifestyles and ideologies from the dominant business elite. Separation of the sexes was the key to this endeavor.

Together with demonstrating how various classes get articulated to Islamism in different ways, the appropriation of Islamic capitalism by workers also shows that the Islamist project of rendering religious knowledge the true oppositional knowledge in Turkey had been successful among certain sectors. Religious workers like Gökhan gathered around potential Islamic capitalists because of their credentials in the areas of Islamic law and theology. What made these capitalists trustworthy was their access to Islamic cultural capital, which the increasingly religious working populations of Turkey perceived as the source of salvation and liberation. In sum, workers were mobilized by the Islamist project to boost alternative capital accumulation rather than to alleviate inequality and poverty.

So, a deregulated economy and the transition to a market society did not give rise to solid associational activities challenging or negotiating the market. Instead, young tradesmen and professionals cursorily opposed the economic system unsystematically, workers and others fleetingly invested their hopes in the RP's nebulous program, and eventually pious people from all classes committed psychologically and financially to what appeared to be a communal rejection of pure market relations. But this rejection would only amount to the integration of civil society to the unregulated market with the rise of the Justice and Development Party (AKP).

· · ·

Islamists were only partially successful in building an integral Islamic society. They spread Islamic patterns of everyday life, but (as Islamic political society's grip over civil society loosened) these became hybridized with instead of hegemonizing other modern and traditional life patterns. They were, however, apt in creating an Islamic urban space, which was going to later create a challenge for the conservative project of the AKP. Finally, while it seemed to some actors that the religious mobilization of the 1980s and 1990s was going to lead to Islamic economic relations, it instead led to the deployment of Islamic lifestyles for capital accumulation. Islamic civil society was thoroughly uncoupled from Islamic political society and alienated from religious utopianism. The AKP would then transform this historical irony into a passive revolution.

Part 3

POLITICAL SOCIETY AND
CIVIL SOCIETY RECOUPLED

5 THE EMERGENCE OF MODERN ISLAMIC POLITICAL SOCIETY

WHEN I LEFT Sultanbeyli in the summer of 2002, the recently established Justice and Development Party (AKP) was in an embryonic state. The 1997 coup's almost total disestablishment of Islamic organizations weighed heavily on the district. When I returned in 2006, the AKP had already solidified its hold over the district after it won the municipal elections of 2004 and took over the Sultanbeyli mayoralty from the Islamist Felicity Party (SP).

Social changes such as the naturalization of market relations—to be analyzed in Chapter 6—had a solid political foundation: Islamists' transfer to the system's political cadres. Following the AKP's election victory in 2002, Kemalist journalists and politicians intermittently voiced their suspicion that the AKP was still an Islamist party. As "proof," they claimed (despite a cosmetic change in the national showcase of the party) that the party apparatus remained unchanged in popular neighborhoods and provincial towns—deeply Islamist. Contrary to these claims, the party's success rested on integrating Islamic activists and appropriating many strategies from the Islamist tradition, while at the same time shedding the thorns of religious mobilization—a politics of absorption. It was only thanks to this absorption that other changes in political society (such as rationalization and professionalization) could be implemented with as little trouble as possible. Yet, the process of absorption was still plagued by ethnic divisions and specters of radicalism.

ABSORPTION OF ISLAMIST STRATEGIES

Under the AKP's leadership, unions, hometown associations, teahouses, and mosques fostered demobilization. Ultimately, political society interacted with civil society to build consent for the Turkish state. The driving force of the passive revolution was the integration of antisystem cadres and strategies into the system. Even the partial mobilization fostered by this absorption demobilized larger sectors of society. Islamists who openly challenged this process had only a marginal voice in Sultanbeyli. But could there be a way of making a radical use of the absorption?

Incorporation of Islamists and Center Rightists into the AKP

Ex-radicals, those who used to reject party politics in the 1980s, had joined the AKP en masse. Those who had been already absorbed by the Welfare Party and those who had kept a distance even to that party were also incorporated. The AKP integrated the former radicals to the existing system, while at the same time opening the doors of the system to the hitherto excluded radicals.

This created hopes among the radicals for some Islamic transformation, but they also realized that this would have some limits. In addition, the integration naturalized the system, the state, and the position of the power holders. One of the ex-radicals who had joined the AKP said:

> The system has again won by taking the radicals' demands and integrating them. It has won by tolerating the radicals. Maybe this is what being a great state is all about. Now, the radicals are transforming the system from inside. Now, some changes can be made within democracy. But we have to understand that this can never be done against the will of those who control the system. They have set up the system and they control the opposition much better than we have ever understood.

So, even in a former radical's thinking, there was a tension between accepting the AKP as a party of the system and seeing it as an agent of Islamic transformation. This ambivalence made the party appealing to people of various ideologies.

Yaman (see Chapter 4), who had remained a radical and a nonpartisan much longer than most ex-radicals, more directly linked his transformation to the emergence of the AKP. An independent radical during his years as a teacher in the 1980s, Yaman had always rejected mystic communities, political parties, and even radical Islamist organizations because these all proposed authorities other than God. In the 1990s, he started to sell clothes in a small store. He began to question some of his ideas but remained a radical. The decisive change came later:

It all became clear for me in the 2000s. I started to understand that as long as there is the rule of law people will be comfortable. Living in Istanbul also changed me. Betrayal, the theft at my shop, and my [Islamist] partner's swindling opened my eyes. As I became engaged in trade [in the 1990s], I also saw that interest banking is a necessity, even if an Islamic state is established. The banks that say they are applying an Islamic alternative are actually charging 7 percent interest rather than 3 percent. It is still interest! After all that, I liberalized even further. I even went into party politics, which I was opposed to. I went into it in 2004, during the municipal elections here. There will always be party politics anyway. At least, by being there, we are preventing tricksters from going into politics and corrupting it. I realized that as an individual living here, I have a responsibility to the region. That was one reason why I joined the AKP, as well as my readings of Soroush and Jabiri,[1] which taught me that there is no such thing as a distinctively "Islamic" state—the rule of law and democracy are sufficient. My goal now is increasing the number of moral, honest, and virtuous people. I no longer try to Islamize these people, as faith is between them and God. We [the ex-Islamists and the AKP] are going to build the Madina-i Fazıla, the city where virtuous people live, with this new method.

One of the fundamental factors speeding up the change was the establishment of the AKP, which became a vehicle for the already liberalizing ex-radicals. Yaman's involvement in business after his years as a teacher had already raised doubts about the relevance of Islamist doctrine. But reading liberal Islamic sources with his circle of friends and joining the AKP (that is, the interaction of civil and political society) dealt the last blow to his past radicalism. He gave up the idea of an Islamic state and redefined his aim as building a virtuous city through civic (rather than religiously radical) party politics. In 2006, Yaman occupied one of the top positions in the AKP.

As Yaman's narrative demonstrates, the liberalization of the radicals was overdetermined, that is, it had many causes that cannot be easily disentangled. But still, these social factors (adapting to Istanbul, increasing involvement with business, and reading liberal Islamic as well as radical sources) already had an influence on the lives of radicals during my first visit. What changed was the emergence of a political leadership that could channel this flux in a definite direction. In other words, the AKP guaranteed that these social changes took a democratic, institutionalized, civic, and neoliberal direction.

Another former radical supportive of the AKP government explained as follows the reason he was content with the party:

> There is no longer an attack on people's religion and faith. . . . Erdoğan takes his veiled wife everywhere he goes. This is a very big gain [*kazanım*] for Muslims. . . . There is no difference between the AKP and the [Islamist] SP [Felicity Party]. They are from the same circles. All the Sultanbeyli administrators of the AKP come from the RP [Welfare Party] tradition.

So, even former radical Islamists had come to the same position with the construction workers and nonradical religious people: For them, the Islamic cause was now first and foremost about the lifestyles of the leaders; it was no longer about the system or the state. It is also telling that this radical Islamist believed that the AKP was part of the Welfare Party (RP) tradition—a very common reason so many ex-radicals and workers supported the AKP. That the same men had occupied most of the top positions in the RP, the Virtue Party (FP), and the AKP, and that they still had veiled wives were proof enough for them; they were less concerned with the thorough mainstreaming of these men's concrete agendas and policies.

On top of these ex-antiparty radicals, the RP-FP's district leaders also transferred in large numbers to the AKP. Bahri, a Kurdish tradesman, was typical of this switch. He had come to the district in 1990 because there was cheap land. He first worked as a hardware dealer then as a real estate dealer. He now lived and ran his store in a predominantly Kurdish neighborhood of the district. He was around fifty-five years old, wore a skullcap, and had a thin mustache. I met Bahri a few days before the AKP's local congress, which would witness a confrontation between Turks and Kurds (see later discussion in this chapter). He was going from shop to shop along Sultanbeyli's main boulevard, complaining that they were being marginalized because they were Kurds and trying to organize the vote for the Kurdish list. I asked him why he had transferred from the FP to the AKP. He said there was no better leader in Turkey than Erdoğan: "Erbakan made a lot of mistakes. He was agitating people before really doing anything. When the RP took this district, he said it was a conquest. He really exaggerated everything. He then talked about the Just Order, which was another exaggeration." Likewise, other previous RP leaders and supporters complained about how their old party attacked the system unnecessarily. The AKP did not have such grandiose visions (conquest, a Just Order, Muslim unity worldwide, etc.), which made it a better party.

Along with the transformed old Islamist guard, a completely new type of character was starting to occupy the top positions in the AKP. These were more technocratically oriented, "moderate" people who mostly came from the center right and right-wing nationalist political parties. Thus the patterns of recruitment in the district exhibited the same tendencies in the overall national structure of the party and its top leadership: The local party was a coalition of Islamists, the center right, and nationalists. In other words, this multidimensional face of the party was not a facade to trick the mass media and the public, and one could see its reverberations even at the local level.

Toygar, a Turkish marketing consultant from a mixed eastern city, exemplified this trend of coalition building. He had a business degree and came from a right-wing nationalist background. Despite his young age (he was in his early thirties) he held a key administrative position in the party. He defined the party's political line in a different vocabulary than that of the ex-radical Islamists:

> This generation is beyond old political rifts. We are neither rightist nor leftist. We are in this party because of *responsibility*. What is important for us is do-ability [*yapabilirlik*]. . . . Once upon a time, only idle [*işi gücü olmayan*] people dealt with politics. Now, politicians have a career. We can classify society into four layers. At the bottom, there are swindlers and thieves. Above that, there are those who earn their lives honestly [*namusuyla geçinen*], but who can barely subsist, and who have no property. Above that, those who live for values and who want to build strong families. At the very top, those who no longer worry about subsistence and live for personal development. These also serve their environments as a part of their personal development. They have careers. Previously, politicians came from the first two layers. But now in the AKP, we are all from the very top layer. . . . Sultanbeyli is going through an evolution from ignorance to education with the AKP. But there are those who resist this, especially from the Left. Therefore, our struggle is against the Left.

The AKP emphasized professionals and professionalism in its discourse and practices. Those such as Toygar came to hold central positions especially in the third, Turkish-dominated local administration of the AKP. This was also one of the fundamental differences between the (Islamist) SP and the AKP. Some of the local administrators of the SP were still workers. The AKP activists thus used this language of class struggle against the Left and implicitly against the Islamists. The language of pragmatism (the denial of ideology and emphasis on practicality) went hand in hand with hostility toward the Left. But this discourse was not used in public (and this conversation was not taped). Such open disclosure of class struggle occurred only in private circles.

This double incorporation of Islamists on the one hand and center rightists and nationalists on the other did not lead to a superficial coalition. Center rightists and nationalists absorbed Islamist strategies, and they too became absorbed into the emergent, redefined Islamic movement. The ex–center rightist politicians I talked to used an Islamic discourse, had intensified their religious practices, and had learned ways of doing politics from the Islamist tradition. For example, a couple of them were active in the elders' commissions. Just like the RP activists, they jointly dealt with the spiritual and material affairs of the elderly. They provided food and clothes for them and also took them to prominent mosques in Istanbul and to visit the tombs of *şeyhs*. This reproduced the Islamist strategy (analyzed in Chapter 3) of replacing the demolished welfare state with religiously inspired bottom-up welfare services.

But there were grievances from within the party against the absorption of militancy. Even active members had concerns. I talked to a twenty-eight-year-old laboratory assistant from the Black Sea region after a tiring evening of meetings of the AKP's youth commission. He had returned from a full day of work and spent the evening and the night at the party headquarters. He did not think everybody was as sincerely dedicated as him:

> The party came to where it is on the back of the oppressed masses. But now it forgets them. Those who became administrators bourgeoisified. They forgot religion too. There is a serious this-worldization. They came here by using the poor. But now those who lead the MÜSİAD [Association of Independent Industrialists and Businessmen] behave as if they do not know those people. They do not even say hello to them.

One could opine that the class location and age of this laboratory assistant explained his reaction. However, such criticism came from even among the well-to-do and elders of the party. A forty-eight-year-old top administrator of the AKP said: "Today, Muslims are face-to-face with a choice. They are going to choose either social justice or democracy, the polarization between the rich and poor, and this-worldization." "This-worldization" was a common term I heard over and over from both Islamists critical of the AKP and even from a minority among the members of the party in 2006. A small voice within the party *nonpublicly* protested against absorption into secularism, capitalism, and democracy.

Mass Demobilization and Mobilization During the Passive Revolution

There was a challenging mix of mobilization and demobilization after the AKP's empowerment in 2002. There was less street action, but preachers more openly incited people to Islamize the life around them. Yet, both the remaining street action and what preachers now understood from Islamization actually took out the thorns of religious mobilization. In this sense, the passive revolution was characterized by "the mobilization of demobilization."

Traces of demobilization were readily observable in everyday life. In teahouses, the focus of everyday conversation had shifted from politics to sports. The ratio of subjects related to hometowns remained more or less the same as in 2000–2002: people talked frequently about who is from which village, who is a co-local, and so on. People didn't pay attention to newspapers as much as they used to. For six months, I encountered no collective reading of any news (which was quite commonplace in 2000). In the municipality, in the shops, and in teahouses, people used to discuss politics around axes such as "people versus the rulers," "religious people versus secular elite" and so on. Now political conversation was focused on who was going to be a manager, who was going to take a certain bid, which member of the municipal council had an unregistered building that he would illegally save, and so on. Similar topics were a concern in 2001 but not as much. In 2006, the only mass political issue in everyday conversations was the Kurdish issue. The empowerment of their political party had shifted the attention of pious people to abusing power, rather than realizing their religio-political projects and dreams.

This loss of interest in politics led to a further decline in street action but not to its end. There was still mobilization, but it tended to be ritualistic and symbolic more than political and strategic. Most importantly, street mobilization no longer targeted those in power in Turkey but attacked the safely distant Western elite.

A global crisis erupted after a cartoonist in Denmark depicted the Prophet Muhammad disparagingly in late 2005 (Müller and Özcan 2007). In 2006, Muslims throughout the world organized protests not only against the cartoonist, but also against Western and pro-Western governments and media, which they thought should have discouraged or banned such religious attacks.

During this "cartoon crisis" there were only feeble protests in Turkey despite favorable opportunity structures (declining repression and the empowerment of a sympathetic elite).[2] In Sultanbeyli, the protest was organized so weakly that even many of the people attending the event learned about it haphazardly. During and after the rally, people were complaining about how they heard about it at the last minute, how they came across it while walking down the street, and so on. One day when the whole world was simmering with protests, the bus I was on had to stop and make a detour because of a protesting crowd (and the police vehicles surrounding them) that had blocked the main street. "*Tekbir*" and "*Allah-u ekber*" chants were coming from a distance. Less than five hundred men had convened around the Atatürk statue. They had gathered after the noon prayer around the central mosque and had marched up to the statue, which is about two hundred yards away. The demonstration was organized by Bem-Bir-Sen (the municipal branch of Memur-Sen, the Islamist trade union of public employees). There was a large presence of the Felicity Party and the Great Unity Party, and a certain hometown association of the Black Sea region. Most of the placards called for a boycott of various brands linked to Western (and a few Turkish secular) businesses.

The speaker's comments focused on Europe's double standards, the attack against the Prophet, and Muslims' respect for other religions. It was quite a short speech. Only one sentence in the whole speech referred to an authority in Turkey. "Muslims who still remain silent, what more are you waiting for? We expect Prime Minister Erdoğan not to remain restricted to two words." He did not specify what the prime minister needed to do. When he said "Erdoğan," three people booed. However, the people around shushed them.

At the end of the rally, people said "may God be content with you" to each other and "may God be content with the organizers of this rally" with mild and warm smiles on their faces. Just after this, the speaker said: "May God be content with our citizens who have joined us. May God be content with our security forces." There was an atmosphere of peace, rather than conflict. This was like a fraternal gathering rather than a contentious demonstration, despite some contentious slogans (such as "Denmark, don't lose track, don't force our patience" and "Let the hands that reach out for Islam break"). The speaker's last comments, and the collective silencing of the protest against Erdoğan, emphasized the unity of state (police and government) and "nation." There was aggression only against the unreachable foreigners. The speaker concluded his words by saying: "We gathered here and made our reaction known. Please let's disband quietly without intemperate acts, and return to our work and shops." About thirty young people started to chant slogans, after which the speaker repeated his warnings. The youth fell silent, and the crowd dispersed.

After the demonstration, I discussed the event with a top municipal administrator, who was also one of Sultanbeyli's politically influential shopkeepers. He said, "The Islam in Turkey has always been moderate. There is no burning and destruction like in the demonstrations in other countries. It has always been like this. This comes from Turkishness." When I reminded him of the contentious demonstrations before 2002, he argued that those had foreign roots. Just like him, many of the radicals who had participated in those demonstrations also thought in 2006 that both the demonstrations and the radical ideology underlying them came from Arab countries and Pakistan and were not true to Turkey's social texture.

It is remarkable how this demonstration, along with the other demonstrations over the cartoon in Turkey, had no palpable national target. Foreign governments, companies, and press were targeted. Erdoğan's criticism was elusive and a harsher mass reaction to him was repressed. The mobilization reinforced the unity of state and nation, rather than opposing state and society. The opinion makers of the district emphasized the "Turkishness" of the demonstration, which they argued lay at the basis of the difference from the contentious and "foreign" Islamist demonstrations of the past. This was a shift from the 2001 demonstration (analyzed in Chapter 3) when the government and police were fiercely attacked. But both demonstrations were significant shifts away from the pre-1997 demonstrations, which attacked not only the reigning governments but the whole regime and demanded radical transformation.

More or less the same patterns were repeated during other street actions. The following Friday, about half an hour after the noon prayer, 150 young people between ages fifteen and twenty, some of them in high school clothes, marched from the central mosque to the second main boulevard of the district at a running pace. The common chants were "Let the hands that reach out for Islam break" and "Damn Israel." This again presented a contrast to pre-2002 protests, which had national targets.

Given that there were Islamic street protests during the AKP government, and that the link of the party to the (European and transnational) targets of these protests was common knowledge, one might ask: Why weren't people (especially supporters of other parties at these rallies) protesting the AKP? Why didn't street action go further and protest the religious restrictions that the 1997 coup had introduced? Why didn't the unemployed and the poor massively protest government policies, as they did in 2001?

Established popular prejudices against non-Muslims came in handy here. For example, Felicity Party activists were not publicly reacting against the AKP because of its reinforcement of bans against certain religious associations, foundations, and dressing. A standard line was that if the AKP liberalized religious organization, Christian missionaries would establish foundations everywhere, walk around in special clothing, and Christianize the people. The AKP therefore remained beyond attack even though it did not lift certain religious bans, as its religious supporters (and even some of its religious opponents) believed that it could not do much without hurting the interests of Muslims. In forging this belief, various parties resorted to the fear of Christians. (By contrast, this was deployed for mobilization before 2002, as, for example, when imams told their audiences to revitalize their faith and fight for the Islamization of society lest Christians culturally take over once Turkey becomes a part of the EU.)

Moreover, even its Islamist opponents saw the AKP as a Muslim party (mostly because of its practicing leaders). Hence, they suspected people who attacked it *publicly* of having anti-Islamic concerns and even non-Muslim backgrounds. On one cold February day, Refik, a construction worker in his fifties, and his friends were talking about the latest developments at the teahouse he usually went to. Refik said that all the latest incidents (the cartoon crisis, the decision of a high court against a teacher wearing the veil on her way home, and some talk in the media about increasing unemployment nationwide) were all conspiracies intended to remove the AKP from power. These were all planned out by Jews and people who had Jewish mentalities, he said. He emphatically added that we should not allow this to happen. All the people around him echoed his concerns: "We should not," they said. After this, Refik said that he was going to vote for the same party in the next elections, and several other workers repeated the same. It is interesting that the day before, when I was hanging out at the same teahouse, Refik had a fatalist tone about his and other workers' impact on politics. But now he was brave, determined, and persistent. The day before, he was talking about the AKP as if it were just another party; now this party had become something worth fighting for. My presence there might have been interpreted as another part of the Jewish conspiracy. (Refik had mentioned the media's discussion of increasing unemployment nationwide as a conspiracy against the AKP. However, unemployment was not discussed in the media in those last few days: they had heard about it from me.) Unlike in 2001, workers refrained from action against a political party that impoverished some of them, partially because they interpreted any sign that hinted that the economy was going badly for them as a part of a global Jewish conspiracy. Worker or not, the crushing majority wanted to make sure that even if there were protests against religious restrictions, these did not hurt the "Muslim" party.

Friday sermons also produced this mass demobilization. But they did more than that. They redefined Islam in a way that restricted but still deployed religious activism and subjectivity, reproducing the mobilization of demobilization. Several weeks after the cartoon crisis had passed, the Friday sermon at the central mosque was about the verse that contained the well-known *"emr-i bi'l-maruf ve nehy-i ani'l-münker"* (commanding the good and forbidding the evil) phrase, but the imam did not utter these words. He only read the verse in Turkish and commented on it:

> God has created us differently from all other living beings. He has given us reason. We can differentiate between the good and bad, the right and wrong with it. This gives us some responsibilities. But reason by itself is not enough. Therefore he has sent us prophets. We should apply what those prophets have brought us in the light of reason. What does the Kur'an-ı Kerim order? "Let there arise out of you a band of people commanding the good and forbidding the evil." So, we are encumbered to correct our children, spouses, friends, and relatives. Also, what has our Prophet ordered? "When you see an injustice, correct it with your hand; if you can't do that, correct it with your tongue; if you can't do that, correct it with your heart." We might not be powerful enough to correct some of the evil around us. We are going to condemn these with our hearts.

"Emr-i bi'l-maruf ve nehy-i ani'l-münker" is a phrase from the Arabic original of the Kur'an.[3] The phrase holds a privileged place in activist interpretations of Islam: Islamists argue based on this phrase that each believer is charged with reorganizing society and state.

After the prayer, I went to the teahouse where Fikret usually hung out and joined his table. With him was his friend, a thirty-year-old right-wing

nationalist who was in the parking lot business. He expressed some concerns about the sermon (the sermon was the same in the Ulu Mosque, the
largest in the district, where they attended service):

> I started to get worried because of the sermon. It said "correct with your
> hand" and some people could understand this in a dangerous way. The imam's
> tone was heated too. It was really unnerving. But then he calmed down and
> because of the general direction of the sermon, I understood that this was a
> controlled sermon dictated from the center. There was no need to worry.

Indeed there wasn't. In interpreting the famous verse, the imam had told the
people to correct the people around them but not society or the state as a
whole. This was one of the milder interpretations of this verse. But nevertheless, it was still an active one. It still preached the Islamization of one's immediate surroundings. Centrally appointed prayer leaders had not given such
sermons in the central mosque five years before. This was yet another sign of
Islamic mobilization. But, even such mobilizing sermons in 2006 were meant
to normalize and integrate the previously radical mobilization. Since people
would not easily forget this verse of the Kur'an, which was central to their
lives until only a few years ago, it was better for the new AKP regime to keep
it under control. So, even the seemingly more oppositional sermons in 2006
were a part of the passive revolution.

The mobilization of demobilization also structured the individual along
with these institutional and mass levels. Individual activism and Islamic engagement changed face during AKP rule. So did the pious person's relationship with and perception of the state. Due to the AKP's empowerment, religious activists and pious people felt more in tune with the state, they even felt
like they were a part of the state. Hakan, born in 1955, was from the Black Sea
region. Unlike most of the other prominent ex-radicals of the district, he had
graduated from a regular public school, not an İHL (High School for Imams
and Preachers). He became an Islamist during his years in college at one of
Istanbul's best engineering schools. After he graduated, he became a contrac-
tor in the construction sector. During all these years, he gradually shifted
from radicalism to the Welfare Party (RP), then finally to conservatism. However, he still put a positive spin on his past involvement:

> There has never been any development of Islamic consciousness [şuurlanma]
> in this district. The only thing that has happened is that pious people have

started to send their children to schools in the 1970s, starting with the Milli Salvation Party mobilization. Before that, they did not do this. That was why I was sent to school. In these schools, children learned how to do business and how to establish companies. Actually, the Welfare Party was very beneficial to this society. It changed the society's perception of women. It made people read. It made people participate in social movements and in politics. But the AKP took off the Milli Outlook shirt. AKP activists frequently say this. What does it mean though? It means that they have gone beyond the RP. The party first took people to its side, now it is changing them. The RP was the process [sic] of including these people, but now there is a thorough change. You cannot change people by excluding them. This society has very recently left behind a Sultanate system. If you try to impose something, you get a lot of reaction. But look at the change the republic and the AKP created: People were not even able to approach the palace during the Ottoman Empire. Now common people say, "Even I can rule this society." [Laughing] when friends gather, I also say this jokingly. I say, "I can be the head of the state too."

Hakan's story of absorption—his (and his social circles') previous mobilization that has turned into demobilization—exemplifies the way Islamists have mobilized hitherto passively resisting (pious) people against the system to then incorporate them into the system. But there is more to his story than this absorption. Hakan's imagination of himself as a possible top ruler was the crux of the hegemony built by the AKP. Through the empowerment of praying people, men on the ground had started to feel that this was *their state too*. Nobody in Sultanbeyli in 2001 thought that he could be in control of the state. Perry Anderson (1976) argues that bourgeois hegemony is constructed not primarily in civil society or in the process of production but at the level of the parliament, through creating the impression that everybody is equal. This is what the AKP has accomplished. The emergence of pious authority figures at the national level made an imaginary identification with the rulers possible, once again demonstrating the centrality of political society to the establishment of consent.

Islamic Opposition

The Islamist opposition to the passive revolution, led by the Felicity Party (SP), was marginalized in the district. The SP, rather than creatively renewing its platform and strategies, partially reverted to (the already defeated) old-style Islamism. It could not make use of the transformation in Turkey. The party became more rhetorically aggressive, more militaristic, more nationalist, and started to rely more on religious dogma when compared to the Virtue Party (FP). Those like Mahsun (see Chapter 3) were reintegrated to the party's top administration. At the same time, the SP also denied radicalism and stayed away from any desire to change the system.

I regularly visited the SP headquarters in Sultanbeyli. The activists of the SP based all their arguments on religious sources, especially religious sources in Arabic. No one from the AKP quoted the Kur'an frequently while doing political or intellectual work, while this was standard among SP activists. As the AKP decreased the role of religious language in its strategies, the SP emphasized it more. At the SP headquarters, there was also strict discipline about the regular prayer. As well as calling the headquarters a "military base" and party bureaucrats "commanders," the activists also called the main room, which was painted green, a *masjid* (prayer place). When prayer time came, the whole building became dead silent. The party members interrupted work, took their ablutions, and prayed communally. Members of various positions in the party rotated to perform the role of the prayer leader. So, the simplest functionary led the prayer from time to time. As these rituals (which also had been enacted in the FP five years before) were no longer a part of the AKP routine, there was no equalizing gesture between administrators and others in the ranks of the AKP. In contrast to 2000, SP activists denied having ever been influenced by radical Islamism, by Sayyid Qutb, or by transnational Islamic movements. Several of them complained that all the "fake radicals" had ended up in the AKP; radicalism had never benefited the Islamic cause.

The following is another example of how the SP failed to organize people. I came across Metin, a longtime member of the Islamist party, while walking on one of Sultanbeyli's busiest shopping streets. He was still selling clothes but now in a better car than in 2001. But still, this was the model in the market that was most fuel efficient. He called it "a poor man's car." He had three daughters and two sons. He also had nine grandchildren whom he was trying to raise as pious Muslims.

He immediately took me to the watch repairer across from his vehicle. The watch repairer was talking to a teacher and a shopkeeper friend of his about how to guide their children after school. What were these kids going to do after they graduated? Metin said:

You are talking about educational issues. Look, here is a teacher from the United States. He knows these issues much better than us. Now, listen to what I will say. [Turning to me] my hoca, you would know these better than I do. So you can add to what I am saying. . . . There can be no true education in the city. You have to take your children to zones populated by trees. Then you have to feed them really well. Look, you are poisoning yourselves with cigarettes. I have never smoked. And it is not correct for a Muslim to smoke. The children should also live in smoke-free environments. Then, they have to be instructed in small classrooms. All the teachers have to be practicing Muslims. I would not trust my children to others: They would not set good examples.

The teacher (laughing): These are macro solutions. And where are you going to get the funding from?

Watch repairer: We are trying to save our children here. What are they going to do if they cannot enter the university? What are they going to do if they are still unemployed after university? We know what you are saying, but we have to find solutions to these problems.

His attempts to convince them to build an Islamic cultural center thus failed. Then Metin returned to his vehicle and the two men asked me questions about the United States. An increasing number of Sultanbeyli residents were interested in getting things done, accessing education for their children, and finding employment for them more than in building an Islamic society. If the two goals conflicted, they went for the first. The party that insisted on the latter lost in the presence of another Muslim party that emphasized getting things done.

After a while, I left and went to talk to Metin. During the rest of the day, Metin guided people about the correct ways to practice Islam, just like he had five years before. For example, when he saw two unveiled young women shopping at the Islamic clothing store across from his car, he went there and said: "Were your grandmothers veiled?" They said yes. He then asked: "Were your mothers veiled?" The answer was affirmative again. "So, why do you not wear the clothes of your grandmothers, but that of the Greek and the English?" One of the women answered: "We want to, but we can't." They hastily walked away without explaining why they couldn't. After the incident, Metin bragged: "This is how we should work on the veil." However, this direct way of working on the veil was now restricted to his marginalized party. I did not see any AKP member take an active and imposing stance, either regarding the veil or any other Islamic issue.

People who said they had changed were almost all from the AKP or were related to it. The counterpart of this was that those connected to the Islamist SP had not undergone a dramatic change in everyday practice (except a superficial shift to the extremes of nationalism, dogma, and militarism). They also resented the term "change" when political and religious issues were in question. Metin still used his business for ideological purposes and imposed his own beliefs on others. These are two practices that the AKP has nearly eradicated. Metin still said "property belongs to God" and tried to act accordingly, while AKP members frequently repeated the sentence Erdoğan had popularized: "money has no religion and belief." In short, regarding the transformation from 2001 to 2006, the most important variable was the change in political organization. The emergence of the AKP had reinforced the already existing patterns of bourgeoisification and the impact of the 1997 coup. One could easily detect the importance of this party by looking at those who had stuck to the old party.

Together with this legal opposition to the AKP, there were also small illegal groups fighting against the global secular system. As in 2001, these groups were marginal and hardly visible and therefore had little impact on hegemonic and counterhegemonic politics. But, different from five years before, the main Islamist party (SP) had isolated itself from these radical currents completely, further marginalizing them in the district.

The Search for New Patterns of Radicalism

Are the hands of those who want to build an Islamic society and state completely tied in this environment where militants either join the AKP or are marginalized? Not necessarily. Some groups tried to make use of the passive revolution and build a revolutionary politics based on what Antonio Gramsci has called a "war of position." Gramsci differentiated between the classical Bolshevik strategy based on a frontal attack against the state ("war of movement") and a strategy that he thought western European communist parties had to follow: engaging in a protracted fight in the "trenches" of civil society (war of position) to gradually surround and take over the state. This strategy does not reject a final frontal attack but reduces its significance.[4] Therefore, there is no complete break between a revolutionary politics based on the war of movement and a revolutionary politics based on the war of position: Radical Islamist movements of the 1980s and 1990s also resorted to the war of position, but this was secondary to the frontal attack on the state they prepared for. In the early 2000s, some movements underwent a strategic transformation and in 2006 they emphasized the war of position over the war of movement. This was a very difficult path in the overall context of conservative, democratic neoliberalization, for every move in the war of position could be absorbed by the passive revolution. How did militants carry out such a war?

First, it has to be understood that those who strove to remain Islamists themselves had partially been influenced by the passive revolution, liberalization, and marketization. But they were still trying to accomplish Islamization, even though not with the same fervor and conviction.

Some of these attempts were less organized and systematic, as in the case of Yaman's and Numan's circles and the Furkan Center (see Chapter 3). Necmi's goal regarding the people around the Furkan Center was to constitute a core group that would have influence in a major political party. So far, this project has not worked out: even though all were affiliated with the AKP, they had no impact on the party as a group. In contrast to the Sufi communities, and like the radical groups of yesteryear, Necmi's group fluctuated between having many leaders and having no leader at all. Its *sohbet*s sometimes ended in noisy theological or political quarrels. It was even difficult to tell whether the group was a modernist Islamic one or a radical Islamist one, as Necmi and the others sometimes seemed to go in other directions. They had neither reached consensus on a definitive political goal nor on the means to reach these goals. Many ex-radical groups in the district were in a similar, confused situation.

The X group, the activities of which are analyzed in Chapter 3, was among the political groups that sought a new, working method of radicalism without neglecting the structural changes in Turkey. Under another government, the X group, which was crushed by the military intervention of 1997, might not have been able to revive itself. So the AKP government had actually allowed some Islamic revival. The group also supported the AKP government though with awareness of its disadvantages for Islamization. Moreover, the AKP appointed one of the group's ex-members as a top official at the national level, winning the sympathy of the group.

The circle had established a new educational association. They still had about a hundred members in Sultanbeyli, but they were proud of their influence in the district: about 1,500 people had come to the opening reception of their association. In 2006, the association was at the center of their activities. It was mostly teachers and high school students who frequented the association's building on a regular basis. The students chatted, read Islamic magazines, surfed the Internet for Islamic content, and worked on their Arabic and their reading of the holy book when they were there. As opposed to the teachers in the established religious communities, the teachers here were mostly of working-class origin. Until a while ago, the crushing majority of the members of the group were workers and peasants. But now there were more and more teachers, doctors, and judges. Because of the town of origin of the group, they were a mixture of Kurdish and Turkish elements. Over the summer, volunteer teachers taught thirty students the Arabic alphabet and the Kur'an.

Demir (see Chapter 3) explained why the group switched from emphasizing armed struggle to focusing on struggle in civil society:

> The activities of the group were underground in the 1990s. But now, we are completely legalized. The people of this country are obedient. They are loyal to their state. Soldiers are sacred for them. This won't change for another fifty years. Maybe unionization and the development of civil society [STKlaşma] can break this in the long run. We understood this only after 1998. Before that, our thinking was imported [from the Arab world] and we could not conceive of this reality. Now we are thinking more locally.

Whereas the sources they focused most on were foreign in the 1990s, now they read more local Islamist authors, such as Mustafa İslamoğlu. But the traditionalists of the district still criticized them for depending too much on translated sources. The group thus underwent a "hegemonic" transformation: they still wanted an Islamic revolution but aimed to carry this out through weakening loyalty to the state by using legal means and civil society. Its members also emphasized translating universal truths into local realities.

The group's other political and religious activities also changed thoroughly. Its members started to go to the Friday prayers after 2000 in order not to be cut off from the community. Some members of the circle even became state-employed imams. The group no longer demanded an immediate Islamic state. It demanded a "just state" because its leaders, as members repeatedly told me, "understood that the Islamic state cannot be built immediately." Group members started to work on the education of women and children, which they had neglected before.

Moreover, group members started to see the strict separation of the sexes as a deviation from the essence of Islam. On one warm summer evening, I visited Demir for dinner. His wife came in to the living room and said welcome. She also brought us soda before dinner. But Demir himself brought dinner on a tray, and she did not join us for dinner. Such lax separation of the sexes had been a common practice in the non-Islamist, traditional families of Sultanbeyli five years before. Back then, Islamists reacted to such looseness sharply. The radical contenders of the group interpreted their recent relaxation as a sign of growing traditionalism and a move away from Islamism (in sociological terms, a sign of absorption into the passive revolution). According to the group's own members, this was a more flexible understanding of Islamism (in our terms, a war of position).

Yet, this relaxation was not standardized throughout the group's members. During our visit of an old Kurdish street vendor member of the group, conversation centered on an association that had split from them. In that association, their ex-comrades put curtains between men and women during meetings so that they would not see each other at all. Demir reacted to this practice: "This is an Ottoman custom. There wasn't anything like this in the times of the Prophet. We still sit separate, but at least our wives say welcome to our friends." At this point, the old host looked away, as we had seen no females at his place. One of his sons, another member of the group, had brought us tea. Separation of the sexes was thus still contested terrain within this circle.

However, there were more uncontrollable aspects of the change. In the new atmosphere of integration with the system, the group's members were also integrating with markets as producers and consumers. This was leading to bourgeoisification, while the group was still striving to define itself as revolutionary. Rasim (see the Introduction) commented on how the group suffered from this:

The Kur'an says, "Pray and give your alms." Some of our friends pray, but they don't do the latter. However, these are not two separate aspects of our religion; they are always mentioned together. If you do not do one, the other has no meaning. Now, there are a lot of Muslims, they give thousands of dollars for their son's education, but when it comes to giving a few pennies to hungry people, they say they're out of money. They run after houses [pursue property]. After they have a house they want a summer resort. After they have that, they want more houses. Our friends formed a hometown association, but it does not serve our cause. It only serves them to form networks and chase bids. How will we fight these tendencies? We have to start from the family, and we have to change the whole culture. You know Ayatollah Khomeini. He lived in France for years, but he didn't relax, and he kept on fighting for the cause. He eventually returned to his country for the revolution. And after the revolution he realized that people were lax. But he warned them and said to be so was wrong. He said, "Our generation has not arrived yet. It will come thirty years from now. Until then there are many things to do." This is what he understood from the revolution. The revolution is not an overnight thing. This is what we are doing today. We are working on the family and on education. Just like he said, our generation will arrive thirty years from now.

Some other radical groups interpreted this focus on the family, education, and culture as a conservative strategy that attested to the deradicalization of the group. However, the group's activists wanted to see these activities as part of a long revolution, as an updated and localized version of the Islamic Revolution in Iran rather than an alternative to it.

This dynamism, which sometimes bordered on confusion (between conservatism and a war of position), had its counterpart in the group's innovative strategies. The groups' members restructured *sohbet*s in such a way that could lead to a cultural breakthrough or to further divisions. I attended one of the group's sohbets in the neighboring region Samandıra. Several activists lived with their families on the many floors of an apartment building, the basement of which they had transformed into a *medrese*. The host for that night was an İHL (High School for Imams and Preachers) teacher. The audience of fifteen people was mostly composed of teachers and workers. An engineer in his early fifties was among the vocal figures. Most of the men had plain trousers and shirts and thin mustaches. Only a couple had beards. One of these had baggy trousers and a quite long beard. Along with me there were two visitors, Ferhat and Kamil (a previously anti-Western imam who had switched to a pro-Western position after 2002; see the last section of this chapter). Ferhat was a fifty-five-year-old Kur'an school teacher with dark hair, a sandy, short beard, thick eyebrows, and a serious face. After graduating from an İHL, he had received his college degree from a prominent theology school in Turkey and then gone to Pakistan for further education in a medrese.

This group of fifteen people (excluding the guests) gathered regularly and read exegeses. They read one verse and its interpretations each Friday night. That night, the verse was about the miracles of Jesus, including his making (*khalq*, in Kur'anic Arabic) of a bird from mud.[5] Before starting, the host informed us about the structure of their meetings: First, they read the verse in

Arabic and Turkish. Then they read four different interpretations from four exegeses (Qutb's *Fi Zilal al-Qur'an*, Mawlana Mawdudi's *The Meaning of the Qur'an*, Muhammed Ali Al-Sabuni's traditionalist exegesis *Safvet al-Tefasir*,[6] and Muhammad Asad's modernist exegesis *The Message of the Qur'an*). They evaluated the differences for an hour. They then performed the night prayer, which was followed by snacks. They finally read chapters from the Prophet's life.

After this introduction, Rasim read the Arabic original and Turkish translation of the verse. He then turned the floor over to the guests, rather than following the regular structure. Kamil gave a long and hard-to-follow warning speech. As in his regular sermons, he liberally combined and mixed Arabic and Turkish while speaking but used more Arabic than usual, probably to influence and overpower the educated and/or politically engaged audience. The main idea of each long sentence was intelligible to non-Arabic speakers but not the details (nobody in the room, other than these two guest scholars, was fluent in Arabic). He talked in a soothing, soft voice:

> The Turkish version of a verse is not even one tenth of its Arabic original. When it is translated to Turkish, it first loses its quality as a direct word of God. Second, the structure of Arabic is not the same as Turkish. Therefore, when someone who does not know Arabic reads the Kur'an, s/he might find it superficial. But those who know Arabic never have this impression. The translation [*meal*] you have has translated "*khalq*" of the bird as "to create." However, only God can create. Here, "khalq" means bringing into existence [*vücud*] with God's permission, not creating from nothingness. When you do not know Arabic, you are prone to traps like this.
>
> Rasim: This is the Ateş *meal*. Our Z. Hoca told us to read it. We have to go by his word.
>
> The host: You are right about the importance of Arabic. But not everybody's capacity and conditions are suitable to learn Arabic. Therefore, one needs to make use of the science [*ilim*] of those who know Arabic. Yet we cannot always find a hoca who knows Arabic. When we can't, we resort to the best intermediaries we have: We look at exegeses.

After offering this explanation, the host started to read Qutb's exegesis. Like the others who had read the other exegeses, he had prepared what he was going to talk about beforehand, and he did not directly read from the text. This task was circulated among some members of the group, constituting them as responsible subjects. Before moving on to the next exegesis, the host offered yet another explanation:

> Asad has a different way of looking at things. He usually doesn't believe in miracles. He explains them based on reason. For example, when the Kur'an talks about Jesus healing the blind, this actually refers to his healing of a society the spirit of which has gone blind [*ruhları körelmiş*]. When the book talks about him turning mud into a bird, this means that he has turned the corrupted Jewish society into a spiritually exalted society.
>
> The engineer (laughing): He is really pushing it. This is unbelievable!
>
> Ferhat (hardly controlling his anger): These thoughts cannot be accepted. Asad has been raised in the West. He writes these to convince the Westerners. This is a completely rationalist approach and has nothing to do with science [*ilim*]. When this exegesis was first published, I read it and noted down fifty criticisms. [Smiling] I will give these to you so that you can make use of them. [Frowning again] Actually, you should not read this in public. Why are you doing this? This is confusing and harmful.
>
> The host: We are not reading it because we agree with it. But we are trying to learn different approaches.
>
> Ferhat (with a gesture of disapproval): You will maybe agree with me when you come to the parts of the book where he says Christians and Jews will go to paradise.
>
> The host: Well, don't think that I believe this text just because I'm reading it.

After this contentious episode, another teacher took over and read passages from Asad. The above conflict over the correct method of learning religion reproduced the tensions between radicalism/modernism and traditionalism on some levels. This formerly radical group was in favor of revealing different interpretations (including radical and modernist) to the public. The traditionalist religious scholars were in favor of hiding especially rationalist and modernist interpretations from the public. But interestingly, this methodical flexibility did not lead to rationalization: The leaders of the group rejected Asad's rationalism.

At this moment, the call to prayer was read and the group performed the night prayer collectively. After the prayer, Kamil beefed up the scholars' criticism: "The exegeses you are reading are not the perfect sources. This should be your method: A verse is explained by another verse. When it is not, you should look at *hadis* [the Prophet's saying and deeds]. When this is not sufficient, you should look at what the scholars are saying, to *ijma*." But some in the room raised objections to this traditional method. The engineer especially was very determined:

> There are so many invented hadis. Is this really the right source?
> Kamil: By now, we know which are invented and which are not. There are so many things in the Kur'an that are not sufficient by themselves. *Salat* is mentioned in many places, but without hadis we cannot know how it is performed. Therefore, there can be no religion without the Prophet.
> The engineer (mockingly): But, there are so many hadis that the Prophet cannot have said all of them! His life would not have been long enough for all that. Also, our Prophet did not talk so much, you know.
> Kamil (calmly smiling): But everything is a hadis. The way he wakes up, the way he speaks, his orders, his explanation of the Kur'an. When you add all this together, it of course amounts to a lot.

This contentious atmosphere, along with the engineer's irony, was a good example of the fragmentation of religious authority, which scholars have pointed out (Eickelman and Piscatori 1996). Especially the emergence of radical movements had reinforced this fragmentation. But the transformation of the X group also attested to new developments regarding religious authority.

The host tried to soften the increasing tension by saying, "It would appear that some people here have a problem with hadis. But this is definitely not the case." Ferhat interjected one final comment before the snacks: "There is one more problem. All of the exegeses you are reading are translations. But there are beautiful ones in Turkish. Why aren't you reading Elmalılı?" The host responded: "We are reading those too. We are not restricting ourselves to these four." Because of all these debates, there was no time for chapters from the life of the Prophet, which would no doubt lead to yet more discussion. The sohbet that had started after the evening prayer around 9 p.m. was concluded after midnight.

The X group had thus developed a critical way of working, but this criticism reproduced aspects of tradition. There was one significant shift away from its past sohbets: group members now invited traditionalist scholars and engaged them in debate. The very structure of the debate (posing questions to them, respecting their interpretations even when not in agreement, recognizing the status of Arabic, etc.) reproduced their authority. But this did not mean that they were leaving their claim to "lay authority" on religion. Rather, their way of working had become more dialogic in the Bakhtinian sense of openly incorporating rival voices into one's discourse: they attempted to integrate traditionalist language and authority into their own revolutionary project. Five years before, all the radicals I met were extremely harsh in their rejection of traditionalists and traditionally licensed religious scholars. Now, just like they were still critical of the republic but had softened their tone and started to listen to the other side, their interaction with the traditionalists had also changed.

It was also significant how they attempted to resolve the issue of internal authority that had troubled all other radical groups. The top national leaders of the group assigned certain texts, but the local members could include other readings in their meetings. So, central authority and local flexibility were combined. Another democratic aspect was added to this by reading several exegeses and comparing them as a group. But the case of the engineer, his liberty to openly challenge the group's position on hadis, shows that this method might also produce future rifts.

The X group had noticed the marginalization of radicals in Turkey, and it had developed methods to cope with it. It was trying to integrate traditional patterns of authority while also being open to modern and rationalist influences. Of course, the question is whether this newfound flexibility will only better absorb these ex-radicals into the system while allowing them to entertain the illusion that they are still revolutionaries.

As these ex-radicals themselves realize, their dialogic strategy would take several decades to produce revolutionary results. It is not for this book to evaluate whether an Islamic revolution is indeed possible a few decades from now in this country, as these activists would like to believe. However, what Sultanbeyli demonstrates is that whereas radical groups that push for an Islamic revolution either through armed struggle or mass uprisings have been marginalized, the X group has been gaining ground. The analysis of the X group also allows us to study revolutionary Islamic forces without attributing conspiratorial goals to the totality of the AKP. While avoiding facile approaches that insist that the AKP has a hidden agenda of Islamization, we can still recognize that there are organized activists who are trying to make use of the social transformation in Turkey to build an Islamic society and state in the future.

THE CHANGING PATTERNS AND DISCOURSES OF AUTHORITY

A transformation in the conception and practice of authority was squarely interwoven with the changes in political leadership to have a deep impact on life in the district. The local authority structure had thoroughly changed when I visited Sultanbeyli again in 2006. Most importantly, the Justice and Development Party (AKP) had replaced the increasingly ineffective Virtue Party (FP) municipality. The new municipal authorities emphasized professionalism and blamed previous municipal authorities for being unprofessional. Despite this seeming rationalization, the magic of Erdoğan's figure was still central in the district.

The Blame Game

The lack of professionalism was not the only AKP grievance against previous municipalities. Both the residents and the new authorities distanced themselves from the years of dual power, which they now saw as responsible for Sultanbeyli's underdevelopment.

Time and again I witnessed residents attack the old municipal authorities of the district. Five years before, poor people especially said good things about the RP (Welfare Party) and FP (Virtue Party) municipalities, about how they provided land for them, and so on. But in 2006 most people complained about how the municipality allowed them to buy land cheaply but how now they were paying dearly for that. As the process of legalization was delayed, it created new price hikes for the residents and the municipality at every turn. This increased the tensions and led the residents to blame the past administrations more harshly. Many residents also thought that the previous municipal authorities created many unnecessary tensions with the state and national authorities. As they now had their lands and homes, they no longer wanted a clash with the state. They wanted more tactful authorities who could negotiate legalization with the state—one reason why they had shifted their votes from Islamist parties to the AKP.

It was not only ordinary residents who blamed the municipality. Municipal employees attacked it too, but they directed their attacks more to the past rather than the present. Ahmet was a short, joyful, and a rotund man from the central Black Sea region. He had a thin mustache, plain pants, and a plain shirt. He was the son of a doorman. His family came to the district in 1990 after spending several years in Üsküdar, a conservative district of Istanbul. During the 1990s, he worked as a secretary for the vice presidents of the municipality. Back then, he was an ardent Islamist, but he later shifted to the AKP line. Now thirty-seven years old, he was carrying out the same task in a lesser office. He was also the president of his co-local association. I talked to Ahmet about the problems of the district while he was going door to door, raising funds for his association. He vehemently attacked the RP administration and Sultanbeyli residents:

> Devils in the guise of Robin Hood destroyed this district. They encouraged the construction of these buildings, which was wrong. They took from the rich and gave to the poor. They made us settle on public lands and on private lands of the rich. It seemed that they were giving us something, but indeed they were destroying our future. Since the whole district developed without a plan, we could not receive any infrastructural service. And now, we do not have the right to demand any clean water or electricity or a sewage system. We do not have that right because we knew what we were doing was not legal. These lands [referring to all of Turkey] were taken with the blood of believers who fought for us in the Dardanelles [in 1915]. But we are just devouring these lands. Now, you will see a lot of people in the media and among the politicians presenting us as victims [mağdur]. But we are definitely not victims. We brought this upon ourselves. Now we have to suffer the consequences. We want a lot of things from the state, but in order to get something, you have to give something. The people here have given nothing to the state. Therefore they do not have the right to demand anything.

The representation of the district, its past, and its authority figures had completely changed by 2006. Even the image of Robin Hood was used in a different way and for different purposes. This new representation attests to the establishment of hegemony: A fake Robin Hood had fought against the state and pillaged the nation's land, for the sake of which martyrs had shed their own blood. Ahmet, like many residents of the district in 2006, thought that the redistribution of land was wrong, as "you have to give something" to the state in order to have rights and property. By blaming the district's authorities and residents in this way, Ahmet sacralized the nation and legal property. This self-blaming discourse regarding squatting was widespread in 2006, demonstrating an ideological capitalist success rarely seen anywhere in the world.

This also led to the justification of inequality. Residents blamed the scarcity of good schools and educated people in the district on development without a construction plan. They thereby rejected the existence of systematic inequalities by blaming themselves (their class) and the now-defeated Islamist mobilization for low-quality education. In short, this new representation of Sultanbeyli naturalized the nation as the political unit, social inequalities, and duties toward the state. This was possible because the new AKP mayoralty attacked the remnants of dual power, which had already been demolished by the 1997 military intervention and the local government.

Professionalization of Authority

The blame game did not consist of empty words. The structure of authority in the district changed. The appointed governor lost his centrality, and the elected municipality started to hold sway. Yet, the elected municipal leaders themselves were different kinds of people, and they appointed different kinds of officials in the municipality. Lawyers, urban planners, engineers, architects, computer analysts, and doctors now staffed the top offices in the municipality, replacing Robin Hoods, religious lawmakers, and preachers. Along with this change in the authority figures, the attempted naturalization of their authority also changed. The authorities no longer claimed to be "of the people." The emergent rationalization I pointed out in Chapter 3 was thus more organized and systematically put into practice by the AKP in 2006.

When I told him my research topic (mentioning somewhere the relation of urbanization to politics and religion), the new mayor Alaaddin Ersoy, a pediatrician in his fifties, reacted nervously: "We have no links to religion and politics. I was trained in the positive sciences. I cannot discuss theology. And ask the politicians about politics." Right from the start, Ersoy denied that he was a politician and presented himself as exclusively an expert. I tried to soothe his worries by saying that I was of course going to discuss these other topics with other people, and that I was just trying to give him an overall sense of my research. The beginning of my interview with him immediately signaled his difference from Koçak, who had presented himself as a man of religion and politics. The main theme of Ersoy's self-presentation was the professionalization of authority:

> We meet every day with the vice presidents, every two weeks with unit managers, and every three months with all the personnel. We listen to and learn from what they say. We built a hierarchical system here, which was lacking before. An ordinary employee or an ordinary resident cannot meet directly with the mayor. First s/he has to see the unit manager, who relates the problem to a vice president if needed. Only then will I hear about the problem.

Unlike municipal authorities before him, Ersoy emphasized hierarchy and formalization of authority instead of emotional links and common practices between the rulers and the ruled.

Actually, some of the top administrators of the municipality and its council members no longer lived in the district, which further weakened these links. Some residents criticized this situation. Even supporters of the AKP like Yasin voiced these criticisms:

> Those who rule the district are alien to the people. They are not from here. Ersoy knows nothing about the people. He does not have tight connections with society [*toplumla içli dışlı değil*]. His deputies are also from outside of the district.

During the six months I spent in the district, I heard similar criticisms in teahouses, schools, workplaces, and even in municipal offices (from visitors). But the new mayor knew how to answer this criticism:

> We are managing a city. When you go to a hospital, you look at the work the doctors do, not at where they sleep. People should be judged by the projects they accomplish. Our leader Erdoğan has three red lines: ethnic nationalism, regional nationalism, and religious nationalism. The criticism you are talking about is based on regional nationalism. Until today, most of the municipal council members lived in Sultanbeyli, and you see where Sultanbeyli is. For fifteen years, none of the men who served as technical vice mayors had a career related to managing a municipality. Some of them were minibus drivers. We do not look down on them, but one needs to have a [professional] career [in order to manage a municipality]. We are trained as scientists [*bilim okumuş insanlarız*] and Sultanbeyli needs experts.

While Koçak, with his long beard and discourse based on religion, stood for the Islamism of the 1990s, the thin mustache of Ersoy and his emphasis on hierarchy and professionalism symbolized the AKP's new position. Karakaya (the mayor before Ersoy), with his silence and low profile, was emblematic of the transition phase and the FP's lack of character. One of the Islamist leaders of the district summarized the transition in the authority figures as follows:

> Koçak destroyed the forest. But he also gave Islamic names to the streets. Of course, he also built those streets when there was nothing here. Karakaya is an ignorant person. He is Erbakan's man [Erbakan'ın torpillisi]. Otherwise he could not have come to that position. He is immersed in women and money. Ersoy is rich. He is also haughty. He sees himself as urban and the residents as peasants.

This change in the authority figures of the municipality was not an isolated change restricted to urban management. Authority patterns were changing in other institutions of the district too. The AKP, in fact, coordinated this change, which infiltrated the capillaries of political society. In 2006, the party was silently carrying out a national campaign to replace previous municipal and party administrators with wealthy and educated ones. A woman activist explained how this campaign was changing the face of the party's women's commissions:

> We take every step by keeping in mind the EU accession process. We know that our illiterate members work day and night cooking, collecting clothes, and carrying food and clothing from door to door. We don't want to be unjust to them, but we have to emphasize culture because of EU accession. We have to make sure that we have at least high school graduates at the head of the women's commissions, without insulting hard-working women. We are trying to elevate the level of Sultanbeyli's women by sending them to special literacy and career schools, so that there will be more qualified women in the commissions.

Other activists too trumpeted the increase in the number of educated party members. This was actually by order of the prime minister, they said. He wanted high school and university graduates to be the main body of the administrative staff. So, the conservative leaders attempted to naturalize this overall professionalization by using Erdoğan's name.

The Persistent Magic: Erdoğan's Charisma

Prime Minister Erdoğan's charisma was the magic that kept things together in this swiftly disenchanting world. While his family is from the Black Sea region, Erdoğan was born in Istanbul (1954) and raised in Kasımpaşa, a poor and rough neighborhood of the metropolis. His upbringing in Kasımpaşa bestowed him with a masculine and energetic style. A once-professional soccer player, he owed his popularity to years of interaction with the popular sectors during his long career as an outstanding organizer. He served as the Milli Salvation Party's youth organizer and street mobilizer, the RP's Istanbul administrator, and Istanbul's metropolitan mayor, positions that forged his popular appeal. Journalists at the national level, as well as Sultanbeyli residents, define him as *mert* (chivalrous, manly)—a quality that might be traced back to his experiences in Kasımpaşa, sports, and youth mobilization.[7]

In Sultanbeyli, many people referred to their love for Erdoğan as one of the main reasons why they supported the AKP. His pictures were everywhere. The residents followed his speeches carefully. They took his words very seriously. From time to time, national television channels pictured him visiting his poor neighborhood of origin, Kasımpaşa, and going to his childhood barbershop to have his hair cut. Such moves reproduced his image as "one of us," while at the same time he was becoming a part of the Turkish elite. AKP supporters frequently contrasted Erdoğan's modesty to Erbakan, who had allegedly pillaged the RP treasury and amassed incredible amounts of gold. Though not as popular as him, other ex-Islamists in the cabinet (Abdüllatif Şener, Bülent Arınç, Abdullah Gül, etc.) were also seen as true Muslims and "of the people" (*halktan, halk adamı*).

Many AKP activists told me a standard story about joining the party: they cried when they heard Erdoğan read the poem that caused his imprisonment.[8] They then decided that they had to do something about his imprisonment, that they could not remain silent in the face of injustice. Erdoğan's victimization made him a hero. The most prominent activists said they respected him because he was a good orator, had strong communication skills, spent time in prison, and was a veteran politician who served in every phase and rank of mobilization.

Even former radicals saw themselves in the prime minister. One ex-radical activist claimed that Erdoğan represented all the activists who were once radicals with his masculine, sincere, charismatic stance and his popular roots: "The radicals see him as one of them, distanced from the aristocracy." Those radicals who had not joined the Welfare Party were disturbed by Erbakan's allegedly "aristocratic" and condescending attitude. They could now join the AKP because the prime minister was "one of them." One could argue that Erdoğan's appeal emanated from the multivocality of his figure: educated radicals, as well as uneducated construction workers, identified with him.

During the local congress of the AKP, Erdoğan visited the district. Even though the party had not been very active in Sultanbeyli during those months, its activists worked ardently to gather as large an audience as possible. Thousands of people filled Sultanbeyli's largest gymnasium, which was not big enough to house the Erdoğan enthusiasts: hundreds remained outside. Erdoğan spoke before a tense congress, as a result of which the Turks replaced the Kurds as the party's top administrators in Sultanbeyli. Before Erdoğan entered the gymnasium, people were preoccupied with details of local politics and last-minute maneuvers. Even though it seemed certain that the Turks would take over the Kurds were still hopeful, and both sides were trying to win as many delegates as possible.

Before the prime minister, the minister of economy Ali Babacan (who has an MBA from Northwestern University) gave a speech. Nobody really listened to him. They were busy talking to each other because of the approaching congressional elections. He was applauded only once. Then there was a frantic applause: The prime minister had arrived. Babacan cut his speech short immediately and handed the microphone over to the prime minister. When the prime minister started talking, the whole crowd passionately cheered. People jumped to their feet and clapped with maximum strength. They started to sing the song identified with Erdoğan during his imprisonment: "You Are a Song That Will Last a Lifetime." The prime minister started his speech by talking about other local congresses. He had recently been in eastern cities. He said, "there is no rest" (*durmak yok*) several times and encouraged people to go from door to door for the AKP. When he talked about how the government gave funds for education and distributed high school books for free, the audience cheered wildly again. In the context of a swift transition to a market economy and rising unemployment and impoverishment, his person and his past (combined with a couple of weak provision policies and slogans) cast an aura of social justice on the government.

The prime minister once again proved his skills as an orator. He knew how to control the pulse of the room. Whenever people started talking to each other, as they did during the speech of the minister of economy, Babacan, he switched his pace, changed his style, did a question-answer format, and so on, and again made the people rise to their feet.

Erdoğan spent a lot of time talking about the economy. When blaming the people who resisted privatization in the health sector he accused them of having "the statist mentality," and being "the remnants of the communist regime." He was not going to privatize everything right now, these were "communist lies," but this could be done when the time came. He added: "This is the way things are in civilized countries." It is significant that the Virtue Party did not attack "the communists" (by which Erdoğan meant the whole political Left plus the Kemalists) in the same way. Even in previously Islamist localities like Sultanbeyli, the AKP's authority figures were using a Cold War rather than Islamist language in 2006. Then, when defending extra-national privatization, Erdoğan said, "Money does not have a religion." He also put a lot of emphasis on competition, both in world markets and within Turkey. During the several months I spent in Sultanbeyli in 2006, I saw that this take on the economy was naturalized. Erdoğan's words about the communists resisting privatization, about money not having a religion, and about competition were repeated over and over in various contexts. Moreover, the U.S. dollar, which was the target of so much nationalist and Islamist raving in 2001, had become a normal part of life, thanks both to the AKP's stabilization of the economy and Erdoğan's embrace of international financial transactions. Nonreligious privatization and marketization were thus naturalized through the political work of this ex-Islamist.

However, it should be noted that Erdoğan was not a godlike figure for the residents. There were limits to what he could naturalize. Erdoğan talked at length about the local municipality's construction plan and finally said: "You should support the municipality's project." Nobody applauded this sentence, or any other sentence in this part of the speech.[9] Naturalization was finite, especially when it was immediately obvious that subsistence was threatened. Capitalism at the national level was naturalized, but formal capitalism at the local and immediate levels was not completely. Nevertheless, we should be open to the possibility that the AKP—bolstered by the charisma of Erdoğan—will eventually accomplish this too. After all, men with skullcaps never applauded sentences such as "money does not have a religion" in 2000, but they did in 2006.

Throughout his speech, Erdoğan didn't say "God" more than once. Religious rhetoric was almost not there. In Virtue Party (FP) rallies, speeches used to be imbued with Islamic vocabulary. (For instance, at an FP rally in central Istanbul in 2001, a party leader had opened his speech by saying: "May God's blessing, compassion, and mercy be upon you.") There wasn't even a trace of this tradition in Erdoğan's speech.[10] The people in this sports complex were militants of the Islamist cause about ten years ago. But by 2006 they had become engaged in formalized, professionalized politics, where only services of the government and its deeds rather than its overall orientation and ideology were discussed and praised. Erdoğan's interactions with the audience thus naturalized secularism, professionalism, and capitalism, even if only partially. The AKP leadership's activities linked this professionalization to a transformation in visions of unity.

NATIONALISM AND ABSORPTION INTO WESTERN HEGEMONY

Though there were many mixed feelings and differences among the residents, the overall orientation of the Islamists had moved from an Islamic internationalism mixed with Turkish nationalism to Turkish nationalism mixed with religiously justified integration into the Western world. This went hand in hand with the naturalization of capitalism. Interactions between the Justice and Development Party (AKP) leadership and teahouses, mosques, newspapers, and informal conversations in workplaces led to revisions in Sultanbeyli's fractured political unity. The AKP's absorption of Islamic internationalism into nationalism and the emerging global polity amounted to a passive revolution in the conception of political unity.

Changing Conceptions of the West

In 2006, I observed an explosion of anti-U.S. sentiment because of the war in Iraq, coupled with a growing knowledge and admiration of the U.S. system. I was struck by how the residents' appreciation of the United States had developed in a matter of five years, even though nobody I talked to had visited that country (yet). Another striking feature was the positive direction of the change regarding the sociopolitical characteristics of the United States.

After a youth commission meeting of the AKP, we went to a patisserie with the meeting's most active three male members, who were all in their twenties. The patisserie was an all-male place. One of them was a computer programmer who worked in the municipality. Born in the Turkish part of an eastern city, he was very curious about U.S. society and politics and asked me many questions. He was studying the U.S. suburban geographical model and was very positive about it:

> They have established a wonderful system. Everything is in a separate location. There is no concentration in the urban center. Those suburbs especially

are wonderful. We want to do the same here in Sultanbeyli. We will create a center of education in the least populated and developed part of the district. It will be like the university towns in the United States.

The United States was gradually becoming a model for AKP activists, and this went beyond the old "people of the book" affirmation among the Islamists. The new admiration for the United States was based on more detailed knowledge within each person's profession and therefore went hand in hand with the professionalization in the district. The aim was no longer building an ideal Islamic republic but becoming a conservative empire like the United States.

Changing perceptions of the West not only influenced people's work but also life decisions. For example, I came across several people who wanted to move to the United States. On one warm May afternoon, I encountered one of my colleagues from my first visit to the district, the mathematics teacher Abdullah. Abdullah came from a conservative family. He had flirted with both right-wing nationalism and Islamism in his youth, and in 2000 (when he was twenty-five) he mostly had a negative perception of the United States as a racist country where Muslims and blacks are oppressed. His brother was an Islamist activist who spent his youth working for the Milli Youth Foundation. It was after a national holiday celebration (in which teachers are obligated to participate) that I ran into him, when Abdullah was with his new wife. He had gained a lot of weight, gone bald, and was married to a veiled woman. He was very glad to see me but, as a conservative, did not introduce me to his wife. His brother now worked at an entertainment-based radio channel in the United States making music programs. He had visited England and met a U.S. colleague there; they had married and moved to the United States. Abdullah was planning on joining his brother, as he now wanted to get a PhD in religious studies in the United States. "As you know, the United States is the best place to get this kind of education," he remarked. Five years before, the only positive thing I heard from him about the United States was about the freedom to don the veil. He had changed along with his brother. Abdullah's religiously inspired reaction to the United States had turned into a religiously inspired admiration.

The common feeling about Europe had also moved in a positive direction. The European Union's (EU) anti-Turkish decisions of December 2006 had not passed yet, and the ex-Islamists were quite positive about EU accession. For example, on a day in June, when recently disclosed information regarding secular-nationalist paramilitary organizations' conspiracies was stirring Turkey,[11] I visited Yaman. He told me that we had no choice but to join the EU. This was the only way for Turkey's liberation, he added, since "otherwise nobody can deal with the deep forces in this country," referring to the authoritarian paramilitary gangs. Other previous Islamists also wholeheartedly embraced, as they liked to emphasize, the "Copenhagen criteria" of accession based on human rights and democracy. However, most of them added that we also had things to preserve and that we could contribute to the European understanding of democracy. They wanted to see revisions in liberal and secular European laws regarding adultery and homosexuality. They also thought that the death penalty was indispensable. In that regard, most found U.S. laws more just. One of the major points upon which they did not agree with the existing U.S. system was gender equality. Many people told me that after these points were revised, there was perfect compatibility between their understanding of Islam and Western democracy. The ex-Islamists' desire to preserve certain Islamic ways was thus channeled to the EU accession process rather than to building an Islamic state.

Meanwhile, approval of the Arab world had declined. An almost unquestioning admiration of the Muslim Brotherhood, especially in its Egyptian incarnation, which was widespread among Virtue Party members and nonaffiliated Islamists in 2001, left in its place criticism and sometimes even a condescending attitude. Many activists told me that Turks apparently had nothing to learn from the rest of the Muslim world, as it was only in Turkey that an effective Islamic party strong enough to negotiate with the Western world had come to power. A fifty-year-old shopkeeper, who had preached to me in 2000 about the virtues of Pakistani and Egyptian Islamic movements, said: "We thought the Muslim Brotherhood was a model to follow. But then we learned that it is a low-quality movement. Now *they* are beginning to take the AKP as the model." Such a thorough change of position was more common among the highly educated and the activists.

Yet, the fascination with the American system had spread even among the least educated construction workers. For example, Harun, a fifty-year-old construction worker, told me his opinion about the United States in the following way:

It is a very beautiful country. It is beautiful that they allow every kind of dress inside the classroom. That they go to their churches every Sunday is also beautiful. There is democracy in that country. That they apply the death penalty is also beautiful; it is just. But they oppress the rest of the world. We see what they are doing in Iraq and Guantánamo.

Originally from the Eastern Black Sea region, Harun had switched from the Motherland Party to the AKP, and (along with economy and religion) one reason was the party's ability to read "international developments." In sum, the most common opinion I heard about the United States among the AKP supporters was that they liked the internal structure of the United States and took it as a model but did not like what it was doing outside its borders. The U.S. social model was therefore Islamically acceptable, even desirable, while the violent international dealings of the United States were not. So, how was it that the AKP's pro-U.S. foreign policies did not lead to fury among the Sultanbeyli's residents?

The Justification of the AKP's Pro-Western Policies

Islamic activists justified the AKP's openly pro-Western foreign policies by resorting to religious and nationalist explanations. Even the most ardent anti-West activists had changed their positions. Before the Friday prayer on a crowded day, Kamil (the imam of the third biggest mosque in the district who was famous for his anti-Western preaching five years ago; see also the first section of this chapter) preached as follows:

> We have to learn how to be an average community [*vasat ümmet*], which means taking the middle road and having moderation [*itidal*]. Islam is the religion of the middle road. It is a religion between excess and lack [*ifrat ve tefrit*]. In political matters, find the most beautiful idea by taking an average of all that has been said in discussion. In Christianity, there is a clergy that cuts itself off from the world. They do not work, they do not marry, and they give all their lives to religion. In Islam, there is no clergy, and preachers and prayer leaders are engaged in trade. They do not live off religion. Jews, by contrast, have forgotten worship; they give all their lives to trade. God has made Saturday a resting day for them, but they even work on that day. Of course, in Islam too, we see the counterparts of these. There are some Sufis who withdraw from [*elini eteğini çeken*] everyday concerns. They boast by not being of this world. And there are those others who give all their time to sohbets and *emr-i bi'l-maruf* [implying the Islamists, see this chapter's first section], and who do not work. Finally, there are people who reinterpret Islam and make it a religion

like Judaism by softening its demands [implying the Islamic modernists]. So, in order to be a model Muslim, you have to balance your working life and religious life. You should not avoid the pleasures of this world, but should not go to extremes in pursuing them. The ideal political line in Islam is similar to this. We have to be a bridge between the extremes. We have to make conflicting states reach consensus. We have to be a nation and a state that every other state trusts as an intermediary. Therefore, Turkey should be a bridge between the West and Islam. That is how peace on earth will be established. Islam also teaches us how not to harm the enemy unnecessarily and how to take a distance from friends. We should know that today's enemies might become tomorrow's friends and today's friends might become tomorrow's enemies.

Having attended many of his sermons between 2000 and 2002, Kamil's change of heart amazed me. While such sermons could be heard in the preceding decades in more secular districts, this was a serious contrast to the Sultanbeyli of five years ago. Kamil, known as one of the imams who has Islamized the district, had in 2006 come to preach moderation, which to him meant acting as an intermediary between the West and the Muslim world. He marketed this as the most Islamic line. So, even the radical preachers and mosques had shifted to the center. Along with his naturalization of the absorption of Islam into the globalizing world, Kamil also naturalized (religious) capitalism by constructing the following parallels: as obvious as Islam's superiority to Christianity and Judaism was the superiority of the pious and moderate working life to the avoidance of work and extreme dedication to work. Just like Islam had a natural difference from Judaism and Christianity, so did the AKP's intermediate position from the extreme positions of Western imperialism and religious fanaticism.

However, the absorption of Islam into a national project of integration with the West was not always this smooth. Due to the widespread reaction against U.S. policies in the Middle East, the AKP had to give different messages to different audiences. Most of its supporters in Sultanbeyli believed that the AKP was not as pro-U.S. in foreign policy as it seemed to be. This belief found adherents both among the voters and the top local politicians. Ragıp (see Chapter 3), who had become one of the top leaders of the AKP in the district, attended some closed meetings of academics, politicians, and intelligence officers where the party discussed its foreign relations. In these meetings, he said, there were still some who defended the Greater Middle East

Project (the Bush administration's plan to restructure Middle Eastern regimes along neoliberal, conservative, and democratic lines), but there were also some who thought Turkey should form coalitions with Russia and China (a tendency that was common among both secular and Islamic publics throughout Turkey in 2006 and later). He also said that there was a severe fight between the AKP and the United States in the last meetings in Washington, so the party would have to look for new world powers as coalition partners. Months after the meetings that Ragıp mentioned, the AKP remained a supporter of U.S. foreign policy. While it was one of the main governments supporting the Greater Middle East Project, the AKP successfully created the impression that it was anti–United States among its base.

How could college-educated, politically experienced, intellectually informed people buy into the AKP's charade of anti-imperialism? This had to do with the political and social past of the AKP's national leaders, who had their roots in radical Islamism and the popular sectors. One day, when defending the government's economic record to me, Yasin drew attention to something that he thought was more important than the current economic indicators:

> This government is the most local, the most milli,[12] the most popular, and the most pro-oppressed government Turkey has seen. Look at the cabinet, the ministers all come from the people. They are also the people who follow the most correct foreign policy.
>
> R: So, you see the cabinet's desire in 2003 to allow the U.S. use of Turkey's borders in the war against Iraq as a correct foreign policy?
>
> Yasin: God has protected us from going into Iraq. That desire was this government's biggest mistake. But maybe there was a subtle game there. The cabinet publicly decided to allow the United States. But then, one of the key leaders said, "the parliament will decide." This actually meant "vote against the decision," and the parliament read this directive correctly. . . . If the AKP does not behave completely milli, it is because of the system. When a party behaves milli, they remove it from government. The AKP is the closest party to us, but it has to hide itself.

In the case of some ex-radicals who supported the government, its pro-U.S. foreign policy was thus explained by a "conspiracy theory in reverse" (see Chapter 2 for such theories in Turkey's rightist tradition). Also, Yasin supported the AKP because it was milli, and the conspiracy theory in reverse was not about the party being radical Islamist. This was an important change in comparison to his old position, when he evaluated all parties with respect to their degree of commitment to Islam. Islam was thus further being absorbed into nationalism, and both were unintentionally being absorbed into a national project of integration with the West. Yasin's associate added a more intriguing conspiracy theory to his:

> Today all Muslims are expecting leadership from Turkey. The center of the caliphate is Turkey. The flag [sancak] of Islam is in the Topkapı Palace. When Muslims rise up, we are going to carry that flag. On top of the Middle East there is Turkey: There is no strong state in the Middle East but Turkey. Today, the attack of the United States against Iraq, Iran, and Syria is dissimulation [takiye]. The real target is Turkey. They are collapsing Turkey's bottom so that they can attack Turkey. On the other hand, they are behaving as if we are not the target.

Both Yasin and his associate were Islamic internationalists in 2000. They were extremely critical of the Turkish state because of its oppression of the Kurds. They saw the solution in a transnational Islamic state. Just like Yasin, his associate had shifted his position to nationalism by 2006—a shift much more common among high school graduates when compared to college graduate ex-radicals in Sultanbeyli. The associate even believed in the conspiracy theory spread by right-wing nationalists and Kemalists: Turkey (as the representative of all oppressed nations) and the United States were about to engage in one of the biggest wars of history. But he gave this conspiracy theory an Islamic twist: the war was not between the oppressed nations and the United States but between the *ümmet* (the transnational Islamic community) and the United States. He expected the AKP (and Turkey) to fulfill the role of leadership of the whole ümmet in this great war against the Americans. The AKP believed in this role, they held, but it just behaved as if it were going along with U.S. interests. Thanks to these and other similar intricate conspiracy theories, once-active Islamists remained silent as history unfolded and waited for their trusted leaders to resolve the issues. A contradictory mixture of nationalism, pragmatism, and Islamic internationalism thereby bolstered Turkey's integration to the West.

Aggravation of the Kurdish Question

If the passive revolution marched on decisively regarding integration with the West, the same cannot be said of Turkey's internal integration. In 2006, the district was split along an ethnic faultline. The AKP was still trying to hold the Turks and Kurds together in the manner of previous Islamist parties, but it was running into more and more difficulties. Among the Turks, one of the common topics was the supposed harm the Kurds were doing to Sultanbeyli. A very common urban myth about the Kurds, which wasn't around five years ago, was that each Kurdish family had ten to fifteen children, their fathers were unemployed because they were lazy (and not because they had suffered forced migration), and, as a result, all the children were engaged in crime. They were at the root of the district's social ills. I heard this analysis countless times in the teahouses. Partially as a reaction to this growing nationalism, some Kurds (those not affiliated with Islamic parties) gathered more tightly around the Kurdish nationalist Democratic Society Party (DTP). In line with the Turkish nationalist strategy all over Turkey, Turks fired back by calling this nationalist mobilization "racist," thereby trying to demonize it. In Friday sermons, angry prayer leaders blamed Kurdish nationalists of "racism." No sermons agitated mosque communities against Kurdish nationalism in 2001.

It is noteworthy that the tension was taking on a racializing turn, but both parties were trying to avoid racism. The racism mostly came up in informal contexts. In his interview with me, Mustafa, one of the primary Islamizing agents and merchants of the district in the 1980s and 1990s, characterized religious life in the district as distorted. He held that most apparently pious people were hypocrites (*riyakar*) and were not "sincere." He also added that it could not be otherwise in a district full of drugs and smuggling. He made me turn off the tape recorder here and said this was all because of the "Easterners" (an innuendo Sultanbeyli residents used for Kurds). They had come to the district and made the situation worse. Retaining the same emphasis, he said he supported the AKP's economic policies but pointed out that it was causing more harm to the country than anybody else by raising issues like "the Kurdish question." (In 2006, official discourse still denied that there was a Kurdish question and held that there was only a problem of terrorism in the southeast.)

Hayri, an Islamist construction worker from the Black Sea region, also pronounced his reactions off the record, but went further than Mustafa. As we were finishing our interview, Hayri had started to emphasize the need for democracy. I asked him whether he also wanted democracy regarding issues other than religious ones, for example, ethnic issues. He shook his head:

> That is something else. . . . The people who talk about ethnic rights actually want to partition Turkey. But I want to say this: if they build a Kurdish state, and if the Kurds in my neighborhood stay in my neighborhood, I'm going to force them out. If they don't leave, I'm going to kill them.

It is crucial to note that this spirit was not there five years before, especially among the pious. As racism was still illegitimate in 2006, plans of massacre were mentioned only off the record. The emergence of an autonomous Kurdish region in Iraq, the U.S. support for the Kurds, and the AKP's reforms had changed the context. Similarly in other contexts, sometimes a man in a teahouse exploded and said, "We should bomb that Kurdish neighborhood with napalm" (a quite common utterance in 2006), but others calmed him down and objected that this could not be a solution. Desires for a massacre were spreading, but they were not unanimous.

The growing reaction against the Kurds was not independent from the transition to a market economy and professionalization in the district. In mid-April, I went to Fikret's (see Chapter 4) shop to get a haircut. I told him that the government was unable to solve the "Şemdinli case." In a Kurdish border town called Şemdinli, paramilitary forces had been carrying out bombings. A prosecutor went after these forces, but the secularist newspapers discredited him by disclosing his links to a religious community. The government first encouraged the prosecutor but then left him alone, scared by the reaction of the military. Secular liberal intellectuals in Turkey were deeply dismayed, though religious circles did not seem to mind this affair too much. Pious Turks in Sultanbeyli clearly disapproved of other paramilitary operations in Turkey but had different feelings about the Şemdinli affair, as they thought Kurdish nationalists deserved such action. Fikret's response to my probing, for example, was as follows:

> They [the prosecutor and the government] shouldn't have dealt with it. It was wrong from the beginning. They should have remained quiet. . . . Every state has secret structures like this. Even rich people have these: They have to protect themselves. They have to have back-up. When the law does not work, strong people have to resort to extralegal means for self-defense. Not everything can be done by the courts and the police. Of course, this has to have its peculiar legality. It should not be used for bad purposes. But this state has to protect itself. There are foreign powers that have all kinds of agendas for the [Kurdish] East. And the state has its own projects.

Fikret, one of the former anticapitalist and antistate Islamists of Sultanbeyli, normalized authoritarianism against the Kurds through normalizing extralegal moves of property holders. In other words, this was a double normalization of state and capital. This was coming from a person who was against both in his youth. He went on:

> These extreme events are going to happen while the state is making a transition. This is only an exception. There is probably some [paramilitary] structure behind this, but it will go away. The whole state is being legalized. You know, previously one could become a barber very easily. It was enough to work with a barber for several years. But now, they are changing the system. Now everybody has to get a certificate in order to become a barber. The state is going in the same direction. It is leaving the businesses that do not belong to it. Previously, the state was in businesses like iron, steel, and copper. But now, it is withdrawing from all of these. These [extralegal actions against the Kurds] are the crises we are living through while the state is withdrawing. When the state leaves a void, some people try to fill it.

Fikret made sense of the extralegal violence against the Kurds through naturalizating neoliberalization (privatization of public enterprises) and professionalization (the formalization and bureaucratization of his own line of work). Fikret thereby also normalized the way neoliberalization creates a broad universe of informality while it normalizes certain relations, professions, and property (and postponed the resolution of this informality to an indefinite future). While the growing Turkish nationalism safely reinforced hegemony through the naturalization of neoliberalism, private property, and professionalization, it created problems for a full establishment of hegemony because of the exclusion of Kurds.

Even though there was a substantial and growing Kurdish population in the district, their political and commercial power was small. As in 2001, only a minority of them supported the DTP. Kurdish members of different parties complained about how they suffered from discrimination but usually not in the presence of Turks, as this was a taboo subject. A month after the AKP's local congress, I visited Zaim, one of the party's prominent Kurdish activists. He was in the middle of discussing the district's infrastructural problems with two Turkish members of the AKP's new administration. While these two members were there, Zaim talked about the policies of the party and the history of the district within the boundaries of the AKP's official discourse. But after everybody left, he told me revealing details regarding his history. He had held a prominent role in the first two AKP administrations in the district. But in the third (Turkish-dominated) administration, they had given him a lesser role, which he eventually quit:

> In the municipal council, only I was expressing the weaknesses of the local administration. At the end, I resigned from the party in order not to become a scapegoat. So that there would be no speculations about my motivations, I also resigned from the municipal council. Otherwise people were going to say that I used the party but remained in the council for my benefit. But the real reason is that I was disturbed because my complaints were not being taken seriously since I was born in the East. And of course also because I was Kurdish. If I had been born in Konya, everything would be different. My first language would be Turkish. Then everybody would listen to me and take my ideas seriously. I was born in Muş and this was always a disadvantage starting from primary school. I always had difficulties at school because I couldn't even understand the questions. In fifth grade, I still had to read questions five times before I could tell what they asked.

Despite such common grievances regarding politics in Sultanbeyli and the whole system in Turkey, the Kurds did not form a front against discrimination. They had disparaging perceptions of each other but also complained about how the dominant forces played them against each other. One common, though not universally shared, feeling was the positive attitude about developments in northern Iraq. Kurdish residents said there was a lot of oil wealth there, and now it was going to be used by the local people for the first time. But even here, some had reservations. One day I was hanging out in the store of a Kurdish shopkeeper when a relative of his came in the middle of our conversation, and the shopkeeper recommended that he go to Iraq with his commercial truck. But his relative wouldn't because, even though he was of Kurdish descent, he was a Turkish nationalist, and he did not want to help the emerging Kurdish state. The shopkeeper later told me that his whole family was Turkish nationalists and did not make use of the opportunities in northern Iraq. However, many Kurds did, and there was some modest capital accumulation among Kurdish truck drivers who were occasionally trading in Iraq. Many Kurds who could not qualify for the universities in Turkey had also started to go to northern Iraq to receive diplomas from universities that used Kurdish as a teaching language. The autonomous Kurdish region was therefore not only a distant political hope but also an economic and educational opportunity for the Kurds, which further cut off Kurds and Turks from each other.

Islamic politics, which had kept the two groups together in the past, was also running into difficulties. During my second visit to Sultanbeyli, the local congress of the AKP in March 2006 dramatized these difficulties. When the party was first established in 2001, the AKP's Istanbul organization had supported the formation of a Kurdish-dominated administration in Sultanbeyli. Yet, with increasing Turkish nationalism and reaction against the Kurds in Turkey, the local Turks started to voice dissatisfaction. After a period of confusion, the Istanbul organization informally declared its support for a predominantly Turkish list. There were no ideological, programmatic, or religious differences between the two competing lists in the congress. The division was purely one of ethnic lines (which of course had class and status implications, as Turks of the district were more educated and wealthier). The local newspapers all supported the Turkish candidate. They hardly mentioned the Kurdish one, and then only in a hostile manner. After what some expected to be a tight race, the Turkish list won by a considerable margin.

The defeated Kurds remained members of the party after the congress, but this did not mean that tensions were resolved. In April, Ferit, the former president of the youth commission of one of the neighborhoods, demanded his neighborhood's AKP presidency. When he could not get it, he incited the youth commission and the women's commission to resign. I was at the AKP headquarters on the day the youth commission resigned. Yeliz, a Turkish housewife in her late twenties, said: "Nothing can be done with Ferit. He is trouble. I'm glad that they resigned. One of his relatives is the person involved in the recent high school shootings. His last name is T——. The whole family is trouble. Y—— [this person had just called the party and talked about this incident] is also sympathetic to them because he is an Easterner [Kurdish]." By "high school shootings," Yeliz was alluding to a gang fight in a high school that had erupted because of a love affair and culminated in a Kurdish student killing a Turkish student. The already alarming situation in schools in 2001 (see Chapter 3) had eventually led to a death in 2006. The affair came up in conversations in schools, teahouses, and party headquarters. Nobody discussed it in the context of the decreasing quality of education in public schools or the exclusion of the Kurds, but implicitly or explicitly in reference to the protagonists' ethnic origins and the Kurds' traditions of troublemaking.

There was also an uncovered housewife in her late forties in the room. She had dyed her hair blonde. She was from the AKP's city administration. She said:

> You should not judge this person by relatives. You should not be
>   concerned with whether he is an Easterner or not. Will this person be
>   useful to the party? Will he do business? You should base your
>   decision on these.
> Yeliz: When he was the president of the youth commission, he did
>   nothing.

The others in the room approved what Yeliz said with silent nods. In sum, while the party's agenda was (professionally and pragmatically) transethnic, its practice on the ground molded to ethnic lines.

In June, the tensions were further exacerbated in the central neighborhood's headman elections. Initially, the Kurdish candidate seemed to be winning as the votes were counted in a schoolyard. His supporters were jubilant and started celebrations in the yard. In the middle of the celebrations, gunshots were heard and people started to run toward the school gate, which to their surprise was locked. One of the relatives of the Kurdish candidate was killed. The Kurds held the Turkish candidate's family responsible for the killing. It was rumored that the relatives of the Kurdish candidate called him that night and asked him to leave Sultanbeyli if he was not brave enough to avenge the killing. The eventually victorious Turkish candidate was accused of inciting the killing and imprisoned for several months, after which he was freed and assumed the post.

Chapter 6 will show that the district was experiencing urbanization from above concomitant to this ethnic polarization from below: the party wanted to transcend ethnic and hometown differences and build unity in the district. This chapter emphasized that, on the ground, ethnic differences were gaining a lot of importance, and the next chapter will reveal that hometown differences were not necessarily losing their significance. While the AKP could not neutralize ethnic differences, it was able to neutralize Islam and articulate it to an emergent project of integration to a capitalist globe. The next chapter will also demonstrate how the AKP either demolished or absorbed elements of Islamic space to pave the way for further marketization of society. The absorption of the leadership and authority patterns went hand in hand with the absorption of alternative religion and space.

6 MODERN ISLAMIC CIVIL SOCIETY TRIUMPHANT

THE POLITICAL SOCIETY that emerged as analyzed in the previous chapter reintegrated civil society to the secular state and the capitalist economy. In 2006, the ongoing repercussions of the 1997 coup were observable in the further secularization of life in the district. However, the Justice and Development Party (AKP) had capitalized on the surviving elements of Islamic civil society to give an unforeseen twist to this secularization.

The civil-political changes in the district were unfolding in the overall context of national-global economic changes or, more specifically, the AKP government's further opening up of Turkey to international competition. A number of the few existing factories in the district closed down and moved to China, leaving hundreds of workers unemployed. Textile workshops were also leaving the district or going bankrupt. Deindustrialization was at its peak. Yet, it did not become a political issue: No major political party used it against the AKP, as other parties did not have prescriptions for preventing deindustrialization either. Nevertheless, the expanding construction sector and trade in Turkey created new opportunities for other residents of the district.

The thorough marketization, neoliberalization, and individualization I witnessed in 2006 received no organized, critical response from society. Why was there no pro–social justice reorganization in civil society as a response to marketization in Sultanbeyli? This chapter demonstrates that Islamists were able to build a modern Islamic (and neoliberal) civil society, effectively pacifying resistance to neoliberalization.[1]

CONTESTED SECULARIZATION

Cultural centers, networks of friends, mosques, religious communities, private TV stations, and Islamic schools unintentionally cooperated to reduce the role of religion in life. Under the leadership of the AKP, these nodes of civil society redirected a much more pragmatic, nationalist, and rationalized religion to venues such as business, the care of the self, and the revitalization of the Turkish state.

Islamization of Top Institutions, De-Islamization of Everyday Life and of Peripheral Institutions

In 2006, the former Islamists prayed less, did not discuss religion at length, and used Islamic language much less in their daily conversations. Many even confessed to being confused about whether to call themselves Islamist or not.[2] An indicator of the linguistic transformation was the change in the use of the Islamic greeting *selam-un aleyküm* (peace be upon you) instead of the secular *merhaba* (hi). Islamists used to start and end their conversations with *selam-un aleyküm*. Even the phone conversations started and ended with this greeting. But in 2006, people didn't always start with this greeting, and they rarely ended with it.

Another Islamic phrase people used less and less frequently was *inşallah* (God willing). The frequent use of this word used to imply that God's permission is required for every event. While an infrequent use of this word is a part of Turkish custom, its frequent use was an Islamist intervention. During 2000–2002, some Islamists mentioned it in almost every sentence.[3] In 2006, while some still used the word frequently, daily language was no longer suffused with it.

This change in speech patterns was paralleled by a change in outward appearance and other daily practices. A lot of people had shaved off their beards. Some previously radical Islamist men had even dyed their hair, which would have been unthinkable five years ago. Also, while alcohol sales were just starting in 2000, in 2006 they were widespread in the district. Pious residents still did not consume alcohol, but now—with no Islamist movement agitating against it—they were less concerned with its legal sale.

Middle-class activists performed the daily prayer less than they used to. However, the workers I interacted with more or less stuck to their routine. Veysel (see Chapters 3 and 4), exemplifying this general trend, had come from the Friday prayer when we met for the first time in 2006, and he still put aside time for the daily prayers. But this was still as far as his religiosity went. Just like five years before, he was not engaged in religious reading circles, did not read any religious sources on his own, did not attend religious *sohbets* or any other similar activity. This is what the religion of the construction workers and the other working poor mostly looked like. Five times a day was the limit. There were workers doing more than that, like Hüsnü (see Chapter 3), but those men were members of certain Sufi communities or were in commanding positions in the Islamist party. Since both the communities and the mainstream Islamist party had lost influence and members, even fewer workers engaged in religious activities beyond the daily prayer and the fast.

The tendency among the middle-class activists not to perform their prayers was not absolute. For example, during the local AKP congress (see Chapter 5), a lot of men rushed to the nearby mosque when the call to the noon prayer was read. I realized that even people who no longer regularly prayed joined them. (Yaman, for example, went even to the Friday prayer quite rarely, but he joined the communal prayer at the congress.) So, praying communally together was still an important symbolic act. Yet, this is not very different from the center right tradition, where politicians are usually not very pious men but take care to show off their piety in public. This demonstrates how the dominance of the AKP had (in line with the center right tradition in Turkey) reduced religion to being symbolic: religion no longer *organized life* but was still an important political "resource."

While praying less was not always associated with other major changes in one's life, in the case of Necmi it was a part of a major shift in the direction of the modernist interpretation of Islam. As I pointed out in Chapter 3, Necmi came from the Welfare Party tradition, but he moved away from Islamist ideas after the military intervention in 1997 and started to organize an Islamic modernist group in the district around a cultural center called Furkan. By 2006, his hopes that the AKP would be a major modernist Islamic force were not fulfilled, but at least he was happy that the party had appointed an Islamic modernist theology professor (Mehmet Aydın) as the minister responsible for religious affairs. When he was talking about Mehmet Metiner (one of the major modernist Islamic thinkers in Turkey) in one of Furkan Center's *sohbets*, Necmi smilingly said:

> My friend was working with him in the metropolitan municipality. He noticed that Metiner misses the prayers. I was shocked to learn that a person so high in

Islamic thinking [*tefekkür*] could be weak in Islamic practice [*amel*]. But I am no longer angry at him because these days I am in the same situation.

Necmi added that this situation allowed him to develop a better understanding of Metiner's ideas. Necmi was actually sorry that he was not praying as often as he used to but glad that he had stopped worrying about Islamic eti quette at every step (a worry, emphasized in Chapter 3, that was central to building an integral civil society). In his youth, he complained, he was obsessed with which side of the bed to get up from, which foot to use when exiting his home, how to behave in the restroom, how to shake hands, and how to sit and behave when with friends. When taking his *gusül* ablution,[4] he took care not to leave any area on his body "as large as the head of a pin" dry, as İlmihals (manuals for doctrine and ritual) had taught him. He also paid attention to the size of the bath: if the area where he was taking a bath was larger than 1.5 by 1.5 meters, then he made sure he was not naked, because the angels could see him. "Today I wonder why this isn't 1.8 m, but such questions never occurred to me before," he said. Now, after the example of the modernist thinkers, he thought that the sincerity of the ritual mattered more than any of these. The others in the Furkan Center were not as dismissive as Necmi about these ritualistic details, but they still affirmed the general tone of this critique.

The Furkan group had shifted from reading and discussing the works of the modernist Islamic scholar Fazlur Rahman to those of another modernist, Muhammad Asad. Asad's works, especially his recently translated *The Message of the Qur'an,* gave rise to controversies between modernists and traditionalists in the district (see Chapter 5). Sultanbeyli's religious notables were furious with Necmi because of his promotion of Asad, just like they were angry at him for his promotion of Rahman five years ago. Sohbets in the Furkan Center sometimes started and ended with communal prayers, just like other sohbets in Sultanbeyli, but not with the same regularity.

These ritualistic changes had their counterparts in religious instruction too. Numan (see Chapter 3), one of the dedicated radical Islamist teachers of the district, had quit trying to instill his beliefs in the pupils. He no longer strayed away from the official curriculum as long as the students did not ask questions. "I am not doing missionary work," he joked. This was a significant change from the days where he, like other Islamist teachers of the 1990s, used to spread the word in the classroom. The noncurricular questions coming from the students, in turn, were not of a theological or political nature either. They mostly asked about supernatural appearances and creatures like the *jinn*. Numan thought that this obsession came from the religious education they got from their families and TV series such as *Sırlar Dünyası*. It is significant that after the 1997 military intervention, the private TV channels of religious communities had become even more influential. These channels aired very popular programs that blended the styles and themes of U.S. series such as *The Twilight Zone* with popular supernatural beliefs. Consequently, the religious interests of children started to revolve around supernatural rather than theological or political themes (we will see later in this chapter that supernaturalism had a slightly different fate among the adults).

Meanwhile, traditionalist venues of instruction, such as the *medrese*s, now found themselves in an intellectual environment where they had to take Islamic modernism seriously. When I had engaged a respected medrese instructor, Muhsin, in a conversation about Islamic modernism in 2002, he was very dismissive. Yet, I noticed that this time books by Fazlur Rahman and Mehmet Aydın, the most prominent Islamic modernist scholars discussed in Turkey, were also in his library. I did not remind him of our conversation about Islamic modernism four years ago, and just directly asked him what he thought about Aydın, who was now on the bookshelf. "He has very beautiful ideas. I respect his ideas. He is also a knowledgeable Muslim. And I am saying this even though he is an Islamic modernist. I do not agree with his thoughts." Muhsin was now more careful about criticizing the modernists, and he had to position himself with respect to them. The modernists had started to set the terms of the debate in even the underground schools of peripheral neighborhoods.

There were, however, persisting patterns of ritualization in the district. For example, many mosques still held lessons every Sunday morning. Teachers from surrounding secular schools, as well as the imams of the mosques, gave lessons on subjects as varied as Arabic and exegesis. Nevertheless, some mosques had moved their lessons from Sunday to Friday, leaving Sundays as a vacation day for imams and teachers. This de-Islamization of the weekend, which would have been unthinkable in 2000, attracted reaction from some.

All this does not mean that former Islamists no longer believe religion has an important role in social life. A young AKP activist made this very clear to me as he explained Islam's regulating role: It provides morality, values, and keeps the community together. So I asked him about why the AKP opposes this regulating role in the state and in economic matters. He responded dispassionately:

> Religion should not be intermixed with everything. The state has its own way of functioning. You cannot rule the state like a religious body. I'm going to use a metaphor, but it won't be exact. The state is like logic, and religion is like emotion. Logic predominates in politics, but sometimes you need emotions.

This activist in fact partially displaced my emphasis on AKP-led secularization by using the overdetermined metaphor of emotion. He pointed out that religion does figure into politics but not to the detriment of logic; its influence on the state is emotional rather than regulatory. There is thus no one-dimensional certainty about secularization among the AKP activists. We could say that the top activists in this district wanted individual, communal, and social lives to be religious, but the state and the economy should use religion only as fuel and not be shaped by it thoroughly.

This would allow us to interpret several signs of Islamization throughout Turkey in 2006. The public television station TRT (known as one of the bastions of secularism) featured many programs on which religious scholars and intellectuals discussed Islamic topics. A parliamentarian from the governing party declared on a private TV channel that Islam has rules governing the minute details of everyday life, including restroom behavior. More specifically, the parliamentarian argued that it was un-Islamic to urinate when standing up: one ought to be seated. We can add to all this the restriction on alcohol sales and the appointment of conservative men with veiled wives to top positions, which would both be unthinkable in a country ruled by hard-line secularists.

These developments had their counterparts at the local level. While between 2000 and 2002 I had not encountered any proto-Islamist messages in official mosques, I did come across some in 2006. Actually, there was no change in the conduct of the mosque participants: Many people yawned, itched, half-slept during sermons, and arrived late. Only a minority listened to the preacher attentively. This popular, undisciplined behavior demonstrated the limits of Islamization both in 2000 and in 2006. What changed was the content of some sermons. One Friday, the preacher in one of the central mosques of Sultanbeyli said:

> A lot of political systems have come and gone. At the peak of each of them people have said, "This is the best system; this is the highest point that humanity can

reach." All of those systems have collapsed or are going to collapse. Communism, capitalism, pharaohism are systems of oppression. Do not obey them. The system of the Muslim person is Islam. It is Islamic law. That is to say, it is shariah.

Official mosques are usually the mouthpieces of the secularist state, and sermons do not pose Islam as a system against capitalism—let alone propose shariah as a system, which is banned in Turkey. Such developments worried secularists in the country, but a bottom-up analysis shows that these changes have to be interpreted in an overall context of the partial de-Islamization of everyday life.

Murat, one of the former Islamist radicals of the district, related the following story, which underlines the contradictions of the changes occurring under the AKP:

> The other day we were sitting together with a group of men. A very old man among them stood up and went to the restroom. He had his coat on. One of the men said, "Is he going to urinate standing up?" I asked him what would happen if he did. He said, "His prayer will not be valid." I told them even a handful of excrement would not render a prayer invalid. These are all *bidat* [theologically unacceptable innovations].

Murat based his argument on written sources of Islam, while the old men around him depended on what they had learned from imams and what they had heard from the AKP parliamentarian who had spoken on TV against urinating when standing up. This was the paradox of AKP rule: even when the elected rulers went in a more religious direction, society did not necessarily follow. Indeed, angry old men echoed the conservative parliamentarian, but newer generations (including middle-aged former radicals) were moving away from dogma.

The Changing Nature of Religious Activity Among Mystic Communities

Changes in Yasin's religious life give clues about changes in the Sufi communities in the district. As pointed out in Chapter 4, Yasin's radical position regarding mysticism had already started to change in 2001. However, this was mostly a change in political position and was not reflected deeply in his practices. Now, his everyday life and its relation to mysticism also changed.

I had come across no displays of mystic activity in Yasin's office five years ago. Even though his life had not become thoroughly mysticized, in 2006 there was at least some activity along these lines in his office. One day a very old, long-bearded man with a wand came and sat with us. He sang several hymns. They were about belonging to a lodge, obeying a mystic leader, death, morning and night, the meaning of life, and so on. But he was too old to stay awake, and he fell asleep from time to time. He eventually woke up and began to sing again. When he sang, the other people in the room fell silent and lis tened to him respectfully. Yasin said in an affectionate tone: "Look at this uncle, he came here, and he sang hymns. He created an atmosphere that gave us peace of mind. He made us rest. It is beautiful to deal with *tarikat* when one grows old. *Tesbihat*,[5] *zikir*,[6] these are nice things when one is old."

When I pointed out these changes, Yasin underlined that he was not the only one to change: the mystic communities were also changing and adapting to the age, which softened him. The mystic communities were now working like "civil society organizations," in his own words:

> The İskenderpaşa community has quit classical tarikat work. They are work-
> ing on the environment and other social issues. This is good too. We need this
> too in an Islamic state. If you had apportioned the tasks, it wouldn't be this
> good. A lot of different communities are doing what they need to do.

It is interesting to see how this differentiation is naturalized, especially by someone who believed in 2000 that everything has to be controlled by the Islamic state (the Friday sermons had to be distributed from the center, etc.). Yasin still believed in an Islamic state (and he believed that the AKP was building it), but he thought that this would happen spontaneously, with each community and social group discovering its true tasks, rather than through an authoritarian political program. I propose that this differentiation of tasks is not a spontaneous process (as in modernization theory, and as in Yasin's own account). The differentiation occurred because of political processes, especially (1) the military intervention of 1997, which put restrictions on Islamic activism, and (2) the establishment of the AKP, which regulated the adaptation of activists to these restrictions.

Yet, the largest group was still the conventionally mystic Menzilcis. They still held well-attended Saturday *sohbet*s in their main mosque in Sultanbeyli. The conventional Mahmud Efendi group, however, shrank after the military closed down their Kur'an schools. They had weekly sohbets in the district center. They also had neighborhood sohbets. Very influential hocas came to the Wednesday meetings, but despite that only twenty-five to thirty people showed up.

The more conventional communities had become restricted to the elders. Even their women's groups, which were very strong before the 1997 intervention, lost adherents. This also happened because the elders lost power in the family and could not recruit new members to their communities. (So the same mechanisms that caused radicalization fifteen years ago now created secularization.) As the mystic communities lost power and the AKP came to power, the (government-controlled) Directorate of Religious Affairs became more legitimate, the people turned to it more, and they started to hang its calendars on the walls as a sign of respect and acceptance (also concomitant with the Islamic turn of the directorate). More importantly, the books of Turkish scholars (the Ankara School, Yaşar Nuri Öztürk, etc.),[7] along with the translated sources, started to circulate among the educated, who now believed that the local scholars were more valuable and profound. Hasan (see Chapter 4) proudly said, "The people expressing these views are now more courageous in the district, and they have clearer things to say."

All of these transformations crystallized in the changes in the perception and power of the Gülen community (and other historically anti-Islamist Nurcu groups) in Sultanbeyli (see Introduction).[8] Now, ex-radicals referred to Fethullah Gülen all the time, starting their sentences with phrases like, "As Fethullah Hoca Efendi [Supreme Master] has said. . . ." I also saw veiled and unveiled women in their twenties mount buses with books such as *Fethullah Hoca Efendi Konuşuyor* [Supreme Master Fethullah Speaks], a sight that could not have been conceived in 2000.

The first Nurcu group in Sultanbeyli was established in the mid-1990s. It ran a small medrese with only three to five students. It was quite isolated. But now Nurcu groups opened up to the public. Even people from the AKP and Felicity Party (SP) went to their seminars.[9] However, some of them (the so-called Readers) were still against sending their daughters to high school and college. Including the seminaries of the Gülen community, Nurcus had about ten medreses in the district in 2006.

So, why did ex-radicals change their anti-Nur position and start to populate their classrooms? Yasin accounted for his increasing sympathy in the following way:

Previously, Islamists did not take the real conditions of Turkey and the world into consideration. They directly opposed the United States. But sometimes in order to do something, you have to take the conditions into account. Fethullah Hoca always did this. Erbakan Hoca always opposed the United States. What happened to him eventually? Now Islamists approached Fethullah Hoca's understanding.

Based on his transformed opinions about the community, Yasin did not recoil from chastising me: "Why don't you visit Fethullah Hoca in America?"—blaming me for not becoming an affiliate of a group he was viciously opposed to five years ago. But, among many other reasons, I had a reason that he could sympathize with: the community's pro-invasion position during the initial stages of the Iraq War. His partner Hidayet, who had just come in the middle of this conversation, said: "Fethullah Hoca is dissimulating [*takiye yapıyor*]. He knows that the United States will do the opposite of whatever he says. He does everything to trick the United States. In fact, he is taking over the whole world." Yasin seemed to agree with this conspiracy theory and added: "Now, we are thinking small here. But Fethullah Hoca thinks big. He fakes supporting the ban on the veil so that they allow his schools. The graduates of those schools will take over the [Turkish] state. Thanks to those schools, people all over the world speak Turkish." As ex-radicals like Yasin shifted to a more gradualist and Turkish nationalist position, they discovered the virtue of the Gülen community, which had been Turkish nationalist for decades. Yet, they also reinterpreted Gülen's conservative and proregime positions as a secret gradualism.

Even Yasin's antisupernaturalism was now filtered through pragmatism, which also made him appreciate the Gülen community:

> Gülen's followers all believe in *efsunlu* [magical, supernatural] things. In one of their sohbets the other day, they read a passage from the *Epistles of Light*. Said Nursi[10] had gone to Damascus in order to collect some followers there. But three deceased mystic leaders from centuries back came to him and told him to leave. So he decided to leave. I told the group that this was not realistic, because our holy book says that you should not expect anything from the dead. Yet, they believe everything in the *Epistles of Light*. . . . But maybe this *efsun* [charm, magic] is necessary. The Gülen group is able to send people to very distant places such as Central Asia for five years. Educated people give up marriage and do this for their community. They are able to make the sacrifices because of efsun. Their ability to grow and become influential is partially due to this.

The supernaturalism of the group prevented Yasin from becoming a full member. However, he appreciated how the unquestionable power of supernaturalism

created extremely committed followers and allowed the community to pros-
per. Among yet other radicals who did not succumb to Turkish nationalism or
conservatism (like Yasin), the Gülen line still garnered some sympathy because of its discipline and international success. Some former radicals went to
their weekly lessons or monthly meetings irregularly. Most of the people who
used to be against the community were no longer so.

Just like ex-radicals had shifted to the Nurcu line, so had members of other
mystic communities. Tahsin, an active member of the Welfare Party in the
1990s, was now active in the AKP. His whole extended family had switched
parties with him. A tall, sandy-haired, slim, and quite busy real estate dealer
with a thin mustache, Tahsin was a member of the Menzil community in
2001. But for the last four and a half years, he had started to join the sohbets of
the Gülen community. He said, approvingly, that most of the sohbets were
based on love and understanding. There was a change in the methods in all
communities, but especially in this community, which made him switch his
allegiance. Now believers had started to spread Islam by using "the language
of the Prophet," the language of tolerance and reason, rather than "crude politics" and dogmatism. He was recently in Edirne, a town close to the Greek
border. There, like in most other places, there was a tension between the Gülen
community and the Felicity Party. They did not understand Gülen. They
blamed him for supporting the 1997 coup. They blamed him for being apolitical. Actually, his community was more political than any other, according to
Tahsin. But Gülen had a different way of playing politics. Some were angry at
him because he was in contact with Christians. But actually, he taught a lot of
Christians Turkish and how to sing the Turkish national anthem. Ten in every
hundred Christian students eventually "come to Islam" due to Gülen's activities, argued Tahsin (echoing many other people in the district). He preferred
this community to his previous one because it was able to combine tolerance
and systematic work, which eventually converted Christians and spread Turkish. In sum, rationalism, pragmatism, Islam, and nationalism came together
in the discourse of many Muslims as they accounted for their switch to the
Gülen line.

Yet, not everybody in the district sympathized with the Nurcus. Especially
some radical Islamists were still highly critical as they found the Nurcu communities pro–United States, pro-Vatican, and interest-seeking rather than
belief-seeking. Mehmet was a rare case among key AKP leaders who had an
openly anti-Nurcu position. A tall, plump, dark-haired merchant, he was also

exceptional in that he retained his radicalism while rising up in the party hierarchy. Mehmet calmly argued that Sultanbeyli residents were quickly fall-
ing prey to alcohol, gambling, and drugs, and the religious communities, including the Nurcus, were doing nothing about this:

> The communities have no such goals as saving people from vice. All of them
> became corporations. They all have TV otations and firms. If you look at their
> sohbets, most of the people who go to them do so in order to form business
> networks. The only other thing they are concerned with is raising people for
> their own community [through their schools and family networks]. They are
> not concerned with the larger society. [Plus,] there is no systematic question-
> ing, and there is no scientific thought in these communities. Worse, they
> think that Said did not write the books with his own *heva* [ambitions, pas-
> sions, desires]. He wrote them with inspiration from God! Just like them,
> other communities also have unquestionable leaders. Süleymancıs would not
> question their founder Tunahan, others would not question their founder
> Kotku. [Moreover,] none of them carries out *emr-i bi'l-maruf ve nehy-i ani'l-
> münker* [see Chapter 5, endnote 3].

Invoking the *"emr-i bil-maruf ve nehy-i ani'l-münker"* phrase, Islamists argue
that all Muslims should be politically involved. They blame Sufi communities
for keeping people busy with unnecessary rituals and preventing Muslims
from carrying out a fundamental religious task (political involvement). Other
radicals also condemned the Nurcus for being hostile to transnational Islamic
currents and abusing people by blinding them with supernaturalism. Together
with these rationalist and radical criticisms of Nurcus, there were others who
kept their distance because they found other mystic leaders better orators and
more gifted with supernatural powers.

Notwithstanding these less commonly voiced criticisms of the Nurcus, the
change in their influence can be interpreted as the routinization of charisma
throughout the religious field in Sultanbeyli. The groups that were able to
gather big crowds due to the charisma of their leaders (groups such as Menzil,
Mahmud Efendi, etc.) had started to lose out in the spiritual competition after
the 1997 military intervention. Only the groups that were able to combine the
"remembered" charisma and magic of their dead leaders with systematic work
(Nurcus and, though not analyzed here, the Süleymancıs) were able to grow
in size and influence. The major difference of my understanding of routinization from Weber's account is the following: I argue that routinization occurs

in a context of political struggles rather than simply through the universal rationalization of religion. The military intervention that dealt a heavy blow to the Mahmud Efendi circle, and the later empowerment of the AKP that bolstered one type of religiosity, were decisive factors. The AKP did not necessarily favor some communities over others, but it created the right sociopolitical atmosphere for the further blossoming of more rationalist Sufi communities.

Islamization of Elite Life

The developments narrated below, both in and outside the district, show how there was paradoxically a convergence between secular and Islamic camps in Turkey, concomitant with polarization.

I encountered many signs of Islamization of elite life during my flights to and from Turkey. While before 2002 I came across no Islamic practices or religious conversations on airplanes, these had started to become part of the flight experience after that year. First, there was an institutional change. Turkish Airlines, controlled by the government, started to include Islamist newspapers among the newspapers it distributed to passengers. I also started to notice changes in the passengers in 2006. For example, on one flight from Istanbul to New York, the man sitting next to me performed the prayer (while sitting) twice. Two men sitting across the corridor were talking about Fethullah Gülen. One had recently accepted an invitation from him but did not have the time to go. They were the typical Westernized, professional types one sees on Turkish planes, with business suits, clean-shaven faces, and relaxed attitudes. Their clothes were much fancier, their accents more Istanbulite, and their conversation louder than the observant man sitting next to me. So, even nonobservant, wealthy, and professional people had started visiting this religious leader. Boundaries hitherto impermeable had started to be permeable on both sides.

Such permeability was also visible in Sultanbeyli. While the party ranks and the district elite still mostly consisted of people who had been raised in this peripheral district, people from the urban elite of larger Istanbul had also started to hold key positions in the party. One of the most active members of the women's branch of the AKP demonstrated this newly emerging pattern.

Semra was the wife of a businessman who owned a factory in the neighboring region of Samandıra. She was born in 1950 in a central Anatolian city, whereas her husband was from the Turkish part of an eastern city. She was mainly a housewife but had worked in a beauty parlor and as a teacher in Sultanbeyli. She held a degree from a professional school. During most of her marriage, she lived with her husband and children in one of the richest neighborhoods of Istanbul. For several years, they had been residing in a three-story apartment building behind thick and quite high walls in Sultanbeyli. They also had a garden behind the walls. They had a big garage downstairs and lots of balcony space. Semra had a necklace with an Ottoman sultan's monogram. She had long, dyed blond hair. When I visited her at home, she was wearing a business suit that reinforced her businesswoman-like appearance, similar to the one she wore when working at the AKP headquarters. The walls of their living room were all decorated with verses from the Kur'an. There was a big, flat-screen television and also several fancy ornaments throughout the room.

Both her roots in the urban elite and in secular environments facilitated Semra's different approach to Islam. Originally, she was not very observant, but she was not antireligious either. She found it abhorrent when her neighbors in her former wealthy neighborhood intervened in the religious lives of their domestic workers, for instance by trying to dissuade them from fasting. She was deeply touched when she started to interact with Sultanbeyli's pious residents in the 1980s and found them more accommodating than her neighbors:

> They offered to fast instead of me because I was sick. I encountered here the constructive side of pious people who appear rigid [to nonreligious people]. As a result of this, I started to do research on religion. I read twenty-two different exegeses by different hocas.

She was currently reading Mahmud Efendi's exegesis, as he was influential in the district and his followers had shaped the political structure:

> When this exegesis injects Islam into the people, it is very beautiful. For example his explanations of the *besmele*[11] and *Fatiha* [the introductory chapter of the Kur'an] revitalize faith [*ihya ediyor*]. But when he interjects political, organizational things, those are harmful. He frequently says: "You are going to burn in hell if you don't do this or that." But Islam is not a religion of fear. It is a religion of love. . . . The wrong understanding of Islam comes from a historical tradition that lets people use religion for their own interests. [A former top authority in the Sultanbeyli municipality] is one of Mahmud Efendi's followers, and he has given out land for free to his party's and community's followers. He has thereby used religion for his own political interests.

Semra's interpretation of religion was based on a distinction from political, populist, fear-driven, and self-interested religion. By opposing herself to Mahmud Efendi, she constructed her religious position as apolitical, property-respecting, love-driven, and disinterested. Other ex-secular, elite members of the AKP also differentiated themselves from both rigid secularism and Islamism. They were alienated from the antireligious prejudices of the old secularist guard, had discovered in (or attributed to) popular sectors an accommodating religiosity, and sought to develop this in a way that naturalized individualism, depoliticization, and legal property. The AKP had paved the road to a new elite religiosity.

In short, the political party re-created civil society in its image. These changes in cultural centers, schools, *medreses*, televisions, mosques, and Sufi communities were not dictated by the AKP, but the party created the necessary environment for them. It reshaped civil society by acting as a model and providing cues regarding the terms of religious correctness, rather than imposing it. This thorough transformation fostered convergence in the lifestyles of the poor and the rich.

MOLECULAR URBANIZATION

Political society and civil society likewise interacted to transform the use of space, though there was no perfect harmony between them. The change in the land tenure structure set the context for much of this change. While the municipality was already working on a reconstruction plan during my first visit, there were serious doubts about whether it could put this into effect, given the tight connections between the municipality and the people whom the plan would harm. After the Justice and Development Party (AKP) came to office in the district in 2004, the municipality started to implement the plan more boldly when compared to the previous officeholders. According to the reconstruction plan, there would be no new informal construction and the existing informal buildings would be destroyed. The AKP took a gradualist approach and was implementing the plan slowly, rather than destroying the informal buildings all at once. Still, this gave rise to a lot of uncoordinated, individual resistance from the residents (e.g., people shooting at and wounding the officers demolishing their houses).

In short, the AKP municipality was slowly legalizing and commercializing urban space. Paralleling this transformation was a change in the use of social space and spatial symbolism. Under the leadership of the AKP and the municipality, mosque communities, networks of friends, restaurants, businesses, and offices refashioned their spatial practices.

The Creation of Modern Urban Space

On a warm spring day, an uncovered woman with heavy makeup and tight clothes passed through the yard of the central mosque with confident steps. The yard was filled with the usual mosque community waiting for the next call to prayer. Nobody even turned and looked, let alone protested her trail. The mosque yard is located in the busy main square, with the main gate facing the main boulevard, and the two side gates opening to the two other major streets. The woman had probably saved herself a minute by using the two side gates of the yard, rather than walking around the walls that separated the yard from the streets. Yet, such avoidance of the accustomed detour would have been unimaginable for women in 2001. Even though there was no physical reaction to this situation, I later heard many mosque-goers complain about the increasing visibility of women around the mosque before and after prayer times. They saw this as interference with worship but did not take any action against it in the absence of political leadership.

During the same month of April, the secular establishment was carrying out a campaign against a financial expert the government had appointed. Yasin, who no longer took off his shoes in front of his office, proudly pointed out Fethullah Gülen's declarations in the daily *Vakit* against this campaign: "Now they deal with people's shoes. They target the new president of the central bank because he takes off his shoes in front of his door. Gülen has very firm proclamations against enforcements like this." It is telling how Yasin, his partners, and his customers had to take off their shoes in front of his office five years ago but had now quit this practice. Most offices of the municipality, as well as private workplaces throughout the district, had gone through the same change in the last five years. Now, the district's Islamists were only defending the practice of taking shoes off in front of one's apartment in the case of a distant comrade. This major spatial step back also fell in line with Gülen's rising prominency: Yasin and others were now comfortable with a religious leader who defended some religious freedoms in some contexts, rather than one trying to transform all aspects of life in an Islamic direction.

Spatial changes in the district had such bottom-up sources, but they were also intricately linked with changes in the authorities' spatial interventions. The alternative space that the Islamists had created was partially what earned the district the label "the Islamic Republic of Sultanbeyli." Central to Sultanbeyli's spatial symbolism was the municipal building, the windows and color of which resembled those of a mosque. The building was highly visible from the highway.

After the AKP took control of the municipality, it initiated a conscious eradication of Islamist "symbolic space." The municipal building built by the Islamists was demolished by the ex-Islamists. Another indicator of the change is that there was a special prayer room on the fourth floor of the new, temporary municipal building in 2006. People went to this room instead of praying in their own rooms like they did five years before. In 2006, the AKP was also in the middle of building what it considered a "modern boulevard": a pedestrian street where residents could stroll and shop. This, in the mind of the new leaders, would eventually replace the chaotic and traffic-jammed boulevard of old Sultanbeyli.

Ersoy, the new AKP mayor, explained the spatial changes they made in an interview with me:

> Cities are famous for their squares. Our district is famous for its *gecekondu*s [shanties]. The modern boulevard will be a place where people can breathe and shop. Of course, since some of the district's *esnaf* [tradesmen] have no urban consciousness, they oppose it. They only have commercial concerns, and no aesthetic and architectural concerns. . . . We are turning Sultanbeyli into a beautiful place. We have already saved the buildings on the main boulevard from looking derelict by making the shopkeepers fix their window frames and plaster their walls. We are now doing the same thing around the highway.

The brick scenery (described in the introduction of Chapter 3) was indeed almost gone from the highway. The AKP's new official urban discourse emphasized aesthetics, consumption, urban consciousness, and appearance, in contradistinction to purely commercial interests, shantytowns, and ugliness. Another top administrator echoed the mayor:

> If we change the physical structure, people's ideas will change. If we build parks, cultural centers, and tunnels, people will change too. That these weren't built before was all because of the previous administrations and their populism. If they had done the right things, if they had restricted the building of houses, this district would be one of the richest places in Istanbul rather than a *varoş* [a poor suburb].

Therefore, one of the goals of changing the spatial structure was changing the people. The AKP had bequeathed one of the central tenets of modernist social engineering: Create a new city, and you will have created a new man (Scott 1998). The most frequent target of criticism among the new municipal officials, as duplicated here, was (the now defeated and despised) Islamist populism. This account also naturalized neoliberalism by producing the belief that if all administrations were modern, then there would be no poverty in the district. If there was poverty in the district, it was only because of the faults of populist local administrations. This assumption was in line with one of neoliberalism's fundamental propositions: decentralization and rational, effective local rule will heal inequalities temporarily caused by the market.

The residents of the district interpreted these spatial changes in different ways, demonstrating both the transformation the residents were going through and the production of new cleavages in Sultanbeyli. Some connected this spatial transformation to the characteristics of the new leadership. According to this interpretation, Ersoy (the new mayor) was a tyrant. For example, the argument went, he had fired those officials who did not obey him unquestioningly and flatter him. Shopkeepers on the main boulevard were especially critical of the boulevard's modern refashioning, as they thought their business would be adversely affected. They even came together and published a one-page advertisement in the pro-AKP daily *Yeni Şafak* to criticize the reconstruction.

The demolition of the municipal building was much more symbolically laden and multilayered. The official line went as follows: the two top floors had been demolished because they did not conform with the earthquake regulations. The columns of the rest of the floors would have to be renovated, but that would take too much energy and funding. Constructing a new building from scratch would actually cost the same. Therefore, the municipality decided to build a new one. However, backstage, AKP leaders and followers gave different explanations. One media consultant for the municipality joked, "We were going to build two minarets on the sides of the building, but then we gave up," referring to the mosque-like appearance, which he implied did not suit a municipal building. Even though this consultant was a religious person, like others he had moved away from all-encompassing religion and accepted the separation of religion and architecture. Another media consultant related this story:

> When the bulldozer started knocking down the building, a worker said that
> Koçak had sent us his greetings. The workers said that they would not be able
> to demolish the building because it was too strong. I said, "It is high time that
> you quit this [magical] nonsense."

The workers demolishing the building had attributed a magical sturdiness to
the building, hence to Koçak and his Islamist project. But the new municipal
officials mocked these beliefs. So, both the still pro-Islamist workers and the
AKP officials saw the demolition as an action against the past of the district.
Not only the building's mosque-like appearance but also the fact that it was
built by the previous mayor disturbed the new municipal leaders. Nevertheless, some AKP leaders told me that they had difficulty in explaining even to
their families and other informal contacts why they were doing this. There
was still a perception among some residents, even those sympathetic to the
AKP, that the demolition amounted to rejecting one's roots.

An AKP activist (an accountant in his thirties) connected the creation of
modern space with other social and political changes in the district.

> We are building fifteen new schools in the district. A new generation is taking
> over Sultanbeyli. This generation is more urban and more social. The AKP
> gives trust and honor to people, and this ability comes from Islam. But this is
> why Islam is important here, not because we have extremist fantasies. The
> windows of the municipal building resembled mosque windows. This at-
> tracted a lot of attention from the highway. Therefore we demolished it. Now
> we are building a modern building.

Again, this characterization of the demolition was not public, and this accountant did not mention this in a formal interview but during an informal
conversation with me at his friend's car store. It was interesting to see how the
demolition is discussed in the context of trust, honor, and urbanism. While it
was especially Islamic spatial symbols that gave trust and honor to an earlier
generation, the generation in whose name the accountant spoke supposedly
found trust and honor in an Islam that does not shape architecture but fills
one with the desire to be urban and educated. As if embodying this new generation, the accountant had a business suit, a clean-shaven face, well-trimmed
hair, and polished shoes despite the dust-filled environment of the district.
Quite tall with an erect posture, he spoke calmly and with an unshakable
confidence. There were other accountants, lawyers, engineers, and teachers of

his generation who resembled him in bodily presentation, but the accoun-tant's generalization certainly did not reflect the situation of the workers in their thirties. It was characteristic of the AKP discourse and self-presentation that businessmen and professionals (and especially the financial experts) met-onymically came to stand for the whole population. As the theory of hege-mony would put it, the AKP marketed particular spatial interests as the spa-tial interests of the whole population.

It was not only explicitly Islamic architectural symbols that were under fire. Another significant shift away from the Islamist line was the overt or covert approval of high buildings. A municipal official stated a common perception in these words: "Land use here was completely misguided. All over the world, homes are now being built up toward the sky, but we in this district keep on spreading all over the land. We are disturbing the ecological balance." Isla-mists in Sultanbeyli once held that buildings should not be higher than mina-rets, as this would be competing with God's authority. In 2006, it was rather small and unassuming buildings that were perceived to be irresponsible.

The Transformation of the Gender Regime

Interactions between political and civil society also revamped the gendered dimension of urban space. There was an explosion in the number of women walking the main boulevard, whereas this had been a man's land five years before. There was an explosion too in the ratio of unveiled women. Even the veiled women wore much more colorful clothes and veils, and they applied heavy makeup. In the restaurants I frequented five years ago, there were fam-ily sections upstairs (this meant that women should go to those sections rather than sit with men). Even those family sections used to be mostly empty and the restaurants mostly populated by men. In 2006, the family sections were frequented more. But women sat and ate even in the main areas.

There were two new high-quality clothing stores (as well as a solarium) on the main boulevard. I shopped in one of these, where the female clerks treated me very warmly and said "please come again." They were not covered. Fe-males did not treat males like this in this district in 2000, when there were few female clerks and all of them were covered. As mentioned in Chapter 4, Friday sermons warned men about the female clerks in other districts. But now, the welcoming and warm female clerks were in Sultanbeyli.

The residents of the district talked to me about what now seemed to them to be a distant century and told me that in the early 1990s there was only one leftist family whose women were brave enough to walk around without head-scarves. But now everything had changed. Back then people who came from outside of the district eventually covered. Some of them even donned the *çarşaf*. The trend in 2006 was in the reverse direction.

Shopkeepers who sold Islamic clothing reported that the women who were walking without veils on the main boulevard were from conservative and Islamic families. Their sales of *çarşaf* and *pardösü* (long coat) had decreased dramatically. But the rival clothing stores that carried revealing dresses were expanding. Some residents explained this change by institutional measures:

> The daughters of conservative families are influenced by the headscarf ban. The only way out for a covered young girl is going to an İHL [High School for Imams and Preachers]. But those schools decrease your chances of going to college. They want to cover their heads again once they have an occupation.

One resident also related the change to the schooling situation but added to this the changes in the mentality of conservative families:

> I came here nineteen years ago. I know women who did not pass in front of these doors without çarşaf. Actually, almost everybody was in çarşaf. I remember that some of them put their little daughters in çarşaf. Now these daughters turned twenty-five and they are not even veiled. Now many families believe that sending girls to school is *farz* [religiously mandatory]. Nineteen years ago, they did not believe in the value of schooling. The same people did not pray behind prayer leaders who did not have beards in the 1980s.

While in this account people still retained their religiosity and only their understandings of religiosity changed, other residents argued that the daughters of conservative families were actually much less pious. Some complained about how the daughters of some formerly Islamist families started to go out with boys and not only uncovered their heads but wore T-shirts that left their midriffs exposed.[12]

These changes in the spatial gender regime were not restricted to the street, bazaar, and informal places like restaurants and cafés. Workplaces and official buildings went through a similar change. In one Islamic clothing store, I was shivering during an informal conversation on a cold March day, and I had to leave after talking for about an hour. In 2001, there was a stove in the front section of this store, where we as the male contingent were seated during my visits in 2006. When they were not busy helping customers, the female employees sat in the hardly visible back section of the store, as they did when I used to visit the store five years ago. This section, buried at the very back corner of the store was about twenty feet deep and was quite dark, even though spacious. The men, by contrast, usually sat around the front desk on better chairs next to the store window. The internal design of the store had mostly remained the same, but two female employees had protested the heating situation and said: "If you don't get us a stove, we will resign." As he had no money to afford another stove, he gave his to the employees, which meant an end to receiving guests for long periods of time in the front of the store. As this man was actively engaged in party politics, he had to be involved in informal networking all the time. This was a possible blow to his political career. Nothing like this could have happened before the liberalization of Islamism. Women in this district could not have easily found this kind of courage in themselves and demanded moving the stove.

There were more women working in the municipality in 2006 when compared to 2000.[13] In 2005, when I briefly visited the district, the women worked in separate rooms from men. In 2006, they were mostly in the same rooms. For example, there were three female professionals in the municipality's Office K, which was separated into two rooms. The two women I saw in the first room were not covered. Another one was in the second room, and she was also unveiled, but much more outgoing and enterprising than the other two. The other two seemed to be silent in the presence of men, attesting to the persistence of patriarchy. The third woman was a little more active because her husband shared the same room. Even though there was one woman working in the municipality's Office K in 2002, she was veiled and her demeanor and speech emphasized modesty and reservation. In 2006, there was a different picture: women could behave as they do in regular, secular public offices in Turkey (where there is also a mixture of proactive and reserved female behavior).

Gender segregation was broken at the very heart of the main Islamizing agent (or former agent), the political party. In the local congress (March 2006) and neighborhood meetings of the AKP, there were some women who sat in female-only groups. But most of the audience was mixed. This was in deep contrast with the old tradition in the district, where any public meeting involving both sexes was designed so as to separate males and females. Some congresses of the AKP in Anatolian provinces in 2006 created much turmoil because of gender segregation among the audience. While some people in

Turkey tended to see these as a step toward an Islamic state, they seemed to forget that before the AKP was established, most of the congresses, rallies, and other public meetings of the Islamist party were *completely* segregated. But in 2006, the media had to go around looking for a segregated congress. It was indeed significant that the governing party in Turkey had held segregated meetings in the provincial towns of Turkey. However, it was also significant that this had happened only in a restricted number of localities. The same kind of spatial change marked the use of the party headquarters. While women tended not to come to the headquarters except for women's meetings during the time of Virtue Party rule, women came in and out of the AKP headquarters throughout the day as easily as men.[14]

Despite all these changes, there was an important spatial continuity in the district that still empowered the AKP differentially with respect to other parties. Among rural immigrant families, people who are not an immediate part of the family network are seen as outsiders and they are not quite welcome in people's homes. Especially when there are only females at home, outsiders are seen as dangerous. This social barrier makes it quite difficult for political parties to mobilize people by going door to door, either during election campaigns or during membership campaigns. However, "when the person who knocks on the door is a covered woman," many people from the conservative as well as secularist parties have told me, rural immigrant women are more likely to respond and talk to them. The covered female activists of the party were what differentiated the Welfare Party from the other parties in the 1980s and 1990s. A central technique was thus handed down from the previous Islamist party: deploying covered women for activism, so that other covered women could feel comfortable and open their doors. This was key to the success of the AKP. It was only through this mechanism that the AKP could detect those who were resourceful and who were poor and demand funds from the former to give coal, food, and educational fellowships to the latter. The AKP's absorption of Islamist strategies allowed it to sustain political mobilization in the largely untransformed back neighborhoods of the district and use their support to fuel the "modern" transformation in the district center—that is, to support the Islamist elite's inclusion into the ruling elite or, in other words, the passive revolution.

Hometown Identity
One of the aspects of the district that did not go through dramatic change in these five years was the salience of place-based identity. The first question

most people still asked when they met a stranger in the district was, "Where are you from?" In the coffeehouses and teahouses, the typical conversations still revolved around how long it takes to get to one's hometown from Sultanbeyli, what the bus fare is, and where exactly one's village or town is located.

One day, when leaving the central teahouse frequented by pious construction workers and Islamic activists, I saw Gökhan (see Chapters 3 and 4). As someone who had been active in the Islamist movement ever since his early youth, an outsider could expect Gökhan to shed his regional belonging in favor of his ideological belonging. Yet, his roots in a western Black Sea village were still of utmost importance to him. He was quite dismayed that I said hi only on my way out and took this to be a regional insult. He said: "My hoca, this is not the way to do it [hiç olmuyor]. You come, you only spend time with those from Gümüşhane [an eastern Black Sea province], and then you leave. You should stop by here too." The "here" in this sentence referred to his table composed of his co-locals, but also sounded as if it signified a different region of Turkey. Failing to honor his table was failing to honor his province. Also significantly, the eastern Black Sea men I was talking with were teachers, and Gökhan was a worker in the municipality. There were mostly municipal employees of different ranks at his table. He did not emphasize the class and/or occupational differences between him and the teachers, but he did emphasize the regional differences. He could have said, for example, "You only spend time with teachers, and you neglect municipal employees," but he did not. Hence, both the conversations in the teahouses and the friendships in the municipality were still based on hometowns, which were (along with gender, religiosity, and ethnicity), rather than occupations or classes, still the most meaningful axes of classification.

It was not only informal venues that were structured around hometown identity but formal ones as well. Co-local associations frequently organized dinners and meetings, they had their own teahouses and coffeehouses, and the political parties still had to mobilize these associations for votes and funds in 2006. At the same time, there was a discursive change: almost everybody in the district now emphasized how "we" should go beyond hometowns and think of ourselves in terms of national identity and also belonging to the district. As Chapter 4 emphasized, this was the discourse especially of the Kemalist parties in 2001. Now, the AKP shared this discourse too. But this was in tension with other elements in the party's discourse and practices. Many of the Virtue Party's leaders had carried with them to the AKP hometown-based networks they had formed through decades of political activity. The party's strength was partially based on these links that had been established during the former decades.

The AKP did not only depend on existing co-local networks but built new links with new immigrants. On one day during the membership drive of the AKP, three men came to the party president's room. They were from a village of Tokat and came as the representatives of their newly established co-local association. They did not have any specific demands, and the visit was meant to initiate links between the party and the association. The most vocal among them were Kemal, a construction worker in his thirties, and Ceyhan, another construction worker in his sixties. As we were speaking of this and that, the president turned to me and said:

> Look hoca, their village has settled in three parts in Istanbul, one in
>   Kartal, the other two here. They carried the whole village here.
>   [Turning to them] but you are not living [reproducing] the village
>   here, right?
> Kemal: No, we are not. But we are trying to make our traditions live.
> Ceyhan: My president, you were going to stop by our village on your way
>   back from Erzincan.
> President: I couldn't. [Turning to me] I promised, but I couldn't do it. I
>   was too busy.

When the president introduced me as from Erzincan, Kemal said:

> Of course, as a president, you should have no hometown.
> President: No, I don't have one. But it makes me happy that my hoca is
>   from Erzincan. If he were from Tokat, it would make you happy too.

As they were leaving, they invited the president to the inauguration ceremony of the association.

In this give and take, everybody was trying to prove that hometowns have no importance for them. But at the same time, they were emphasizing that they are important. Also, this incident shows that residents evaluated the president's credentials and integrity in terms of his recognition of their hometowns. When a leader fails to properly recognize someone's hometown, his integrity is compromised and he has to apologize not only to the people of that village but also to others in the audience. In sum, the AKP danced around provincial identities, contextually articulated certain aspects of these identities and left others out, while at the same time restructuring the whole district in a modern urban direction.

The destruction of Islamic space and the creation of modern urban space was thus at times a result of cooperation between civil and political societies, and at times resisted by civil society. There was more cooperation between civil society and political society in naturalizing market relations (outside the question of land tenure).

THE NATURALIZATION OF CAPITALISM

So, how do these developments in the realms of religion and urban space relate to the naturalization of capitalism? This section demonstrates that everyday conversations, mosques, municipal debates, teahouses, workplaces, and media channels integrated people to an emergent market society and that this happened under the leadership of the Justice and Development Party (AKP). But Sultanbeyli did not experience a full blossoming of civil society. Unions and other associations that could negotiate or rechannel market forces were still absent or weak, and this also had to do with specificities of AKP hegemony.

The Victory of Privatization, Work, and "the Economy"

In Turkey, privatization had been going on for twenty years, but the pace after 2002 has been mind-boggling. There was immense popular support for privatization from all sectors of society. The construction workers, public sector workers, truck drivers, and retired workers of Sultanbeyli, along with the shopkeepers and businessmen, had all become ardent supporters of privatization (which was not the case five years ago). This had to do with the fact that Prime Minister Erdoğan, who was deeply loved in the district (because he was a practicing Muslim and "looks like us"), promoted privatization whenever he could.

Speaking more generally, the leading agent of the transformation from a social justice orientation to a market orientation was without doubt the political party. A few years ago, Islamist politicians used to say "we are both against capitalism and communism," arguing that the Islamic economy would take the best of both systems but be fundamentally different from both. Now politicians said their "understanding of the economy includes some aspects of capitalism, but no elements of communism," which was against their program. One of the crucial capitalistic elements they pointed out was "getting rid of the *memur* [civil servant] type, who has one eye on the clock and always wants to quit work when the clock strikes five. Even in the public sector, people will work with contracts rather than having tenure as memur." Civil servants in Turkey started to lose status and economic power with the neoliberalization of the 1980s. Under Turgut Özal's rule, "memur" became a bad word with connotations like laziness and corruption. For AKP activists, one of the defining elements of economic reform was a wholesale attack on memurs, which was interrupted after the death of the Motherland Party's Özal. In other words, the AKP's project was liquidating anybody who did not conform to the work ethic through administrative reform.

The Sultanbeyli mayor from the AKP, Alaaddin Ersoy, also exemplifies how the naturalization of neoliberalism finds its clearest expression in the bosom of the AKP. During his interview with me, Ersoy said:

> The poor of this district are different from the poor of California, who have no future. The poor here have the dynamism and enthusiasm necessary for upward mobility. In Western cities, the poor sleep under bridges. Here, they have their own apartments or houses. They also want to build more stories that they can leave to their children. Family and neighbors support people here, making upward mobility possible. Unlike in New Jersey, nobody dies of hunger here. The traditional family structure and Turkish-Islamic thought are predominant here, making people help each other regarding education, health, and housing. People should have strong beliefs so that they can bear difficulties. Today, everywhere in the world, there is a turn to faith. But this is faith shorn of superstitions. Psychiatrists also point out that people need strong beliefs to face difficulties. And we have strong beliefs, praise be to God.

While contrasting Sultanbeyli to his caricature of California and New Jersey, Ersoy also deployed that most American of socioeconomic ideals: mobilizing family, religion, and community ties to fight poverty, while at the same time encouraging competition and upward mobility in a free market through a religious-cum-scientific discourse. As in U.S. conservative discourse, science (here, psychiatry) and "pure," original, rational religion could peacefully coexist to bolster economic performance.

There was also an everyday life dimension to the internalization of capitalism that again occurred in the atmosphere the AKP created. The residents now saw the market as a part of the divine order, which was not the case five years ago. Below is a conversation between two former radical Islamists of the district. Yaman (see Chapters 4 and 5) had recently become a member of the

AKP. Numan, the religion teacher quoted previously, approached the AKP with some caution. During a discussion in his store, Yaman said:

> We [the Islamists] used to say that even standing in the shade of a bank is a sin. . . . Now Islamists get in line to put money in the bank. They are now after the money they have not earned all their lives [because of Islamist activities and beliefs].
>
> Numan: Doing this is one thing. What annoys me is that the former Islamists see this as a right.
>
> Yaman: But if they don't do this, if they don't see it as a right, they will lose their heads. We fought all our lives for an Islamic order. We could not achieve it. This is not a light load to carry. . . . The situation of Islamists is like this: if we [as the family members who run this clothing store] have a loss at the end of the month, I gather my children and say, "What can we do? This is our *nasip* [that which is allotted one by God]." If I don't approach the situation like this, I will lose my head. Just like this, I see the present condition of the Islamists as our nasip.

This interaction exemplifies the naturalization of capitalism at several levels. As Numan's interrogation shows, there was still an Islamist rejection of the interest banking system that circulated in the district. But the system was nevertheless naturalized through a sense of loss, defeat, and also fate (implied by "nasip"): Yaman insinuated that the absorption of Islamists in the system was just like *the cycles of a business month*, which were themselves naturalized or, even stronger, sacralized, through the word "nasip," a divinely arranged share that one cannot object to. Yaman's approach naturalized market society as well as Islamists' recent integration to it. This presents a parallel to the Reformation when Protestants rechanneled their religious energies to the market after political stalemate and defeat, strengthening the emergent capitalism (Gellner 1991). Even though scholars like Ernest Gellner think that the same historical pattern cannot be repeated in the case of Islam (because of its all-encompassing theological system), the transformed conduct of the former radicals in Sultanbeyli manifested a rechanneling of religious energies to the market. This again establishes the relationship between hegemonic struggle and religious transformation: The partial secularization of Islamists is not simply and only a sign of the construction of an alternative modernity but of their absorption into capitalism.

Just as we were on this topic, a girl in her late teens entered the store. She had on a very colorful and somewhat tight dress and headscarf. She was extremely self-confident. She spoke very fast and waved all of her limbs nimbly as she spoke:

> Hi Numan hoca, hi Yaman *abi* [big brother].
>
> Yaman: Hi.
>
> Girl: Abi, I want a job at X Inc. [a subcontracting firm working with the municipality]. I heard that a partisan reference [a recommendation note from a party leader] is required. Abi, can you write a reference?
>
> Yaman: My daughter, you have a job, don't you?
>
> Girl: Yes, I work at the optometrist.
>
> Yaman: You at least have a job. What more do you want?
>
> Girl: Thank God, I have a job. I also have a salary of 1,000 YTL. I have become independent of my family. I am very content. But I am not happy with my job.
>
> Yaman: Nobody's happy with his/her job.
>
> Girl: That's true, but at least people have a better social environment at X Inc.
>
> Yaman: You can also keep on working at the optometrist.
>
> Girl: I have community ties too. I'm a good member of the Nur community. Those who have my ties all got jobs at firms like X Inc. Why should I remain at this job?

Throughout this conversation, Yaman nervously tore pieces from the paper covering of the empty mineral water bottle in front of him. As a response to this last question, he said nothing and kept on tearing pieces of paper. After getting this implicit and negative answer, she also asked some questions regarding preparations for university entrance exams. She then left the store. After she left, Yaman said:

> You can no longer get a job without pulling strings. This girl is actually making a 1,000 YTL a month [approximately $650]. If she gets a job at X Inc., she is going to make 700 [approximately $450]. She wants this job because of the insurance and the security.
>
> Numan: And that security is there only until the municipality changes hands.

As the AKP held both national and municipal power, and as upward mobility in Turkey depends partially upon political ties, religious people were at the moment particularly aggressive in using these opportunities. There was nothing new about this link between politics and upward mobility, but this interaction was indicative of some of the changes that religious people in Turkey were going through. Ignorant of these changes on the ground, the secular elite in Turkey was in panic during the last two years of the AKP's first governmental term, perceiving the insertion of pious cadres into the state as a gradual transition to an Islamic state.

The most important dimension of these changes was that the link between the Islamic party, Sufi community, and business was naturalized: young female workers now had uncontestable career rights derived from belonging to the party and community. No job was good enough in itself: one needed to have upward mobility. The salience of another concern—happiness at work—was also telling. Not long ago, happiness at home was at the center of life for the majority in Turkey (including both the seculars and the religious conservatives). People perceived work as a means to reach this more fundamental goal. Moreover, the girl mentioned above saw being independent from the family as a virtue. I had not encountered such an individualist stance five years ago, except in two young university students. The exception had become the rule, thanks to the interaction between political society and civil society, party and community.

The centrality of work in one's life was naturalized not only in everyday interactions but also through religious channels like the Friday sermon. On one rainy and chilly late winter day, the prayer leader of the central mosque appealed to the antiwar sentiment of his flock to make his procapitalist and nationalist points. The United States had just started the heaviest bombardments in the last three years, against a town called Samara in Iraq:

Now you are going to perform the Friday prayer in this crowded, but nevertheless warm mosque. Outside, there are many men who are praying in the cold. But in Iraq, there are a lot of people praying under a bombardment. They are praying so that this religion can live and God will make the bombardments cease. They are not as lucky as you. You should be thankful to God for being able to pray in this warm mosque. But you should also ask yourself: What can I do with this gift from God? First, God hates laziness. Does God like laziness? [Many people murmured: he does not.] You should work very hard. You should not forget that this is a part of your religion. You should wake up very early in the morning, perform your prayer, and then start to work. Second, you should not forget that you are all one under God. You may be Kurdish, Circassian, Turkish, but before God you're all the same. You should not be divided. Look at what happens to you when you are divided. The people to the east of this country are suffering from this [implying the civil war between the Shia and Sunni in Iraq]. Third, you should keep your thoughts clean. If you have clean thoughts, God will reward you.

Sermons thus instilled the work ethic. There were signs of the marriage of capitalism and religion five years ago too, as the work ethic showed up in a few interviews; however, it was never this central to sermons. A stronger parallel with five years ago was the implicit message, "don't take any political action against the war; just keep your hearts clean." The same imam had given the same message more explicitly during the antiwar protests in Turkey, as the United States was invading Afghanistan. But now, a nationalist message was added to this: don't be divided. However, the conservative imam's nationalism was a mild one, when compared to the extreme nationalist messages I heard at mosques in Istanbul's central districts during the same month, which are more likely to be staffed by right-wing nationalists. The sermon in Sultanbeyli underlined legitimate differences, rather than arguing that everybody in Turkey is Turkish. The imam identified being a good Muslim with working hard and retaining national unity while recognizing ethnic differences (which, as we have seen in the previous chapter, is the hallmark of the AKP's conservatism). Furthermore, I did not encounter any rejection of wealth either in sermons or in teahouses in 2006, which (as I pointed out in Chapter 4) were common in sermons and everyday conversation five years ago.

Naturalization of neoliberalism among workers was more ambiguous when compared to imams, shopkeepers, professionals, real estate dealers, and AKP leaders. Some of the workers I talked to told me that there was no improvement in their own economic situations, and some said things were going better in their own lives. However, even those who were suffering economically themselves were happy to see "a stable economy." This approach to the economy shows the success of capitalist hegemony. If this "stabilization" had happened under another government, these workers would say that they did not believe in such economic indicators. Actually, this was the case with the ruling coalition before the crisis in 2001 (when I was having similar conversations with the same construction workers). But under the current government, they believed the economists and they took the economy as a "thing," independent of their experiences. However, this capitalist hegemony among workers is fragile because if this conservative government goes, the economy might be dereified again.

The reason workers were so dedicated to this government was that it was, in their words, "courageous, Muslim, superior in Islam to the others." Some workers thought that if even these Muslim rulers were not able to correct poverty, unemployment, and the unjust distribution of wealth, it was not because of the system (which was no longer being questioned like in 2001), but because some Jews and atheists somewhere in the system were preventing this from happening. They thought that the Muslim rulers were eventually going to liquidate these Jews and atheists, and then there would be more employment and justice.

In the teahouses where I talked to workers, the most vocal men were usually self-employed laborers who defined themselves as "entrepreneurs" (such as truck drivers). They dominated the conversations at the expense of wage workers. This pattern had not changed in the last five years. This again was the pattern in a group composed of two truck drivers and two workers. The workers were silent until the truck drivers left. When I asked the group about unemployment, the distribution of wealth, and poverty, one of the drivers responded:

> Of course there is unemployment. But it is being resolved gradually.
> Those who make this an issue are being disgraceful.
> The other truck driver: Unemployment cannot be prevented without
> family planning. One person cannot have ten children. This should be
> minimized. For example, three to five is enough. When a person has
> ten children, twenty years from now there will be ten people looking
> for work like me. This is not right. Think about China. In China today,
> you can only have one child. I have five children. The oldest is thirty
> years old. Education, social security, employment . . . these are all
> problems for all five of them. If I had not practiced family planning
> after a point, I would have ten or twelve children. Now my children
> say that two or three children are enough. But there are other types
> who go at a full gallop. Then their children suffer, and become thieves.
> In order to become a civilized country, people need education. The
> primary thing is education.

In 2000, workers at teahouses criticized "interventions in family life," telling me that God would provide for their children if he chose to give them offspring

(*Allah rızkını verir*). With the AKP in charge of the state and family planning, the latter was no longer seen as a secularist intervention. The discourse above, which held the ignorance, the large numbers, and morals of the poor responsible for poverty, was widespread among the secular-educated sectors in 2001. But in the last five years, it had also spread downward. In 2006, pious Turkish workers and small entrepreneurs used it to blame the Kurds (here only implicitly). Five years ago, these workers and truck drivers blamed Kurds for other things (such as terrorism) but never for their own poverty. This is how the increasing unemployment was naturalized and culturalized in 2006. So, more and more sectors found market freedoms combined with state intervention against some populations (especially the poor Kurds) desirable. Nevertheless, the workers who were silent during this conversation started talking after the drivers left and said they thought unemployment was a systemic problem.

Traditional religion's emphasis on patience was now disarticulated from the "Islamic economy" project and articulated to neoliberalism. Workers still talked frequently of patience in 2006, but now they patiently accepted the reigning economic order, rather than patiently and quietly rejecting it like in 2001. For example, a middle-aged construction worker responded in the following way to my questions about unemployment, social security, poverty, and inequality:

> Blacks, Whites, the rich, and the poor are all equal before God. This life is only a test. The hocas we go to teach us that poverty is a great blessing, provided that we know how to be patient. We should be patient and avoid rebellion, know the worth of poverty, and die in that way. There is nothing such as unemployment. The companies have many jobs and many people work with their social benefits. If you want to work, you will find work wherever it is *nasip*. Everything starts with patience. I have been following the lessons of a Mahmud Efendi student for the last four months. The lessons about patience will last another five years. They will teach us patience and fortitude. As I said, everything is a test, and I will be one of those who pass the test, God willing.

Religion teaches how to bear poverty (through seeing it as a blessing and benefit, as a test), and this had not changed over the last five years. What had changed was that even some pro-Islamist religious circles, such as some branches of the Mahmud Efendi community, indirectly supported current economic policies. The discourse of patience, which was used to quietly blame the rich while giving strength to the poor in 2000, was in the claws of a new political project in 2006.

The Changing Rhythm of Life

The residents' use of time displayed both continuity and change when compared to 2001. I did not see dramatic shifts in some residents' daily work habits. Teahouses, coffeehouses, and even workplaces were still full of people leading a quite leisurely lifestyle, without worrying too much about work. Some interviewees (professionals as well as workers) came one to two hours late to interviews, with excuses such as having encountered friends on the way. Yet, others were prompt, immediately got to the topic, talked concisely, and then got rid of me quickly.

However, the overall laxity seemed to cause more tension among the residents when compared to five years ago. During a casual conversation in a teahouse, one worker criticized the others thus:

> When these men wake up, they walk to the window and open the curtains. If they see snow, if they see rain, they say "too bad," and they go back to bed. However, they should be working no matter what the circumstances are. Otherwise they won't be able to find work. Another thing is: I see employers coming here and offering work for 40 YTL per day [around $27]. The workers here say, "We want 60 YTL" and they do not go. But I think that working for these low wages is better than not working.

I had come across similar discourse in one on one conversations and interviews in 2001, but such words were never uttered in the presence of the blamed individuals. The other workers around him said: "His affairs are in order [onun tuzu kuru]. He has a son in France who sends him money." They argued that working was not just when working conditions are not good. So, in some venues, the pro-neoliberal transformation in discourse was not accompanied by as vigorous of a transformation in practice.

However, among some people, I was able to observe a thorough change in practice. One surprising case was Veysel (see Chapters 3 and 4), who had struck me as one of the most relaxed men in the central teahouse in 2000. A construction worker back then, he now worked across the main bus terminal in Sultanbeyli as a steward, at a restaurant where the public bus drivers ate, chatted, and drank tea. He monitored whether the drivers arrived on time, made sure that they left on time, and took care of the situation if there was an accident or a bus broke down. He made three liras per bus every day and took care of eight buses. He was making around a thousand a month. However, he was not happy with the situation because this was a very demanding job: "I wake up, I come here, I return home, and I sleep. I have no holidays. And I do nothing else. It feels like I am in an open-air prison." He told me that he had gone through very hard times since I last saw him:

> We suffered a lot from poverty. I was sick, then my children were sick, and we had no insurance and no money. We had a very hard time finding the medication. We were hungry for a time. After that, I decided to find a more permanent job. Construction was no good. I was working for a day, then unemployed for ten days. So I took this job. But there is no insurance in this job either. When I am sick, we will live a life of misery again.

Veysel's hair was whiter than five years ago, and he looked a little older. But his hair was also nicely trimmed. His shirt and pants looked new, clean, and ironed. He had a bigger belly (a sign of prosperity among the poor of the Middle East). He looked much healthier.

I asked Veysel what he thought about privatization. He gave a standard neoliberal line, very much unlike himself when compared to five years ago.

> Privatization is good. The state is cumbersome. The people working for the state have no interest in their work. But here, we are all after profit. We are always struggling. We are always trying to do something. But the eye of the *memur* is always on the clock. He wants to go home as soon as possible. But I come here at six in the morning, and I go back at seven. This is how one should work.

Veysel had gone from demanding a job in the public sector in 2001 to damning all public workers and civil servants. Yet, when talking about the lack of insurance, he also seemed to be praising public jobs, but he did not do this openly. When I explicitly pointed out to him that public jobs at least have insurance, he simply balked.

Just as we were talking about these issues, a driver called Kerem came. Kerem was about twenty-five years old and had a dirty beard. The other drivers told him to sit down and have a cup of tea. He said: "I have only two minutes." He seemed to hesitate. Veysel told him not to sit down. Veysel then shouted out to the waiter. "Bring a cup of tea in a plastic cup." Kerem sat down nevertheless and started a conversation with his friends. They were laughing and joking

and talking about trivial issues. Veysel shouted again: "Bring that plastic cup."
The plastic cup came, but Kerem went on sitting at the drivers' table. Veysel put
a smile on his face, lit a cigarette, stood up, and went to the next table with a
calm attitude and confident steps. He took Kerem by the arm, pulled him up,
and took him to his bus. Throughout the process, neither Veysel nor Kerem
showed any signs of anger. Veysel had become quite a professional in disciplin
ing. In his case as in many others, the naturalization of capitalism was not only
at the discursive level but at the level of practices as well.

The Limits and Contradictions of Naturalization

Together with these neoliberal shifts in discourses and practices, there was
also ambivalence and resistance to neoliberalization in the district. As opposed to many ex-Islamists, a minority was sharply critical of the AKP's social security reform and not enthusiastic about its other economic reforms.
Those former radicals who could not jump on the train of bourgeoisification
were now suffering financially. There was a dialectical relation between lack of
mobility and political position: The people who were more consistent in their
radicalism had not been able to jump on the train partially because of their
beliefs, and their economic situation reinforced their beliefs.

Although a minority, these people were not uninfluential. A few of them
even infiltrated the party. While the top administration of the AKP in Sultanbeyli mostly consisted of liberalized ex-Islamists, there were a few leaders like
Mehmet (quoted above) who retained their radicalism and made positive references to Qutb and other classical radicals. His difference from the party line
was not only a matter of ideas but also of civic practice. Mehmet ran a foundation, the beneficiaries of which were the working poor. This was a deviation
from the AKP's national line, which emphasized that only the disabled, the
widowers, and the old should receive aid. I asked him the reason for this deviation and he justified it in the language of old-style (non-neoliberal) social
justice:

> They take 380 YTL a month. That money goes to rent, gas, electricity, and
> water. They cannot buy food. We give them food. . . . The real problem in Tur-
> key is the lack of social justice. Workers in Europe get 2,500 euros a month.
> This is how it should be in Turkey.

I then asked him whether his foundation encouraged the unemployed-but-able
poor to find work. He replied that they were only a foundation and were not

systematically involved in things like that: "That is the government's duty. Why should I be doing that?" One of the top leaders of the party thus carried out a quite different practice from the national practice of the party: helping the working poor and leaving it to the government to find jobs and raise wages. It would therefore be inaccurate to say that the AKP, with all its force and all its advocates, pushed for neoliberalization consistently. There were still social justice–oriented Islamists in the party. In his discussion of the political party (which he called the "modern prince"), Gramsci had posited that the party has to standardize culture, ideology, and educational level across all its ranks to be effective. The AKP behaved rather differently and derived its power from being a "postmodern prince": it deliberately escaped standardization so as to maintain appeal to different sectors, demonstrating that hegemony must be reconsidered in the context of the twenty-first century. Yet, such reproduction of radicalism no doubt added to the risks of the passive revolution.

Even more interesting was how the modernization of everyday exchanges coexisted uneasily with traditionalism. On one cold day in February, I couldn't get anyone to do an interview with me in a teahouse, in spite of spending the whole day there with construction workers who used the place as a shelter from the chilly whether. The young people explicitly asked for money; actually they asked for a daily wage for an interview (this had never happened five years ago).[15] But Refik (Chapter 5) stopped me from giving any kind of money or food by saying "you are a guest." Refik was a lifelong supporter of Islamic parties. He was short and had a white beard and sparse hair. He was the moral authority in the teahouse. He had sufficient power to prevent the young workers from taking money but was not powerful enough to make them talk to me.

One could easily conclude from these interactions that the older generation is more traditionalist, whereas the young have been completely transformed in a promarket direction. However, a conversation between one construction worker in his late twenties and another in his late thirties revealed a more complex structure. The latter complained: "The other day I saw that a man smoked when his father was around. But I saw something worse after that: the man rocked the cradle of his baby! I can't do these things near a co-local older than me, let alone near my big brother or my father. Once upon a time, I could not even go to a teahouse where there was an older co-local." The young one agreed with him: "One needs to show respect." Both workers, who had just challenged the authority of an elder and asked for money from a "guest" despite him, discursively reinforced traditional mores according to which one cannot seek pleasure (smoke) or show affection in the presence of elders.

In other words, the construction workers had partially retained their traditionalism. Having several wives was still more or less acceptable in 2006. Respecting elders was of utmost importance (at least at the discursive level). This presented a contrast with the relatively thorough transformation among the businessmen, shopkeepers, and professionals. However, as the above interactions show, the establishment of a market economy can challenge the elder's authority and lead to novel dynamics. Marketization, if still under the leadership of the pious conservatives, might gradually undo traditionalism even among the workers in the coming years.

Rationalization in the construction sector gave rise to a similar ambivalence. In 2001, construction workers were almost exclusively negative about the predominance of large firms in the construction business and the increasing levels of formal control on the sector, which they saw as an unwarranted impediment to the creation of employment. In 2006, they tended to speak more positively but had reservations. A fifty-year-old construction worker demonstrated the contradictory approach of workers to the market:

> In our day, the construction business moves from the individual level to the firm level. Now there are more engineers. There is more investigation. This happened after the earthquake in 1999. I think this is a very good thing. They investigate the concrete, the iron, and everything else. Nothing is allowed before a level of certainty is reached.
>
> R: Would you rather work in a firm like this or on your own, waiting for employment on a daily basis?
>
> Worker: I would rather work on my own, where I have more control. I don't like to take orders.

Despite verbal approval of formalization in the sector, Sultanbeyli's residents still did not desire working for formal construction companies. Displaying what Gramsci has called the "contradictory nature of common sense," informal workers both approved and disapproved of the transition to a formal market. The contradictoriness of common sense was retained even after hegemony was established, again defying Gramsci's modernist expectations.

Perpetuation of Popular Disorganization

Another success of the AKP, and thus of Turkish capitalism, was perpetuating popular disorganization despite transition to a liberalized market. While scholars have posited that the establishment of market capitalism is likely to lead to popular organization (Burawoy 2004; Polanyi 1944), this has not happened in Turkey. We need to understand the dynamics on the ground to analyze the shape of neoliberal hegemony in this country.

Even some staunch supporters of the AKP agreed in 2006 that wealth was not justly distributed. Despite this recognition, another factor that blocks self-organization was added to those in 2001. Now subordinate classes saw the party in power and the prime minister as "their own," and they expected them to solve every problem. The workers, truck drivers, and the unemployed of Sultanbeyli felt that self-organization was harmful, if anything, as could be seen in the example of unions, which were controlled by secularist leaders and allegedly discriminated against the pious (with the exception of the weak and ineffective Confederation of Real Worker Unions [Hak-İş]). The problems were at the top, at the level of the rulers, and they would be corrected there. What is more, the problem of social justice was reframed as one between secular business and pious business, rather than one between business and labor, through an emphasis on the difficulties religious businessmen faced. Therefore, in order to realize social justice, the poor were summoned to side with pious capitalists.

Apart from this new trust in the rulers, the anti-union attitude of some construction workers was reproduced during the five years between 2001 and 2006. Semih, forty-four, was a construction worker who had been employed several times in Saudi Arabia through an intermediary firm in Turkey and worked there for a company owned by the bin Ladin family. His experience was positive:

> In Saudi Arabia, strikes and unions are strictly banned. If you don't get paid on time, you don't protest, you don't take to the street. You work, but you slow the work down. As a citizen, I am against unions. Whenever there are strikes or protests, certain people insert harmful slogans and politicize the environment. It is good that the Saudis have none of this. Especially in the firms where I worked, I've always received my due, from the money and the health services to vacations.

For some workers, especially those who have been to Saudi Arabia and seen an "Islamic regime," the ideal working model was one with full insurance but no unions and no right to strike. They disliked unions especially because of the "risk" of politicization. This fascination with the Saudis and a belief in their justice had remained a constant during these five years among the workers who had been there.

However, in contrast to the general sympathy for the AKP and privatization, anti-unionism was not universally shared. Among some workers, there was an emergent prounion sensibility. Despite this, even the workers who had started to change their beliefs about self-organization were not sure about what to do. Vehbi, fifty, one of the many workers who had switched from the Nationalist Action Party to the AKP, complained about his disorganized sector:

> If people are victimized today, it is because there are no heads in the
> construction sector. Architects have chambers, engineers have
> chambers, tradesmen have chambers, retired public workers
> have chambers, and there are many other examples. But we have no
> chambers. This is one of the shortcomings of the state. But should
> the state establish these, or should the people do it?
> R: What do you think?
> Vehbi: Well, what do *you* think? [Pause.] The citizens who are in the
> construction sector should coordinate this. We can't expect
> everything from the state, can we?
> R: Do you see any attempts in this direction?
> Vehbi: It hasn't happened yet, and I don't think it will ever happen. This
> disorganization [*başı bozukluk*] is benefiting some people [*birilerinin
> ekmeğine yağ sürüyor*].

Vehbi first brought up the state as the agent responsible for organizing the workers, but then he recoiled and emphasized their own responsibility. This kind of discourse was completely lacking five years ago. It is possible that marketization had a positive influence: Instead of expecting protection only from the state, now some workers had started to desire self-organization. Yet, in most cases, self-organization was discussed when I brought the subject up and asked insistent questions: This was usually not a part of spontaneous, everyday discourse. (The back-and-forth questions, hesitations, and confusion in the above conversation indicate that Vehbi had not given much thought to the subject.) Also, an emergent belief in self-organization was wedded to despair and the lack of confidence in its possibility.

Nevertheless, the contrast with five years ago was striking. Construction workers almost never brought up unionization in 2001 (only one of them did), and when I brought it up they just shrugged or were critical. In 2006, they always brought up the insurance issue; a few of them even brought up unionization. This might indeed be the first signs of a Polanyian "double movement" in this second era of marketization. Even *some* within the most unorganized sectors had started to talk about unions positively. However, for the moment this was only talk, and there was no unionization or any serious attempts in this sector.

Apoliticism remained another solid force in the way of self-organization. Among the workers, I still encountered a deep distrust of politics, even among the previously engaged. (Among the middle strata, in contrast to workers, an antipolitics discourse was meshed with political engagement.) For instance, I asked Veysel if he had any political engagement. He responded angrily: "I have nothing to do with politics. Politics is only a self-advantage [*menfaat*] business. When I was doing politics, they divided us as Turks versus Kurds. Is this something good to do? Politics will never benefit me or *anybody like me*. It will benefit *other people* and it always has." (Emphases added to underline the implicit classification of the world along class lines, in opposition to its explicit classification along hometown, ethnic, and gender lines.) But I reminded him of his previous political engagement and insistently asked whether anything was left of it. "My engagement back then had nothing to do with shariah, cutting people, or attacking women with miniskirts. I only wanted a just order. I believed that the Welfare Party was going to build it. I wanted to gain something justly and have a just life. I wanted my share to be given to me and the share of others to be given to those people." This institutional disengagement can be read not only as the lack of popular organization but also the incompleteness of hegemony, for hegemony is the organized, institutional, and active integration of people to the system, such as of the working class through unions and political parties. The AKP had not broken Veysel's and other workers' alienation from formal institutions (remember that Veysel was alienated from associations, unions, and his own Welfare-Virtue Party in 2001). The AKP had also failed to convince Veysel about the future. However, we should not forget that the same Veysel was also a part of the new hegemony and the construction of it with his transformed practice (see the subsection "The Changing Rhythm of Life" above). So, we can argue here that the construction of hegemony is very complex: the same body might work for hegemony and not be totally integrated to it at the same time.[16] This crooked half-integration of the workers, characterized by disorganization and ambivalent hopes in the system, amounted to a passive revolution.

· · ·

Unlike 2000–2002, there was integration in 2006 between the political party on the one hand and teahouses, unions, Sufi communities, and mosques on the other, especially in naturalizing marketization. The passive revolution in civil society—the intermingling of Islamization and de-Islamization, and the persistence of hometown identity amid the demolition of squatter space, all put to the service of neoliberalism's naturalization—was not spontaneous. Just like the Welfare Party's and the radical Islamists' authority and political leadership were central to the creation of an integral Islamic civil society in the 1980s and 1990s, there could be no modern Islamic civil society without the AKP's absorption of Islamist strategies in political society. Islamic civil society and political society were disarticulated after the military intervention of 1997; their incomplete rearticulation culminated in a passive revolution after 2002.

CONCLUSION
Islamic Hegemony in Comparative Perspective

IS THE PASSIVE REVOLUTION unique to Turkey in the Middle East? Have states and Islamic movements developed this unintentionally symbiotic relationship elsewhere in the region? Is there a possibility of passive revolution in other countries?

To underline the significance of political society and hegemonic strategy, this chapter first fully theorizes the passive revolution based on the Turkish case and then analyzes how Islamic politics in Egypt and Iran developed along the axes specified in this book. Comparing Turkey, Egypt, and Iran in terms of the Islamic transformations of political leadership, authority figures, visions of unity, everyday practices, the social use of space, and relations to the economy will demonstrate the differential results of interactions between political society, civil society, economy, and the state.

All three countries started out with authoritarian secularist regimes that attempted to shape everyday lives in accordance with secular, authoritarian, nationalist capital accumulation projects.[1] They all ended up differently. But in each of them, several decades of secularizing state policies gave rise to strong Islamic movements. Turkish Islamism developed a hegemonic strategy and was absorbed into Turkish secular hegemony. Today, the ex-Islamists rule the secular Turkish state with the enthusiastic support of the citizenry. Egyptian Islamism also developed a hegemonic strategy. Yet, despite historical possibilities and strong tendencies of absorption, the secular regime remained intact and repressive (while marginally Islamized). Egyptian Islamism is still the major opposition in the country. In contrast, Iranian Islamism never became truly hegemonic, in spite of a successful revolution. The Iranian Islamists rule the country today relying on repression, state-making, and containment. These differences will not be fully explained, but some tendencies that might shed light on different endpoints despite relatively similar contexts will be discussed.

The differences in the results—a secular state ruled at least partially democratically by ex-Islamists (Turkey), an authoritarian secularist state opposed by a broad-based Islamic movement (Egypt), an authoritarian Islamic state unable to foster consent (Iran)—can first of all be traced back to the differences in the composition of political society. In the first case, a legal Islamic party has dominated Islamic political society. In the second, a movement that resembles an illegal party but that resists becoming a party, and has been challenged by two major radical sociopolitical groups (Jamaa and Jihad), has shaped the political environment. Finally, in Iran, political society is characterized by quasi parties under the shadow of charismatic leadership. However, the differences are more broadly due to variances in hegemonic strategy (variances in ways of building Islamic consent). The differences emerge from asymmetries in the ways political society interacted with the state, civil society, and the economy.

TURKEY: THE PASSIVE REVOLUTION OF THE MIDDLE EAST

This section will propose a retheorization of passive revolution, starting with the three fundamental dimensions of political society and looking at how the three dimensions of civil society are transformed under the guardianship of political society. General propositions regarding passive revolutions are then supported by the Turkish case. This lays out the framework for studying the blockage of the passive revolution elsewhere.

1. Absorption of the Leadership   Movements that seek to challenge existing systems have to establish parties or partylike organizations to articulate oppositional patterns of everyday life, uses of space, economic relations, and relations of authority.

As Adam Przeworski (1985) has pointed out when discussing nineteenth- and twentieth-century international working-class movements, leaderships that do not organize into parties risk dissolution all the time (in an electoral system). Ordinary people whom they are trying to organize have immediate material and identity stakes to which parties are better able to cater. However, this does not prevent groups with totalistic claims from forming outside of parties.[2] These nonparty actors fight for a total transformation that will fundamentally change property, authority, and gender relations while dispensing with the electoral system. However, their utopianism cuts them off from the people they are trying to forge into a collective, which frequently draws them either to the party or to the formation of their own party. The latter strategy can be effective only when there is no already established oppositional mass party.

In cases where there is an established, nonrevolutionary, oppositional mass party, the revolutionaries might join the party and attempt to radicalize it, but they also risk being deradicalized themselves in this process. In the absence of an irresolvable, total crisis of the whole system, the other option is not forming an independent, noninstitutional, revolutionary, uncompromising organization but losing influence and being marginalized. Przeworski has demonstrated this process by analyzing anarchist working-class movements in nineteenth-century Europe. The same process was also in effect throughout the latter part of the twentieth century in the case of many Trotskyist, Maoist, anarchist, and autonomist grouplets in the West, as well as among radical Islamists.[3] Groups that take the path of noninstitutionalization engage in endless bickering, swing back-and-forth between extreme authoritarianism and lack of authority, and (in most cases) accomplish very little. Each group fragments into several factions, which divide into further grouplets.

Ironically, the growing mass party also needs radical groups willing to work with it. Its traditional leaders usually lack dynamism and solid bases among the people except through patronage. The more pragmatic radicals who opt for inclusion contribute dynamism and faith, which function as the oil for the party's rusty cogwheels.[4] Yet, their absorption also radicalizes parties and prepares the way for clashes with the system that have little chance of turning into revolutionary crises, as the established party leadership is neither ready for nor willing to carry out a radical transformation of society.

A diverse Islamic political society in Turkey revolved around a successive chain of legal Islamist parties (Milli Order Party–Milli Salvation Party–Welfare Party–Virtue Party), which displayed this swing between radicalization and deradicalization in its various phases. The Welfare Party (RP), the most open to radicalism among these parties, built an immense organizational infrastructure, which in places like Sultanbeyli was paralleled by the emergence of dual power structures. However, thanks to the ambivalence of the party's Islamism and its Turkish nationalism, this organizational structure acted only to put the brakes on radicalism. Moreover, Islamists could not make use of street action properly in the 1990s (and later), mostly due to top Welfare Party–Virtue Party (RP-FP) leaders' reluctance and corruption, their authority over some radicals and party youth, and their marginalization of the others. The many abortive attempts to establish radical groups and failed street protests caused deradicalization, as the disappointed and disillusioned radicals repented and started to seek Islamic change within the system.

Generally speaking, processes of radicalization and deradicalization (which all oppositional movements are prone to) can lead to several results. First, the intact regime can make use of the indecisiveness of the challengers to crush them totally—including both the bureaucratic leadership and the revolutionaries. This is what happened in 1980 in Turkey, when the regime violently crushed not only leftist revolutionary groups but also the mainstream parties and institutions that they infiltrated.[5] This is more likely to happen when there is a serious imbalance between the strength of the regime and its challengers; and therefore crushing the revolutionaries is viable not only because of their lack of proper arms but because of a parallel weakness in civil and political societies.

A second possibility is that the clash between the regime and the party is inconclusive and the radicals use this as an opportunity to take over the party and turn it into a revolutionary force. This has certainly been the dream of Trotskyists who have resorted to the "deep entrist" strategy in various capitalist countries; however, in none of these countries has there actually been a decisive clash between the party and the system, which partially explains why the strategy never worked. In situations like this, the party leadership can actually absorb some revolutionaries and negate their radicalism: The strategy backfires. A prominent example is Lionel Jospin, who eventually became the leader of the (French) Socialist Party after spending years in that party as a secretive member of a revolutionary organization.

Finally, forces might be aligned so that after the clash, the radicals and the party bureaucrats (along with their constituencies and strategies) join the existing system and consolidate it while marginally transforming it—this was the Turkish path. Taking this final path would imply that there will be a convergence between both the authority patterns and the visions of unity embraced by the power holders and the challengers.

How did this ultimate absorption play itself out in Turkey? At the turn of the millennium, there were many changes in the lives of Islamic activists already pulling them in a market-oriented, liberal, and individualist direction. But it was only with the establishment of the Justice and Development Party (AKP) that these activists decisively quit Islamism and made their peace with the system. The fact that the same people who had led the Islamist RP-FP now led the AKP fostered loyalty to the state, which further allowed former Islamists to take the plunge into the accumulation of wealth and luxury.[6] Yet, these contradictions also created ambivalence in popular support and even criticisms from within the party regarding "this-worldization" and "bourgeoisification," rendering the passive revolution fragile.

During AKP rule, Islamic street action decreased and tended not to target state authority. As an Islamic party was ruling Turkey, there was constant worry that any mobilization that targeted the state would produce anti-Islamic results. The surviving Islamic street mobilization reinforced the increasing Turkish nationalism. Among religious people, there was less interest in ideologically oriented politics at the everyday level too, as politics had come to mean making self-interested use of their party's empowerment. At the same time, mosques and sermons became more activistic, but this activism was restricted to the interindividual level: imams did not incite people to transform society at large. This toned down and restricted activism amounted to what I have called "the mobilization of demobilization." That is, even the existing mobilization reinforced hegemony and popular passiveness. This was all possible because of Islamic activists' and pious people's increasing integration with the state through identification with the party and its leaders.

2. Absorption of Dual Power   Radical projects call into question the monopolization of legitimate violence. New authority figures emerge who enforce laws, officiate at wedding ceremonies, distribute resources, and so on. This leads to a situation of dual power, where virtually two states exist in the same territory. In order to institute such dual power, authority figures need to have different bases of legitimacy than the established ones. These bases might include a more rational organization, a different take on tradition, and charisma. As a result of the differential combination of these elements, the people start to identify with the alternative leaders in a way they could not with the old established elite.

Movements have different ways of instituting dual power. Alternative nodes of power might be built slowly through a very long process, taking over each locality one by one. (This was the strategy of the Italian Communist

Party during the Cold War years.[7]) Or institutions of alternative hegemony might spread like wildfire throughout a country during a breakdown of international order (as happened with councils during the Russian Revolution). In cases where there is an already established hegemony in society, the first strategy is more viable. This also increases the importance of creating model localities and model local authority figures. The emergence of alternative national authority figures also reinforces these patterns. If an alternative, national personality cult is put into circulation against the existing one, it acts as a further basis for mobilization and integration into the institutions of counterhegemony.

In Turkey, the Islamic challenge unfolded through forging alternative authority structures and figures. In squatter localities such as Sultanbeyli, the RP built a dual power structure by distributing land, organizing rites of passage, informally reinforcing religious law, and so on. The charisma of Erbakan and Koçak reinforced these patterns.

The passive revolution in the structure of authority starts with the rejection of dual power. The new elite of the ex-radical movement needs to separate itself from the authority figures who instituted nodes of alternative power and then failed in sustaining them. A substantial chunk of the local and national political discourse now revolves around blaming the previous leaders of the movement and their misguided policies in order to convince ordinary people and the established elite that they no longer intend to make a revolution. This was one of the AKP's main strategies.

As the state cracked down on dual power mechanisms after the military intervention, the hesitantly Islamist FP could resist only passively. The major move of the AKP was sweeping away the remnants of such dual authority structures and spreading discourses blaming the RP, Erbakan, Koçak, land distribution, and squatting. Once a perceived Islamic and social right, squatting became something to be ashamed of during the AKP's passive revolution.

The everyday life patterns and the economic practices of the new leaders partially adapt to the system but partially retain traces of the movement's radical phase. Therefore, the people in support of the movement can look at the leaders and still recognize themselves and their dreams in them, even though the utopian and egalitarian promises are no longer there. Nevertheless, this is a fine balance to maintain and the new authority figures might swing too much in the direction of co-optation. The new authority figures must retain some distinction in order to appeal to the people and attract them to the system so that they can reinstitute the consent the old regime failed to maintain. Yet, the insistence on differences creates tension with the established elite, who read every sign of distinction as the possibility of the awakening of revolutionary forces. The new authority figures go back and forth between the two extreme possible poles (total assimilation into the elite and radical redifferentiation from the elite) as a response to these pressures. Hence the AKP's persistent ambiguity.

Such swings and ambiguities became condensed in the person of Erdoğan, who acted as the organizer of the broadly shared indecisive mood. Rather than emphasizing common practices with the people (the bread and butter of Islamist politics), some local authority figures in Turkey started to emphasize expertise. However, Erdoğan (along with some other national leaders) still appeared as a "man of the people." Circulation of myths about him and his interaction with local audiences prevented the new local authorities' complete alienation from the people. Hence, the AKP gave rise to authority figures as varied as the tolerated Babacan at the national level and the disliked Ersoy at the local level, but the love for Erdoğan (and for other ex-Islamists in the cabinet) was enough to counterbalance these. While the government destroyed remaining institutions of social protection throughout Turkey and modeled itself on the Western world, people still saw in Erdoğan's figure living proof of the AKP's commitment to social justice and Islam.

Though the absorption of previously radical leaders and authority figures was thus at the passive revolution's core, it also paradoxically constituted one of its soft spots. The forces of the old regime were always haunted by the memories of revolutionary activity. Some popular sectors also projected their revolutionary hopes on the transformed, absorbed leaders. The whole political system was bedeviled by mutual distrust and fear. This prepared the scene for preemptive coups d'état and authoritarian conspiracies, which still threatened the AKP's hegemony when this book was finalized in early 2008. Such paradoxes of absorption constitute one reason why passive revolutions tend to be quite unstable ways of establishing and maintaining hegemony.

3. Absorption of the Collective Imaginary   Yet another level of the organic crisis is the loosening unity of the state and the political community. If the reigning hegemonic project cannot deliver on the promise of unity, it leaves itself open to attacks from both inside and outside the state. The internal attack might either take the shape of (1) ethnic or sectarian separatism,

(2) maintaining the old vision of political community but casting it in a different hegemonic light (as the Communist Party fighting for Italian or Chinese *national* unification), or (3) offering a new type of political community (an *ümmet* or a workers' international state). Even when the new hegemonic project offers a new political community, its first test will be unifying some of the promised fragments left divided by the old hegemonic project (e.g., uniting ethnic communities after the fall of ethnic nationalism, which the Iranian Revolution partially accomplished).

If the new political community falters, if it does not deliver very quickly (as states could, for example, during the transformation from empires to nations), dreams and desires associated with the old political community will creep into the new hegemonic project: the latter will be drawn to the terrain of the former. The picture might get even more complicated as yet alternative visions of political community emerge (e.g., a liberal-democratic global community versus a national one). In such cases, the new hegemonic project will be dissolved and absorbed into other (old, national and new, global) hegemonic projects. This might have quite different implications depending on the trajectory of absorption. The once successful (yet defeated) mobilization of the counterhegemonic project might provide fresh blood for the old political community (i.e., result in a more united nation) or other emerging political communities. This would result in the strengthening of unity. If, on the other hand, the appropriate strategies are not carried over from the revolutionary to the passive revolutionary phase, the disunity might become starker.

The RP had absorbed the Islamic internationalism of the radicals into Turkish nationalism. Along with the inclusion of ex-radicals in the party, the RP moved from a Turkish nationalist line to one that emphasized cross-national and cross-ethnic Islamic unity, while still claiming Turkish superiority over and leadership of non-Turkish Muslims. This contradictory unity gave rise to many tensions in the party's ideology and practices. The RP-FP's Turkish nationalism marginalized the Kurds—its dose of Islamic internationalism was not strong enough to integrate them fully. But from the standpoint of many Turks, it was not Turkish nationalist enough and its misguided Islamic internationalism led it to give too many concessions to the Kurds. Islamists thereby failed to establish a vision of political unity that would go beyond Turkish nationalism.

The AKP took the RP's contradictory unity of internationalism and nationalism and deployed it to bolster Turkey's integration with the European

Union. Its supporters also aimed to learn from and emulate the U.S. social system, which they found partially Islamic. The party owed a lot to its ex-Islamist leaders in popularly legitimating integration with the West, which was no longer framed as un-Islamic in civil venues such as mosques and tea-houses.

Yet, due to international as well as national developments, the frictions between the Turks and Kurds worsened. The AKP's further adulterated Islamic internationalism was less and less capable of integrating the agitated Kurds, while its EU orientation led to suspicions among its increasingly nationalist Turkish supporters. Despite all, the AKP's emergent vision and practice of political unity still held these two ethnic groups together, whereas all other major parties were predominantly Turkish or Kurdish. Hence, at the level of political unity, the passive revolution was full of internal contradictions but still somewhat effective.

Civil Society Absorbed

Political society, thus constituted in the process of passive revolution, plays an essential role in reconstituting civil society.

1. Habitual Absorption   In times of organic crises, conventional cultural patterns no longer appear natural and even become unsatisfactory for large sections of the population. In such situations, alternative hegemonic projects challenge the established patterns of behavior and classification, rhythms of life, uses of the body, bodies of knowledge, and rituals in a polity. However, the replacements they propose always meet the resistance not only of authorities but also of ordinary people who have naturalized habits. If this microchallenge is not combined with the provision of material benefits, alternative authority structures, and a trustworthy leadership, it will be rejected outright. When, by contrast, there is some provision along the lines mentioned above, but these provisions are not tightly interwoven, the alternative hegemonic project will be able to transform certain aspects of life but will fail to create a world in its image. This partial success will most likely result in a hybridization of the everyday patterns of the extant hegemony and the counterhegemony.

In the 1980s and 1990s, Islamists attacked secularist hegemony in Turkey and transformed everyday behavior and uses of the body. The political party, municipalities, and radical groups led this attack, thoroughly shaping the activities of associations, foundations, communities, and networks. These activities included teaching people how to pray or the proper way of praying, arranging Islamic wedding ceremonies, encouraging or imposing Islamic ways of clothing and Islamic facial hair, and imposing alcohol bans or making people quit alcohol. They also introduced new bodies of knowledge as competitors against secular knowledge.[8] *Sohbets* and seminars instilled these patterns of behavior in large numbers of people.

By 2000, bourgeoisification and military defeat had ensured that Islamists could not completely transform everyday life in the direction they desired. Political society had lost its guiding role, and without it civil society did not find the vigor in itself to refashion the totality of everyday life. Nevertheless, there was a hybridization of the lifestyle they pushed for with aspects of traditional Islam and modern consumerism, rather than a complete eradication of Islamist life patterns.

As long as a counterhegemonic project is neither completely triumphant nor defeated, such hybridization will be sustained. If defeat occurs through molecular absorption of the project (i.e., a passive revolution) rather than its utter destruction, everyday life will be transformed under the influence of this project in a quite messy way. While the daily routines of the carriers and supporters of the challenging project "normalize," the practices of the dominant sectors will incorporate some aspects that the ex-radicals still hang on to. As a result, the everyday lives of initially warring factions will resemble each other more and more: They will tend to meet in the middle. But hegemony will not necessarily be completely stabilized.

In 2006, I observed a molecular absorption of Islamic life patterns in Turkey rather than their thorough hybridization with competing ones. The AKP appropriated countersystem mobilization to reinforce existing systemic patterns. For example, Islamist activists learned to pray for political purposes and in certain venues only, rather than transforming the totality of life around prayers. By 2006, there was more religion at the official and elite level; paradoxically, this did not create a more Islamic state but infused Islamic spirit into existing political structures.

There needed to be certain spiritual changes so that this absorption could be realized. A bourgeois Islamic civil society slowly blossomed in the liberal atmosphere the AKP created, and the existing Islamic civil society molecularly changed in a modern direction, giving rise to new understandings of religiosity. Islamists mostly gave up antimystic criticism. Islamic television channels shifted to exploit supernatural themes. Cultural centers, networks of friends, mosques, and Islamic schools manufactured a pragmatic and business-oriented spirituality. Religion, still practiced though less vigorously, was more individualized, rationalized, and nationalist. Furthermore, some mystic communities further rationalized, professionalized, and individualized—and these more rationalized became more prominent when compared to the other mystic communities. Finally, some sectors of the secular elite appropriated this emergent religiosity and became more observant themselves.[9] Through the interaction, cooperation, and integration of all these actors (previous radicals, mystics, the liberal wing of the established elite, etc.), Islamic everyday practice became more capitalistic, liberal, tolerant, and individualistic.[10]

2. Spatial Absorption   Hegemonic movements encounter openings in the system when old spatial structures and boundaries start to decay. At these junctures, they impose an unconventional architecture, new boundaries between neighborhoods, a new use of residential interiors, and so on. Their reshuffling of places gives rise to new status groups and new patterns of inequality. Moreover, because space is lived through images and symbols associated with it, alternative hegemonic projects also bring in new images and symbols associated with the places they are trying to transform.[11] In cases of massive rural-to-urban immigration, movements that challenge hegemony also propose new balances in urban space. Spatial identities hitherto stigmatized become glorified and vice versa.

Islamic mobilization in Turkey is a striking case of a spatial hegemonic challenge. The Islamists of Sultanbeyli, for example, built a district based on the separation of the sexes, Islamic architecture, and an Islamic organization of the town square. They produced Islamic space by differentiating teahouses and coffeehouses, giving Islamic names to businesses and streets, and introducing Islamic practices to central locations as well as offices and workplaces. The making of the district as an "Islamic fortress" and its differentiation from secular districts was pivotal to the Islamist strategy of "conquering Istanbul" in the 1990s. The post-1997 hegemonic backlash disturbed the articulation of Islamic bodily practices with new urban space and countered alcohol-free and segregated Islamic meetings with mixed meetings where alcohol was consumed.

We can talk of a passive revolution when aspects of a challenging spatiality are appropriated to strengthen the spatial dimensions of capitalism. In this process, the most threatening spatial structures and symbols are relinquished while others are absorbed.

What the AKP accomplished spatially was the absorption of some Islamist place-based strategies paralleled with the exclusion or marginalization of menacing spatial practices. The AKP subordinated populism and recent immigrants, while silently incorporating co-local networks and associations, the defining moments of squatter civil society. Its version of conservatism partially de-Islamized urban space through cooperation with mosques, networks of friends, restaurants, and other businesses. The interlocking activities of political and civil society eroded Islamic architecture and put an end to practices such as taking off one's shoes in front of workplaces while reproducing a tamed variety of gender segregation. Segregation was unofficially practiced, but in official venues like the municipality or party meetings it lost its prominence. Professional and business-oriented women gained more visibility in this new context of flexibility.

The new urban space that the AKP created emphasized aesthetics, Islamic consumption, and urban consciousness. This was combined with effective local rule, one defining tenet of neoliberalism. All this was made possible by the ongoing popular support for the party, which was in turn made possible by the use of the veil, restricted segregation, and a vibrant civil society. The creation of modern urban space (i.e., the subordination of shantytowns and "peasant mentalities") was built on a solid foundation: mobilization-demobilization of shantytowns and recent peasants, especially through co-local networks. Nevertheless, all this was not sufficient to completely formalize and legalize urban land tenure. When it came to this aspect of the passive revolution, civil society resisted the schemes of political society and the state.

3. Economic Absorption   As hegemony is partially based on economic concessions, the system runs across difficulties when class compromise is forsaken or reordered. This is most likely to occur in times of deregulation, which are characterized by the transition to an allegedly pure free market, the cutting of subsidies, de-unionization, and so on. This is the economic dimension of the organic crisis. Alternative hegemonic projects enter such crises with their own solutions, that is, a new balance of class forces and new sorts of concessions.

In order to differentiate themselves from failed Keynesian and corporatist models, post-Keynesian hegemonic projects cast a wide net that is meant to appeal to sectors disillusioned with old Keynesianism (yet some might have a vague nostalgia); these sectors include those who have suffered from liberalization (e.g., proletarians and peasants), subproletarians who see new possibilities in a free market (e.g., street vendors and construction workers), radical groups and youth with utopian prescriptions, and upstarts who are just learning to make use of the new market openings but are not able to stand up to competition from established capitalists. In such contexts, hegemonic projects take the shape of potentially self-contradictory combinations of welfare provision, radical utopianism, and alternative capital accumulation (consocrated by a sense of spiritual difference from established capital). As opposed to Keynesianism, the written national documents look inchoate due to this potentially explosive combination.

In Turkey, young merchants and tradesmen (together with students) carried out the Islamic assault on post-1980 neoliberalization. However, their redistributive radicalism was in most cases a life stage phenomenon (restricted to school and early postgraduate years), which was gradually dissolved along with their increasing political and market involvement. Interestingly, unlike the students and the tradesmen, workers did not heavily engage in anticapitalist versions of Islamism. One of the reasons for this was Islamism's appeal to unorganized, informal sectors of the working class. The informal structure of their sectors, their understanding of Islam (which was based on "contentment" with one's lot), petty entrepreneur ideology (belief in the virtues of "clean," small business), fluid hierarchies that characterized their sectors, differences from and hatred for organized workers, and patronage prevented these workers from radicalization or even constituting a civil society under their partial control.

Yet, the same workers were cognizant of extreme inequalities and disliked consumerist lifestyles. Some of them thus welcomed the Islamist party's (RP-FP) socioeconomic program characterized by a rhetorically heavy criticism of exploitation coupled with vague and incoherent promises of a "Just Order," though they read quite different things into the program. Akin to Mohandas Ghandhi's mobilization of the peasantry through vague anticapitalist promises and without their participation in the system, Islamists mobilized the subproletariat without empowering them, through multivocal promises such as the Just Order.

In such contradictory situations, how the game will unfold between different sectors and for the economic heart of the movement depends on several factors—such as the relative organizational strength of the sectors (which partially has its roots in the now defunct corporatist or Keynesian system), cultural context (e.g., traditions of self-governance), religious dictums, determination of the sectors' leaders, and international influences. In countries and regions where there is a relative balance between the various classes and also an egalitarian ethos, a new kind of welfare regime might emerge. This path would revive the European social democratic spirit of yesteryear under new conditions. (The "Third Way" might be heading in this direction, together with accepting the broad parameters of neoliberalism. Mexico [Soederberg 2001], Brazil [Petras and Veltmeyer 2003], and Chile are also experimenting with this in a non-European context.) If the radical groups (personified by intellectuals, officers, or the youth) are disproportionately strong with respect to local capitalists and organized popular sectors, quasi-socialist regimes—which subordinate capital accumulation and popular organization to the iron will of leaders—will emerge. This is the recent trend in Venezuela (Hawkins and Hansen [2006]; but see Gibbs [2006] for an alternative interpretation of the Chavez regime). Past experience (including Algerian socialism, Nasserism, Baathism, and Mexican populism) has shown that such populisms quickly slide into authoritarian capitalisms.

Finally, where there is very weak popular organization and radicalism is a temporary life stage phenomenon (as in some of the Islamic world), upstarts will dominate the movement and subordinate egalitarian hopes and welfare provision to capital accumulation. However, at least in the beginning, enrichment will not expose itself as enrichment and will appear to actors from all sectors as a necessary evil—the unavoidable material basis for the construction of a more moral world. The hegemonic project will not vilify private property but will hold that property, despite all legal appearances, ultimately belongs to some transcendental being (God, nation, *ümmet*, party, etc.). Therefore, work on everyday life becomes an inseparable part of this way of absorbing attacks against hegemony.

Nevertheless, as the upstarts become established capitalists, the support of the other sectors and a transcendental discourse will become burdens. Welfare provision will be slackened, and the talk about the universal laws of the economy will replace transcendental and otherworldly fantasies. Radical utopianism will be dropped. The new intelligentsia, siding with the upstarts, will pressure the former radicals and the popular sectors to either adapt themselves to the market or remain silent. Yet, in order to prevent lapsing into a heartless world (a world without hegemony), the hegemonic project will partially reproduce the spirit of the early movement. It will fuse the market with extra-economic meaning. The rules of the market will have a religious significance in spite of the simultaneous rejection of any noneconomic influence on the economic sphere. Through this passive revolution, the formerly anticapitalist spirit of the early movement will become the heart of a heartless world. The success of this path ultimately depends on authority figures and organizations (i.e., on political society) that can synthesize the new economic model with the proper spiritual and everyday work.

In the Turkish case, the Just Order program was not radical enough for the radicals and too radical and unrealistic for the emergent capitalist sectors within the movement. Therefore, despite the sympathy of unorganized workers for the program, the Welfare Party (RP) slowly moved away from it. While the promise of the Just Order gradually lost its appeal in the first years of the twenty-first century, the Islamist strategy of capital accumulation (building initial capital by collecting funds from people based on the promise of an exploitation- and interest-free, gender-segregated, pious world) set the context for the AKP. The absence of a subproletarian civil society, the indecisiveness of youth radicalism, and the increasing strength of pious capitalists ushered in a passive revolution.

As a result of the AKP's passive revolution, political society and civil society—which had fallen out of sync at the end of the 1990s—were reintegrated. Religious people sought upward mobility and happiness at work using the political party, Sufi communities, associations, and networks. The political party, municipal authorities, imams, media channels, friends, kin, and co-locals merged to build bourgeois Islamic ethics through preaching that working hard and privatization are an integral part of religion. The AKP had appropriated certain Islamist understandings of religion (social solidarity, purified religion, etc.) to put them in the service of capital accumulation.[12]

Workers consented to the rule of experts, as these experts and the politicians who appointed them were good Muslims. The rule of experts (or "rationalization") was not simply an outcome of modernity but of the AKP's successful localization of that modernity.[13] As Muslim rulers held the reins, workers were disciplined to the point of accepting family planning and the supreme virtue of secular education, two focuses of the secularist discourse in Turkey that some of them had resisted for decades. This was not only a discursive acceptance of the system, as the daily practices of at least some workers had started to be more work oriented, disciplined, and productive.

In sum, the AKP's empowerment culminated in a passive revolution: the incorporation of subaltern religious elements without the decisive organization of the subaltern. The regime was Islamized but did not become Islamic. It opened up to popular voices but did not become popular. Secular elites retained control, and this was no mere token control. Military, legal, and paramilitary action, especially from late 2005 onward, repeatedly raised the possibility that secularists could remove the AKP from power or even close it down. However, such a fateful downfall would not necessarily signify the termination of the passive revolution. Repression of Islamic politics in the past decade, for example, has postponed and (dramatically) changed the content and form of Islamization but has not brought about its end. Despite this secularist control, the provincial bourgeoisie and the religious orders also prospered. Islam became a defining feature of national unity, without reducing the salience of Turkish identity.

EGYPT: PASSIVE REVOLUTION BLOCKED

Egypt came very close to such a bourgeois Islamic regime but did not go as far as Turkey. After the overthrow of the monarchy, the new Egyptian republic had started out as a secular-nationalist project. The economy had a corporatist and developmentalist structure as in Turkey but with a stronger social justice component. Islam was marginalized in the 1950s and 1960s under the founder Gamal Nasser, similar to the first three decades of the Turkish regime. Even though Nasser initially became a charismatic hero, the defeat of his pan-Arabist strategy, as well as the slowdown of development toward the end of his term, discredited both him and his one-party regime. As was the case in Turkey after the military intervention of 1980, the rulers after Nasser (Anwar Sadat and Hosni Mubarak) coupled neoliberalization (locally called "opening" or *infitah*) with a fluctuating absorption of Islamic activism to cope with the emergent organic crisis.

The Muslim Brotherhood (MB), the central node in Egyptian Islamic political society, made use of the crisis to develop a politics of absorption. The MB was founded in 1928 by Hasan al-Banna and, in its first decades, developed as a sociopolitical movement organizing itself around athletic clubs, evening schools, welfare provision, and anticolonial activism (Lia 1998; Mitchell 1969). The 1950s and 1960s were the most radical years, when the organization propounded a violent overthrow of the regime by a revolutionary vanguard. Privatization and deregulation from the 1970s through the 1990s moderated the MB's position.[14] These reforms brought with them sustained growth in the first half of the 1980s, along with declining real wages and increasing unemployment and poverty (Kienle 1998).

This resulted in bread riots in the late 1970s and in more and more strikes and violence in the beginning of the 1990s. In the 1970s and 1980s, the regime's overall strategy was akin to a passive revolution: the inclusion of Islamic radicals and partial democratization in order to deal with increasing unrest. But with the Islamists gaining considerable power and the specter of the Algerian civil war, the regime rolled back the absorption after 1993 (Kienle 1998).

In the 1970s, the MB strengthened among students, and the public influence of al-Azhar (the major Islamic university) was bolstered. Sadat wanted to use both against the Left (Zeghal 1999). However, Sadat's monopolization of power at the end of the 1970s interrupted the absorption of Islamists. After Sadat's assassination in 1981 and the regime's relative liberalization, the MB started to participate in municipal, associational, and parliamentary elections—an emergent political society, where it played a central role. This taught the MB to play by the rules of the game, just like the Turkish Islamists. In the process of this absorption, the MB gave up its remaining radical ideas and by 1994–1995 declared its support for democracy, women's rights, and minority rights. After this point, the MB even started to use old Islamic modernist arguments in favor of democracy (e.g., *shura* as an Islamic equivalent of democracy) and a plural party system (el-Ghobashy 2005). The organization thereby went against its founder al-Banna's condemnation of parties.

Starting with the 1980s, many former Islamists were absorbed into the state and Islamized the state's policies,[15] though this Islamization was still challenged within the state (Bayat 2007; Ismail 1999; Stark 2005). Concomitantly, the MB gradually de-emphasized its goal of an Islamic state and started to seek Islamic transformation within the existing system. The emergence of a liberal Islamic party (Wasat) in the mid-1990s further liberalized especially the younger generation of the MB, who were willing to compete with this party and learn from its cooperation with the state.

In the late 1990s, innovators were imprisoned and conservatives used repression as an excuse to have their candidate appointed as the top leader of the movement. Only in the beginning of the new millennium did the liberalizing youth have influence again. This influence became more decisive after 2004, with the death of a conservative top leader (el-Ghobashy 2005; Stark 2005). However, even following this liberalization, the Egyptian regime is distrustful of the MB and continues mildly repressing this organization.

Most Islamists in Egypt still call for the full implementation of Islamic law (Bayat 2007). In Turkey, by contrast, Islamists are in the middle of drafting a liberal-democratic constitution. This difference has to do with the interruption of the absorption in Egypt. But also note that today Egyptian Islamists are closer to the earlier Islamic modernist activists than the radical Sayyid Qutb. For instance, they call for the participation of citizens in the making of the law to the degree that public interest is involved (Rutherford 2006). In sum, the process of partial absorption has partially liberalized the Islamist conception of Islamic law and brought it in line with dominant forms of Western thought.

Another difference from Turkey is the divide between rural and urban and between the middle class and peasants within the Islamist movement, which inhibited a monopoly of the MB over Islamism and reproduced the persistence of influential violent Islamist groups. At least until the mid-1990s, the countryside was open to agitation by radicals. Radical armed groups appealed to the urban and rural poor, whereas conservative parties such as al-Ahrar and segments of the MB appealed to rentier capitalists, the labor aristocracy, petty merchants, and professionals (Ismail 1998, 200–201). Hegemony is far from complete when compared to Turkey, where the poor are integrated to the system through a peaceful political society.

As in Turkey, charismatic figures are crucial to political society but play a secondary role to large-scale movement and/or party organization. Qutb and al-Banna, two martyrs, remained organizing symbols for the MB for decades. Even after the organization decisively shifted away from their vision, they remained central to its symbolism (Leiken and Brooke 2007). Their dedication to the Islamic cause and the memories of their torture, assassination, and execution (more than their specific strategies and ideas) reproduced the MB's cohesion. However, radicals still make use of Qutb's ideas and memory to impede a passive revolutionary unification in political society around the MB.

An important change in authority figures from the initial radical decades of the MB to its middle decades was transition from leadership by teachers to leadership by merchants, paralleling the shift from radicalism to conservatism.[16] Yet another change occurred at the beginning of the twenty-first century that witnessed the rise of professionals within the organization, who now share power with the old guard merchants. Paralleling the transformation in Turkey, religion is less and less important in the discourse of the new leaders, in contrast to both the initial leaders and the leaders of the middle decades (Zahid and Medley 2006).

The MB's vision of unity unfolded similarly to that of Turkish Islamists: absorption into the nation state and thereafter into globalization. Hasan al-Banna had a more decisively transnational vision when compared to either

Erbakan or Erdoğan. His point of departure was national, but he did not believe in a nationally confined movement. The later MB switched its priorities. Now, it still addresses global issues pertaining to the plight of Muslims; but, its goals today are national (Abed-Kotob 1995, 329).

Just like in the case of Turkish nationalism, the absorption into nationalism has been followed by absorption into Western-led globalization, though this absorption has been restricted by the blockage of the passive revolution. While the MB is still critical of U.S. foreign policy regarding Israel, the liberal wing of the party is willing to negotiate with the United States, especially regarding Egyptian democratization (Leiken and Brooke 2007). Washington is divided over what to do with the MB, with some policymakers supporting it as a brand of moderate Islam and others opposing it as radical. This ambivalence is important, as the West's stance has been decisive in stabilizing the passive revolution in Turkey. Despite these blockages, the MB evolved from an exclusionary vision of Islamic unity to one that includes Copts in the 1990s. Being anti-West is toned down but not dropped.

These political differences from and similarities with the Turkish case have also shaped differences and similarities regarding civil society. The MB defines its own goal and the goal of the state as enhancing individual piety—including intensified worship, good manners, and overall abidance by Islam (Zahid and Medley 2006). According to the organization, there cannot be a truly pious individual without a pious community and state (Rutherford 2006, 726–27).

As in Turkey, Islamic parties of different stripes enforce cleanliness, correct worship, and Islamic morality through their newspapers, magazines, books, conferences (Ismail 1998, 211–12), and the monitoring of neighborhoods and streets (Ismail 2006). Ever since the 1970s, Islamic groups in universities have been instituting gender segregation (Ismail 1999; Rahman 2002). Unlike in Turkey, courts and official Islam (Azhar scholars, public television) aid Islamic groups here, in order to claim radical Islam's ground and limit its effectiveness.

As in Turkey, here too, religiosity has lost its centrality during the movement's absorption. The MB's old generation is still "religiously correct." However, the new generation values political success over spreading the correct form of religion (Zahid and Medley 2006).[17] Now, spreading religious correctness seems more to be the task of communities (of civil society) rather than political movements (Mahmood 2005). This brings up the possibility that there will be convergence in religiosity among broad sectors of the population, thereby strengthening unity and hegemony.

The weak spot of the constitution of hegemony in Egypt lies elsewhere, in unifying the experience of space. Unlike Turkey, peripheral neighborhoods are not deeply integrated to the state and the market.[18] Until recently, they were controlled by Jamaa and Jihad (Ismail 1998). Even the more pragmatic and business-oriented Islamic activists in these quarters remain opposed to the state (Ismail 2006, 52–57). Rural-urban, periphery–city center divides plague the constitution of hegemony.

The reasons can be partially traced back to relations between the state and economy. Nasser had expropriated landowners and distributed land to peasants. *Infitah* took these lands back and gave them to landlords. Many peasants were pushed off (due to increased rent, eviction, or forced sales). Infitah also abrogated free education. The children of peasants migrated to cities en masse with the collapse of rural development projects, and they became the social base for armed Islamic groups (Fandy 1994).

The lack of spatial integration led to two different kinds of Islamism, to a degree which has never been the case in Turkey. Jamaa (led by university graduates of middle-class and working-class origin, southern, social justice focused) situated itself in opposition to the MB, which supported infitah and landowners against small farmers (Fandy 1994). Southern Egypt became associated with "terrorism." The government distrusted even the official troops of the south and sent in northern troops to suppress the insurgency (Cassandra 1995). This provides a contrast with Turkey, where eastern and central Anatolia and the west of the country are relatively more integrated through civil society, the center right, and Islamism.

These contrasts with Egypt suggest that the Justice and Development Party's holding on to patronage and provincialism despite its public insistence on urbanism (analyzed in Chapter 6) is a crucial part of the passive revolution, as it ensures that the religious immigrants remain loyal to the state, the party system, and the market. This reinforces Auyero's (2001) insight that clientelism is not only a means to procure livelihood but also a component of identity-making, ideology, mobilization, and submission.

The linchpin of the Islamic movement's absorption into the system was its changing relations to the economy. Developing a counterhegemonic position, the early MB propagated Islamic socialism (Ismail 1998, 207). After prosecution by Nasser, MB members escaped abroad and engaged in economic activity, which they continued in Egypt after infitah. Starting with the 1970s, the creation of jobs in the private sector and explosion of foreign trade benefited these MB members; many became rich (Ates 2005). The emigrant money coming from the Persian Gulf escaped state control and was invested in Islamic banks. The financialization of the economy (and the turn away from industrial investment) was thereby legitimized Islamically in the 1970s and 1980s. Trading with the West or on the black market was also deemed Islamic through religious verdicts (Ismail 1998, 213–14).

As a result of these changes, the MB emerged as a proponent of a loose and community-based welfare system contradictorily married to an Islamic integration to neoliberalism. In the 1980s and 1990s, its overall economic program supported the state and community taking care of the poor, narrowing of class gaps, and social security for all citizens. The program of the 1987 election alliance with other Islamic parties supported the shrinking of the government bureaucracy, promotion of the private sector as the backbone of the economy, promotion of giving alms, a noninterest banking system, and comprehensive government regulation and strategic planning of the economy (Abed-Kotob 1995, 326–27; el-Ghobashy 2005). The apparent contradictions here are reminiscent of the Turkish Islamists' Just Order program in the 1980s and 1990s. Similar to the Turkish case, the further liberalization of the MB in the later years resolved these contradictions to the advantage of market forces.

Yet at the same time, infitah drove a wedge between radicals (the losers of neoliberalism) and the MB (the winners). There was no hegemonic combination of the two as in Turkey, signaling the limits of Islamic hegemony in Egypt. Radicalism came as a handy excuse for the regime to block a passive revolutionary route. Starting in the 1970s, the Egyptian regime gave many concessions to Islamism, which amounted to "Islamization without an Islamic state," in Asef Bayat's (2007) terms. However, I would contend that this did not culminate in a full passive revolution, because, in contrast with Turkey, those who have made passive revolution into a strategy (the MB and secondarily al-Wasat) have not consistently shared power. In Turkey, there was a radically novel ruling party in power, but the structures of power were not radically transformed.[19]

IRAN: THE FAILED PASSIVE REVOLUTION

Even though there was an active revolution in Iran, by the 1990s, most of the gains of the popular classes were taken back. However, this did not result in a full-scale market capitalist restoration.

In the 1970s, Iran faced an organic crisis. Failure of the shah's leap forward to industrialize and secularize Iran (Foran 1993) discredited secular authority figures, most of all Mohammad Reza Pahlavi. Spatial contradictions (between the city and the country and within cities) intensified. These were paralleled by internationally imposed, indecisive political openings (Arjomand 1988; Fischer 1980; Parsa 1989).[20] In the meantime, even some secular intellectuals, students, and the middle classes were thoroughly dissatisfied with secular, modern lifestyles and turned to religion as an answer, culminating in an ideological crisis in everyday practice.

The revolution was made possible by the charisma of Ruhollah Khomeini, which united clerics, students, and merchants with sectors such as the urban poor, workers, and the middle classes. There was no proper political leadership (organized in parties or political groups).[21] Islamic and secular guerilla organizations such as the People's Feda'iyan and the People's Mojahedin were active in organizing the revolution (Keddie [2003] 2006, 238; Kurzman 2004, 146–47) but were not strong enough to protect its popular gains against the clerics. Personal and traditional—clerical—authority, instead of organized parties, set the terrain of politics for the decades to come.

The weak link in Iranian political society has thus been the constitution of leadership through parties. After the suppression of Islamic and secular unofficial parties, the Islamic regime gave rise to quasi parties (rather than open ones) in the form of pragmatic moderates, conservatives, and liberals organizing in parliament and civil society under different factions. But these have not penetrated society to the degree the Justice and Development Party has in Turkey. In this context, citizens have been integrated into the system through a chain of charismatic figures going from Khomeini to Mahmoud Ahmadinejad.

The radical quasi party lost ground after the Iraq defeat: its agenda of anti-imperialism, export of the revolution, and militancy was discredited (Ashraf 1990). The conservatives and pragmatic moderates were emboldened and started a general campaign against all tenets of radicalism, including the idea of a classless society. After the end of the 1980s, conflicts shaped up mostly between conservatives, pragmatic moderates, and Islamic liberals. The liberals, many of them disillusioned radicals, were the leading figures of a possible passive revolution: They sought to use their radical past and their (Westernized) Islamic intellectual rigor in the service of liberal democracy and the free market (Keddie [2003] 2006, 266, 270), just like the former radicals in Turkey.

In contrast to Egypt and Turkey, charismatic figures were the main articulating elements in Iranian political society. The roots of revolutionary charisma were in clerical office (Arjomand 1988), unlike the Turkish and Egyptian cases, where charisma both emerged from and was combined with bureaucratic mass organization. Moreover, thoroughly reinterpreted Shiite mysticism conferred on Khomeini a charisma that is not comparable to Erbakan, Erdoğan, al-Banna, or Qutb. Mystic themes such as oneness with God, when combined with official implications that Khomeini was the occulted twelfth imam, fostered extreme dedication—as evinced by crowds in his funeral ceremony numbering in the tens of thousands and risking death just to be able to touch his flesh (Ashraf 1990; Khosrokhavar 2000; Kimmel 1989; Sanasarian 1995).

Along with other transformations, the authority structure of the regime also started to change after Khomeini's death. The deputies of the third *majlis* (parliament) were state managers and bureaucrats rather than clerics. For a while, both traditional authority and revolutionary charisma tended to lose their centrality (Ashraf 1990). After the mid-1990s, this change was bolstered by the rise of Mohammad Khatami—a modest, brotherly charismatic figure (as opposed to the fatherly shah and Khomeini) who promised liberalization (Adelkhah 2000; Khosrokhavar 2004). The rise of Ahmadinejad, yet another charismatic figure, several years later demonstrated that this shift away from tradition and charisma was only temporary.

In sum, in Iranian political society quasi parties are in the shadow of charismatic authority. In Egyptian and Turkish political society, charismatic symbols are in the service of political organizations. What characterizes the Iranian Islamist experience, in comparison to the Turkish and Egyptian ones, is the weakness of party leadership (Khosrokhavar 2004) and strength of charismatic leadership.

The weakness in Iranian political leadership created the framework for the partial success of the vision of unity put forth by the regime—absorption of Islamic internationalism into the nation-state—especially in appeasing Kurdish grievances. As a response to historical Kurdish demands, Articles 15 and 19 of the Islamic constitution recognized linguistic and institutional autonomy. Yet at the same time, during the early months of the revolution, the new regime crushed ethnic uprisings (Khosrokhavar 2004). Later on, the regime was troubled more and more by ethnic demands from Azaris, Kurds, and Beluchis, especially after the breakup of the Soviet Union (Ashraf 1993). Nevertheless, with increasing integration of the state and the periphery through the development of education, communication, and transportation, people's loyalty shifted from primordial belongings of tribe, family, and village to the Islamic state (Ashraf 1990; Khosrokhavar 2000). The revolution thus depended on two central forces for realizing its vision of unity: repression and state-making. Political and civil societies were not mobilized for the purpose of unity, which resulted in only partial consent for the new vision of unity (Godazgar and Fathi 2005).

In this potentially divisive atmosphere, national integrity in Iran owed a lot to anti-imperialist mobilization: Even when the regime faced crises, people lined up behind it to stand together against U.S. embargoes. This became ever more apparent with Ahmadinejad's nuclear program, which mobilized Iranian citizens (even those who did not sympathize with the regime) against foreign meddling in Iran's affairs. As a result, transethnic Iranian identity remains strong and (unlike in Turkey) ethnic movements pose no immediate challenge to the state.

Everyday life transformations after the revolution again depended to a large degree on the state. The state imposed gender segregation and dress codes (veiling and dark-colored clothing for women). It banned music at times. The regime also policed relationships between girls and boys. It outlawed daytime eating during the fasting month. These were enforced not only by the official police but also by paramilitary organizations such as Hezbollah and Basij.

However, these official impositions were not bolstered by as strong a mobilization either in civil or political society. In contrast to Turkey and Egypt, there were no thoroughly organized political parties or professional associations that encouraged Islamic lifestyles.[22] Consequently, people started to act out Islamic lifestyles on the street but engaged in non-Islamic practices (such as the consumption of Islamically incorrect videos, tapes, books, magazines, and CDs) at home and in other closed spaces (Amir-Ebrahimi 2006).

Many studies suggest that both poor and middle-class university students and lower-middle-class women and middle-class women are far from the grip of Islamization (Khosrokhavar 2000; Serajzadeh 2002; Shafaee 2003). But the 2005 elections, which witnessed a conservative victory, suggest another pattern, especially for the fringe neighborhoods. Also, some other studies draw attention to how modernization, commercialization, and the consolidation of individualism went hand in hand with Islamization in the 1990s, rather than undermining it (Adelkhah 2000, 124–29). All this can be interpreted as a rather incomplete hegemony: Due to the heavy reliance on charisma and the lack of political penetration by a party, there is no overwhelming consent to Islamization (except in the urban fringe, which is still mobilized through charisma and incorporation into paramilitary organizations). The unwilling Islamization in Iran provides an informative contrast to the consent for the partial and mild Islamization in Turkey and Egypt, which is built through years of work by political society and civil society, in interaction with partial Islamization by the state.

As problematic as the constitution of hegemony in everyday life was its constitution in the social use of space. In the shah's Iran, the city had unquestionable domination over the countryside, and northern Tehran over southern Tehran. Whereas on paper public places were always open to women, this openness was a reality only in the wealthy and Westernized northern Tehran (Amir-Ebrahimi 2006).

The Islamic republic promised to end urban domination over the periphery and also to segregate urban space along gender lines. For almost a decade, this crystallized as tight gender control of the urban center by paramilitary groups staffed by squatter and provincial youth. With the worsening economic conditions at the end of the Iraq-Iran War, however, the regime had to allow women access to public spaces. Ironically, by opening up the city to all those who don the veil, the regime incorporated more women from squatter areas to the city when compared to the shah's time (Amir-Ebrahimi 2006). Nevertheless, what could amount to a hegemonic integration of women to the system was interrupted again by the rise of Ahmadinejad, who tightened up gender segregation.

On another front, the revolutionary regime initially tried to abate spatial inequality by housing aid. However, as eligibility was defined through formal employment criteria, the informal workers were pushed to the fringes again. Also, most of the housing built for the poor eventually went to middle-income households. It is crucial to note that the solution proposed by some experts to these problems, namely the legalization of informal settlements on the fringes (Zebardast 2006), has been practiced in Turkey for decades. Through an interaction of political parties and co-local associations (that is, an interaction of political society and civil society), each new generation of informal settlements has been gradually regularized. This better integration of the urban poor led to a more hegemonic regime in the Turkish case. Even in cases such as Sultanbeyli, where property is not completely legalized, squatters have at least been integrated politically and culturally, again through a party.

In short, even after the revolution, squatters are not properly integrated in Iran, paralleling the Egyptian case. Hence, there are still two Irans, and two Tehrans—which differentiates the situation from Turkey, where the Justice and Development Party integrated the provinces and the city, as well as the urban center and peripheral neighborhoods. This nonintegration (a failure of political society to interact with civil society) creates the conditions for charismatic eruptions. This is one reason why pragmatic moderates and liberals tend to lose in Iran.

The role of quasi parties in Iranian Islamism becomes the clearest in their relations to the economy. In the first decade of the revolution, Iranian Islamic political society was bifurcated along the axis of support for two different class forces in the revolution: the middle-class sectors of the bazaar and the subproletariat.

The shah's White Revolution had squeezed the small shopkeepers and artisans by introducing large factories and supermarkets (Keddie [2003] 2006). Yet, it unintentionally strengthened them by swelling their ranks: the rural immigrants pushed off their land by the White Revolution found jobs in the bazaar, especially in small workshops that employed less than ten people (Kimmel 1989). These small shopkeepers and artisans were the primary class forces in the Islamic Revolution and the overthrow of the shah (Skocpol 1982, 271–72). The subproletarians (employed in the bazaar or elsewhere) were a secondary class. In the first years of the Islamic Revolution, populist measures won the hearts of the poor: their electricity and water bills were canceled. Luxurious homes were confiscated and turned into dwellings for the poor (Sanasarian 1995). Despite ambiguities and differences within revolutionary ranks regarding capitalism in general, big- and medium-sized capital were under serious attack (Nomani and Behdad 2006, 2–3, 38).

In the 1980s, the radical quasi party included Abolhassan Bani-Sadr (the first president), the Revolutionary Council, the Revolutionary Guard, the Revolutionary Committees, a majority of the members in the first two assemblies, and a few prominent clerics. This party propounded full nationalization, land reform, and equality. The conservative quasi party, composed of the majority of the clerics and the Council of Guardians, and backed by the middle-class sectors of the bazaar, opposed these measures. By the end of the 1980s, the conservatives blocked most of the radical measures. Even though Khomeini seemed to situate himself in the middle and play a mediating role, at most critical moments he weighed in with the conservatives (Valibeigi 1993).

Throughout this process, the conservatives interacted with networks in the bazaar, but the radicals lacked similar backing in civil society, as worker councils were reduced to state organs early in the revolution (Nomani and Behdad 2006, 206) and the urban poor lacked such self-organization a lack of popular power characteristic also of the Egyptian and Turkish cases. Moreover, as the radical quasi party was not a proper political party, it could not reach out to the population and mobilize it for support. Finally, all nonclerical parties (including Islamic ones) that could have backed radical measures were savagely suppressed during the first two to four years of the revolution (Abrahamian 1989; Keddie [2003] 2006).

All these struggles have led to a mixed economy under the control of the clergy (Karbassian 2000), laying the groundwork for a transition to a market capitalist economy, dependent on the clergy's and small merchants' willingness to transform themselves into businessmen. However, Iran did not go very far in liberalizing its economy. Even before Khatami, with the advent of the pragmatic moderate Hashemi Rafsanjani in 1989 the main goal of the regime became privatization, but remnants of a radical Islamic stamp on the regime (public dominance in the economy; labor, tax, and environmental regulations; populist expectations among the regime's supporters) made this difficult (Nomani and Behdad 2006, 48, 53–61). The Khatami plan (the Third Five-Year Development Plan) had most of the necessary ingredients of neoliberalism: privatization, deregulation, and decentralization (Khajehpour 2000). Due to its poor links with civil society (which translated as an inability to overcome opposition within the state), Khatami's liberal Islamic government could not fully implement neoliberalism, but it did succeed in drawing foreign capital to the oil sector (Karbassian 2000). Whatever was implemented from this program led to even more unemployment, poverty, cronyism, and corruption (Keddie [2003] 2006, 323). Ahmadinejad derailed liberalization after 2005, sought to aid the poor, and scared off foreign capital.

In sum, Iranian Islamism, rich in charisma but weak in political organization, has inadequately integrated political society and civil society with the state. The urban poor and radical militants, whose hopes have been heightened by decades of revolutionary rhetoric and policies, are especially still open to mobilization by charisma. This partially explains the rise of Ahmadinejad after years of experimentation with moderate pragmatism and liberalism.

However, there is no independent pro–urban poor civil and political society to exert pressure on the state, and therefore the influence of the poor is restricted to charismatic bursts, which favor conservative rather than radical solutions. The forces in civil society (youth and women's movements along with networks in the bazaar), weak though they may be, mostly favor either liberal-democratic, moderate, or conservative capitalist restoration. It is uncertain how far such restoration can go without proper guidance from political society.[23] The pragmatic conservatives and the Islamic liberals, counterparts of the Justice and Development Party in Iran, have opened the way to Islam's absorption into market capitalism but have not carried this transformation far enough due to lack of political will, unity, and solid links with civil society.

BRINGING POLITICS BACK IN

Scholars have suggested that we study civil society in its interactions with the state and the economy to understand how the active consent of subordinate sectors preserves relations of domination. Political society, I have argued, is the missing link in these studies of consent. Many political scientists and sociologists have indeed attributed a central role to the political party. However, the concept of political society emphasizes that we need to study even the political party in the context of the broader political society, that is, in its interaction with sociopolitical movements, charismatic eruptions, municipalities, and other forms of political leadership. A full analysis of political society should also incorporate how its interaction with civil society reshapes visions of sociopolitical unity, everyday practices, social uses of space, and relations to the economy.

The cases above suggest that the way political society develops and the way it interacts with civil society, the economy, and the state have several implications for social stability and change. Whether a regime will be able to face challenges, how far it will incorporate these challenges, and how repressive an attitude it will take are not solely based on regime type (or the structure of the state plus the socioeconomic structure, as some political sociologists hold). We need to take into account the whole social configuration, of which political society is a key component. We then need to study the way this social configuration interacts with international balances.

The concept of passive revolution can likewise prove helpful in understanding social change around the world. This concept has already been deployed by historians and political scientists. What this book implies is that situating the possibility of a passive revolution in the context of an analysis of interactions between political society, civil society, the economy, and the state can inform us about routes of change. Social change coupled contradictorily with a further entrenchment of status quo is a serious (and under-theorized) alternative to an unqualified preservation of the status quo and major social transformation through revolutions or radical reforms. Political society's interactions with civil initiative and the state deeply influence which of these routes a country is going to travel.

REFERENCE MATTER

NOTES

Introduction

1. "Islamism" is defined for the purposes of this book as a project that seeks to shape the state, economy, and society along Islamic lines. Islamism is best understood in its difference from the conservative understanding of Islam, which assigns a more restricted and subordinate role to religion. Conservative Muslims do not publicly challenge rulers, and the conservative interpretation of Islam usually serves (and is meant to serve) to strengthen the state, which traditional Islam sees as the unifier of the community of Muslims (Ayubi 1991).

2. Nurcu is the general name for several groups that all claim to be the true followers of an early-to-mid-twentieth century Islamic scholar, Said-i Nursi. See also Chapter 6.

3. Scholars have usually focused on Weber's ([1922] 1978) theses on Islam, which posit that Islam is essentially closed to secularization and rationalization. However, alternative interpretations of Weber have pointed out that religion does not play a completely independent role in his writings, and Islam as a religion could also rationalize together with the rationalization of state structures (Turner 1974).

4. The once Islamist, now conservative, leaders and ideologues in Turkey actually shun the label moderate Islam (and call themselves "conservative democrats") in order to emphasize their affinity with the Western conservative tradition (rather than Islamist traditions), escape possible legal complications in Turkey, and avoid the implication that theirs is just another interpretation of Islam (competing with other interpretations such as radical Islamism).

5. The concept of passive revolution, admittedly a slippery one, has not always been used in this sense (Abrahamsen 1997; Soederberg 2001). See Chapter 1 and the Conclusion for an examination of this slipperiness, where I give concrete form and content to the concept through a comparative analysis.

6. The "system" would have to be defined differently in the case of each different radical movement. In the case of Islamism, the system generally refers to secularism, which encompasses a secular state, a secular civil society, and a capitalist economy. "Capitalist economy" is defined as a system of production, distribution, and exchange that is predominantly based on (1) wage labor, (2) accumulation as the driving force, and (3) market transactions (Wolf 1982). While radical Islamism has opposed especially item 2, it has in most cases wholeheartedly embraced item 3 (the misleading reason why some scholars have posited that Islamism has always been procapitalist).

7. Ellen Knickmeyer, "In Turkish Vote, Ruling Party Wins by Wide Margin," *The Washington Post*, July 23, 2007; "Erdogans sieg: Die Türkei soll der Welt als Vorbild dienen," *die Welt*, July 23, 2007.

8. The phrase "informal workers" refer to wage earners in the informal sector who work without benefits and insurance and most of the time without contracts.

9. On the MÜSİAD's positions on these issues throughout the 1980s, 1990s, and 2000s, see Buğra (1998a) and Doherty (2007).

10. Sayyid Qutb (1906–1966) was the Egyptian Muslim Brotherhood's intellectual leader in the mid-twentieth century. See the following chapters for the rise and fall of his influence in Turkey.

11. In contrast to a rounded beard, which more directly discloses an Islamist or conservative Islamic position, a thin mustache might signify either Islamist, right-wing nationalist, or conservative Islamic sympathies. Public employees in Turkey are not allowed to grow beards and therefore those with any of the mentioned rightist leanings grow a thin mustache.

12. Pseudonyms have been used for both the association and the group.

13. "God, protect me from the stoned Devil. I start with the name of God, the most merciful, the most beneficent." Muslims recite these verses known as the *euzubesmele* before they start to pray. The more pious use it before any activity.

14. Some journalists have even discussed whether the AKP's empowerment actually amounted to a Second Republic, especially after its reelection in 2007. The historical significance of these years might account for the profound, if not shocking, changes I observed on the ground.

15. See, for example, Helena Smith, "Secular Turkey in Turmoil as Ex-Islamist Runs for President," *Guardian*, August 15, 2007.

16. Sabrina Tavernise, "Islam Taking Root in Turkey's Bureaucracy," *The New York Times*, May 29, 2007.

Chapter 1

1. See comments in this direction by policy advisers and scholars in "Turkey: Now and in the Future: Panel Discussion," *Middle East Review of International Affairs*, October 3, 2006.

2. There are other culture-based accounts of Islamism that are more subtle when compared to Orientalism and modernization theory but which nevertheless retain the idea of ingrained characteristics. The political culture approach, together with acknowledging the logical possibility of a composite culture, draws attention to the centuries of essentialism that leaves little space for the development of hybridity. Arjomand (2001), for example, argues that as a reaction to the unselective secularist adaptation of the West, some Muslims turned to the exclusionary political culture represented by ibn Taymiyya, a scholar from the thirteenth and fourteenth centuries, to develop what is now the main challenge against the regimes, Islamism.

3. According to political economists, the lack of a tradition of private property, the lack of crystallization along working class and business class lines, and the persistence of "residual classes" and precapitalist tradition set the context for flexible populist movements, which appeal to "the people" as a nebulous category rather than to specific classes (Ayubi 1991, 1994; Colas 2004).

4. For an important exception, see Ayubi (1991).

5. Similar to the resource mobilization approach, in the "frame analysis" approach to mobilization, the focus is on how activists instrumentally package their goals to make them "resonate" with the cultural expectations of their audiences (Gamson 1988; Snow et al. 1986; Snow and Benford 1988, 1992; Zald 1996). There is no problematization and study of these goals and expectations, which might or might not change in the process of mobilization.

6. See Evans, Rueschemeyer, and Skocpol (1985), Mann (1986), Nettl (1968), and Skocpol (1979) for the theoretical premises of this approach. When scholars from this state-centered tradition do focus on the construction of political projects and identities, they mostly remain restricted to studying political work that explicitly targets the state and miss the everyday dimensions of power (McAdam, Tarrow, and Tilly 2001, 55–63, 134, 167–69, 244–46), though Mann (1986) remains a partial exception.

7. Social movement theory assumes that grievances are ubiquitous (McCarthy and Zald 1977; Tilly 1978), whereas they are socially and culturally constructed. The changes in grievances during recent decades in the Middle East demonstrate this clearly. Islamic grievances were not ubiquitous several decades ago. Now they are taken for granted. Hence, statements such as "relatively constant features of Muslim societies" (Hafez 2003, 19), which imply that people in the Middle East always had Islamic grievances, are problematic. Therefore, I am sympathetic to Asef Bayat's (1997) criticism of accounts that have taken the poor to be natural allies of the Islamists and his assertion that the poor only respond to "those strategies and associations that respond directly to their immediate concerns" (Bayat 1997, 159). My hegemonic account, however, also aims to demonstrate that the concerns of populations might be redefined by hegemonic projects and that the poor, though nobody's natural allies, might become Islamists' *naturalized* allies (as happened in Turkey, but not in Egypt and Iran).

8. For a more elaborate evaluation of social movement theory, see Tuğal (forthcoming).

9. Yavuz (2003, 2006) also brings in elements of political economy and social movement approaches into his overall civil society framework, but these are not consistently integrated into a theorization of the movement, and in all his accounts the political party seems to play a derivative role.

10. See Turam (2004) for an analysis of Islamic civil society that focuses on cooperation and interaction between civil society and the state rather than opposition.

11. For the antecedents of my usage of "articulation," see Hall (1985, 1986), Laclau (1977), and Laclau and Mouffe (1985).

12. Organic crises are different from the more frequent conjunctural crises, which are restricted to a level or two of the hegemonic formation. Conjunctural crises include, for instance, exclusively economic crises.

13. See Smelser (1963) for the anomie account that is today largely abandoned by social movement scholars.

14. What I am describing here closely resembles what structural Marxists have called the "accumulation of contradictions" (Poulantzas 1974). However, I do not hold to the structural Marxist position that the economy determines ("in the last instance") the context of this accumulation.

15. This redefinition of political society also fills an important gap in political sociology. Expanding on the historical institutionalist paradigm, Peter Evans (1995) puts state-society linkages (along with the structure of the state) at the center of his analysis and argues that a state cannot be effective without ties to social groups with which it shares a project. Yet, even when historical institutionalism thus embeds the state in social relations, it cannot specify from where such "projects" emanate. Political society is a fundamental bridge between civil society and state, as it constructs and propagates the project that binds them.

16. Also see Chatterjee (2004) regarding teachers as key constituents of political society.

17. However, in attempting to subordinate state agencies, leaders might focus on strengthening the local organization of political society and its links to the national organization rather than attacking the nonelected officials in the local scene.

18. See the informing debate between Laclau (2005) and Hardt and Negri (2000, 2005).

19. There are historical exceptions to the centrality of the party in the making of society. For instance, as Gramsci himself pointed out, intellectuals such as Benedetto Croce may act as the main articulating agents at crucial turning points, in the absence of effective parties. However, such a substitute for parties causes instability or worse: for example, the absence of properly organized parties opened the way to fascism in Italy. The Conclusion will show that a similar predicament continues to trouble Iran.

20. This does not mean that nonparty actors do not organize and coordinate their own affairs or lack creative political visions, as Huntington (1968) and Lenin ([1902] 1969) implied when discussing the transitions to modern statehood. Both authors have failed to see the internal capacities of civil society and its potential to envisage different collective futures, a tendency that historical institutionalism has generally inherited. But what is important for a theory of hegemony is the interaction between civil society and political society, and thus the generalization ("articulation") of all microcoordinational activities. Huntington and Lenin were both right in arguing that political intervention is required to make everything hang together.

21. Inspired by Bakhtin (1981, [1929] 1984)—who held that authors, in their relation with readers, are in the center of the creation of meaning—I bring authority figures and their dialogue with the followers back into hegemonic analysis. This analysis, therefore, is different from hegemonic analyses inspired by the post-structuralist declaration regarding the death of the author (Barthes [1967] 1977; Foucault [1969] 1984), which focuses on discourses rather than actors (Laclau and Mouffe 1985), or at most on actors as signifiers in discourses (Laclau 2005). For the Bakhtinian turn in the social sciences, see Crehan (1997), Gardiner (1992), Nielsen (2002), Smith (1998), Steinberg (1998, 1999), Tuğal (2006), and Wertsch (1991).

22. For an account that integrates the analysis of the margins and localities in the study of state-making, see Migdal (2001).

23. The essential human experience is not unity but fragmentation (Castoriadis 1997). The individual, the group, and greater collectivities are always shattered. If actors do not bring the pieces together, there is no integrated individual, there is no group, and there is no larger collectivity. Each human being carries out this activity by making sense of disparate experiences and perceptions, talking things over, working on reconciliation—only in order to pull together the threads and make them into an individual, a family, or a group of friends. The work of politics is basically the same.

24. Although this reading of the process draws on Benedict Anderson's (1983) work in discussing national unification, it is much more centered around politics than his.

25. The psychological drive for unity also lies at the basis of totalitarian desires, according to Lacanian political analysis (Lefort 1986).

26. Social movements, following Cohen and Arato (1992), and informal networks, following Norton (1995–1996), are included as constituents of civil society. Contrary to both proponents (Putnam 1995) and critics (Chatterjee 2004) of the civil society model, I assume neither that civil society is legal and law abiding nor that it expands individual initiative against communal and state power.

27. Hegemonic projects also involve the regulation of life, space, and relations to the economy by political society and the state as well. Scholarly analyses will have to

blur the lines between the spheres of activity of the state, political society, and civil society. However, regulation of everyday life is much more successfully exercised by civil and political society. When a project rests mostly on the state to carry out this goal, it will have partial success. This has been one of the weaknesses of secularist hegemony in Turkey, and one of Islamism's strengths.

28. Gramsci's focus on common sense can certainly be a starting point for integrating the analysis of everyday life into hegemonic analysis. However, even though he has recognized the importance of habits and practices (beyond mental conceptions), Gramsci has not developed a paradigm within the framework of which everyday practices can be analyzed. It is mostly scholars not forming a part of the Gramscian legacy who have noted the centrality of everyday life to the reproduction of society (Bellah et al. 1985; Melucci 1996; Smith 1987; Swidler 2001).

29. While Gramsci paid a lot of attention to spatial boundaries (especially in his exploration of the meaning of the divide between Italy's south and north, which is central to his *analysis* of Italy), he did not make the social use of space into a central part of his *theorization* (unless we are talking about international space, the difference between the East and West). This omission has characterized his legacy as well, only except recently (van Appeldoorn 2003; Jessop 2006). Yet, the role of space is crucial to the making of hegemony.

30. Foucault (1977, 1980) has underlined that discipline is enacted in space, organization, and control of individuals occurs in space, and therefore, microspace is not neutral.

31. Foucault (along with many post-structuralist scholars influenced by his argument concerning "heterotopias") has studied the importance of microspace in the unraveling of totalities but not its role in the constitution of alternative totalities. Also see Ray and Qayum (2003).

32. The analysis of how space matters in other hegemonic formations should be based on the specificity of each case, as Wacquant (2008) has emphasized. While the urban-rural distinction in other peripheral nations has similar implications with that in Turkey, in core countries of world capitalism, racial distinctions and international immigration play a comparable role.

33. Other scholarly uses of the concept of passive revolution (especially Chatterjee [1986] 2001; Riley and Desai 2007) have inspired my analyses.

Chapter 2

1. This chapter's goal is not providing a full-blown history of the republic but discussing the national context of the Islamic challenge based on the theoretical matrix proposed in the previous chapter. I have attempted a more detailed discussion of modern Turkish history elsewhere (Tuğal 2007, 2008).

2. Also, the CHP underwent a left turn after 1965 as a response to the emergence of a legal leftist party (the Labor Party of Turkey, TİP), radical labor movements, and student movements. For fifteen years, it defined itself as pro-labor, anticapitalist, and anti–United States.

3. Some scholars take Turkey as the paragon of the disestablishment of public religion in a Muslim context (Lerner [1958] 1967; Lewis 1961). More critical scholars have pointed out that the republic has controlled and institutionalized Islam rather than disestablishing it and separating it from the state (Bromley 1994; Heper 1985; Mardin 1983). Recognizing that Turkish secularization combined the separation of religion from politics with the political control of religion (Davison 1998), it can be characterized as the conflictual and tension-ridden development of an "official Islam."

4. There is an intricate and multilayered semiotics around the words *cemaat* (community) and *tarikat* (religious order) in Turkey. Briefly, tarikat refers specifically to Sufi groups, while cemaat is used to designate religious groups of various kinds, including tarikats and their modernized offshoots.

5. See Parla (1985, 1992) for corporatism in Turkey.

6. See the coalition protocol between the two parties, "Cumhuriyet Halk Partisi ile Milli Selamet Partisi Arasında Yapılan Koalisyon Protokolü," *Ankara*, 1974, 9–13.

7. See Cem (1976) for an account of how this anti-Islamist reaction weighed upon the CHP's policies in public broadcasting (which was for a short time under the CHP's control).

8. The MHP had shamanist ideological roots but later reinterpreted Islam to make it fit extreme nationalism. This move proved successful, and extreme nationalism gained some popularity in Turkey (Bora and Can 1991). The military's adaptation of this interpretation of Islam in the early 1980s, together with the conservative reaction against Kurdish nationalism, Islamism, and the European Union made the MHP one of the strongest parties in Turkey in the 1990s and 2000s.

9. There were also many pro-Iranian or otherwise revolutionary Islamist groups in the 1980s and 1990s (including the Islamic Great East Raiders Front [İBDA-C], Hizbullah, Haksöz, the Malatya circle, and Selam), but those who chose not to engage with the RP were marginalized in the Islamic movement.

10. Traditionalism, in this book, refers to the defense of patriarchal, scholarly, and Sufi authority against secular, radical Islamic, or modernist Islamic attacks on and/or reinterpretations of Islam and folk tradition. Traditionalism never exists as a pure ideology: it is always (contradictorily) articulated to varieties of Islamism, conservatism, or secularism.

11. The massacre in Sivas was the third instance of mass violence against the Alevis in the last three decades. Whereas the massacres before 1980 had been organized by the MHP, which perceived the Alevis as the popular base of "the communist threat," the primary suspects in the third massacre were the nationalist Islamist party

Great Unity Party (BBP) and the Islamist fringe organization the Islamic Great East Raiders Front (İBDA-C) (Coşkun 1995).

12. Around this time, the Atatürk cult became popular again, albeit in a more market-oriented, lighthearted fashion, contrasting with the classical, solemn representations of Mustafa Kemal (Özyürek 2006). This came in handy for secular middle-class sectors, which had diversified, professionalized, and integrated into the private sector (as well as still occupying most of public professional employment) over the decades.

13. This does not mean that Islamist parties completely excluded traditionalism and clientelism. They rather played on the center right theme of absorbing local notables into bureaucratic mechanisms through charismatic leadership. Actually, bolder than the center right, they sought to *explicitly* include the Sufi masters as well as the provincial notables.

14. "RP Yemini Değişti," *Zaman*, October 14, 1996.

15. The concept of "integralist" is used instead of "fundamentalist" to refer to movements that aim to Islamize all aspects of life. Fundamentalism, which originated as a concept in the U.S. context of Protestant movements that rejected tradition in favor of early Christian texts (Riesebrodt 1993), is mistakenly used to refer to all Islamic integralist movements. Only a minority of these movements share with original U.S. fundamentalism the urge to reject medieval tradition in favor of early, "pure" religion. There are irresolvable conflicts between this minority (which sometimes calls itself *selefi*) and mainstream Islamism.

16. These intellectuals who coined the phrase "Just Order" were the inhabitants of an Islamic commune, the Akevler Kooperatifi (Çakır 1994).

17. Arrighi (1990) has helpfully applied the Gramscian idea of hegemony as "moral and intellectual leadership" to international relations in the context of political economy. Here, I extend his insight to religious and cultural realms as well.

18. Nazif Gürdoğan, "Ak ile Kara Turnuvasına Yeni Bir Siyasi Katılım," *Yeni Şafak*, August 19, 2001.

19. Rhetorically, there is still some talk of social justice among AKP ranks, but what the party means by this has changed fundamentally. It no longer means redistribution, but support of microcredits and small businesses, and even that within the boundaries of a market-driven society. Other social policies of the party (some distribution of coal in poor neighborhoods, a previous Welfare Party tradition, and the free distribution of educational supplies to poor children) have been marginal to its overall sustenance of fiscal stability, budgetary discipline, and privatization. In this sense, it would not be accurate to say that the AKP is a Turkish version of the Third Way (Öniş and Keyman 2003), as its social policies pale in significance compared to those of self-proclaimed "social-liberal" governments (e.g., contrast Mexico's PRONASOL).

20. Also, the narrative in this chapter is mostly restricted to pre-2007 events. For a hegemonic analysis of national developments in 2007 and 2008, see Cihan Tuğal, "The Hand of the Market and the Boot of the Army," *ISIM Review* 20:40–41 and "Party of One," *The National*, August 29, 2008.

Chapter 3

1. Ümraniye, Kartal, and Pendik used to be leftist strongholds in the 1970s. In the 1990s, they shifted to an Islamist line.

2. All private names are pseudonyms, except where last names are mentioned. Identifying characteristics of individuals have also been modified.

3. While I use Turkish transliteration of Arabic words throughout the text (to remain loyal to the usage in my field site), I have used standard English transliteration in the case of books published in the Anglophone world.

4. In traditional jurisprudence, the world was divided between *dar-ul Islam* (the house of Islam) and *dar-ul harp* (the house of war). The second referred to areas outside Muslim rule. Radicals such as the Egyptian Muhammad Qutb included existing Muslim countries in dar-ul harp, as they had strayed away from pristine Islam.

5. In interviews and conversations, "R" designates the researcher.

6. Real Islam/hearsay Islam was one of the many binary oppositions that Islamists used to differentiate their understanding of religion from the common understanding (also see Chapter 2).

7. "Önce Gül Sonra Taş," *Sabah*, August 23, 1997.

8. "Her Cuma Aynı Görüntü," *Milliyet*, August 30, 1997; "Protestolar Provoke Ediliyor" *Zaman*, August 30, 1997.

9. "Her Cuma Aynı Görüntü," *Milliyet*, August 30, 1997; "Cuma Gösterisine Gözaltı," *Milliyet*, September 6, 1997.

10. *Tekbir* is a word that marks the greatness of God. When uttered in a crowd, it calls for the collective chanting of the phrase "*Allah-u ekber*" (God is great).

11. The mayor (*belediye başkanı*) is the strongest elected officer in Turkish districts. As the chief municipal officer, his or her main tasks include providing the district's infrastructure and regulating land tenure. She or he should be distinguished from the appointed governor (*kaymakam*), who represents the central government in a district and is encumbered with the control of officials at the local level (including police officers).

12. On the days following the street protests, I talked to several FP administrators, and they all dismissed the idea that protests in the district could lead to any favorable results, as the residents were "poor" and "uneducated."

13. Modernist Islam is the theological position that holds that Islam is compatible with rationalism, tolerance, and professionalism. Necmi's favorite Islamic scholar,

Fazlur Rahman (1966), argued that defending Islam meant fighting for democracy, individual liberties, and social justice. Traditional Islam had strayed away from this path because of clerical and political intrigues, as well as medieval conditions.

14. There were other, less important, factors behind the DSP's restricted success, such as the nationalism and less secularist position of the party.

15. "Headmen" are village or neighborhood administrators elected by the people.

16. *Müftüs* issue *fetvas* (religious verdicts), yet these are not legally binding.

17. Erzurum is a province of eastern Anatolia that has supplied many inhabitants, activists, and officials to Sultanbeyli.

18. Even though liberalism became one of the dominant discourses during these decades due to liberal intellectuals' institutional power, a survey in 2007 showed that only 1.5 percent of the population defined itself as liberal, demonstrating that the ideology of liberalism (in its pure state) did not spread among the popular sectors. But as the following chapters will hint at, liberalism later became hegemonic by infiltrating Islamic discourse and politics.

19. Both residents of the district and officials use the word "cosmopolitan" to disapprovingly imply the lack of a unifying culture.

20. Sirman (1990) also underlines how the state becomes a part of local structure through reinforcing male subjectivity, although, in the village she has studied, the state's positive role in reproducing masculinity is more entrenched when compared to Sultanbeyli.

21. For an analysis of the meanings of different types of Islamic covering, see White (2002).

22. Süleyman Arat, "Sultanbeyli'yi Değiştiren Süper Kaymakam," *Hürriyet*, July 26, 2002.

23. İSKİ (İstanbul Su ve Kanalizasyon İdaresi) is the water and sewage provider of the Istanbul metropolitan area. The abuses during the municipal reign of the center left between 1989 and 1994 had caused the water and sewage services of the city to deteriorate remarkably, especially in poor regions.

24. Shafir's typology of nationalisms is based on a study of how nationalists respond to international immigrants, but here it is extended to their responses to non-mobile minority populations as well as rural-to-urban, internal immigrants.

Chapter 4

1. See Qutb (1970, 1993), Kepel (1985), and Sivan (1985) regarding radical Islam. For the influence of radical Islamic ideas in Turkey, see Başer (1999). For the development of similar ideas in the Turkish context, see Özel (1978).

2. According to the Süleymancıs, the Islamists declared that the Süleymancıs were non-Muslims and initiated the fights. According to the Islamists, the Süleymancıs

wanted a share of the central Kur'an school students for their own Kur'an school, and they initiated the fights. The central Kur'an school was officially controlled, but as in the case of many official Kur'an schools in these decades, it was under the influence of the Islamist party.

3. For the alleged frauds in the 1989 elections, see Işık and Pınarcıoğlu (2001).

4. "Every sheep is hung from its own leg," a Turkish proverb, which means that everybody is responsible for his or her own actions.

5. For the prevalence of materialist values in popular religion, see Ginzburg (1980).

6. See Işık and Pınarcıoğlu (2001) for a detailed analysis of the legal issues.

7. The category "subproletarian" is used in the sense of informal, unorganized, lowly paid, irregularly employed workers (Bourdieu 1979; Derlugian 2005), as distinct from "lumpen proletarians," who gain their living through criminal activities.

8. Sirman (1990) points out that masculinity and respectability in the Turkish countryside also depends on securing land for the family, having social and political networks that ensure the family's economic strength, and having the skills to manipulate these ties.

9. But it is also crucial to note in passing that it was from the RP that the AKP learned how to link politics and place-based civil society.

10. For more on the anticommunist and Islamic-nationalist MTTB, see Atacan (2005, 195).

11. This presents a clear contrast to the nearby (and less Islamized) district Ümraniye, where housewives were the principal activists in procuring services for their neighborhoods (Erder 1996).

12. For an economic analysis of this joint investment method throughout the Islamic world, see Kuran (2004).

Chapter 5

1. These are two prominent Islamic thinkers whose books had become popular in the district by 2006. Abdolkarim Soroush argues that Islam and liberal democracy are compatible. Muhammad Abid Jabiri, in turn, is famous for his argument that there never was a distinctly "Islamic state," even in the time of the Prophet. Yaman had already started to read Jabiri when I was getting ready to leave the district in 2002; he had not yet read Soroush.

2. The quite crowded protests in the Kurdish southeast were an exception.

3. Kur'an 3:104. Michael Cook (2000) provides a useful genealogy of the debates around the "commanding the good and forbidding the evil" phrase over the centuries. Traditionally, scholars and Sufis have resisted radical interpretations and argued that commanding and forbidding should be restricted to one's family and immediate community. The phrase does not license ordinary believers to attempt to eradicate evil

from society as a whole. Hasan al-Banna, Sayyid Qutb, and other radicals have revived the activist understanding of this phrase.

4. Therefore, Gramsci also implicitly differentiated between a politics that made "the passive revolution" into a strategy (an exclusive reliance on the "war of position") and a revolutionary politics that made the war of position its strongest component.

5. Kur'an 3:49; 5:110.

6. Sabuni is a Syrian scholar whose popularity was on the rise in Turkey.

7. As Charles Kurzman's (2004) analysis of the Iranian Revolution shows, some aspects of mobilization defy sociological explanation. Charisma, I argue, is one of these, at least partially. While the factors analyzed here might have sustained, reproduced, and bolstered Erdoğan's charisma, I will not attempt to answer whether they have created it.

8. See Heper and Toktaş (2003) for Erdoğan's imprisonment and his career in general.

9. Erdoğan himself was attacked before the 1994 municipal elections for having an illegal building in Sultanbeyli. Çakır and Çalmuk (2001) have argued that people have interpreted this as an attack on squatting, which boosted Erdoğan's charisma among the popular sectors.

10. The decline in religious rhetoric in public speeches paralleled the near disappearance of religious references in the AKP's program, especially when compared to that of the FP.

11. For the wars of intelligence and conspiracies in 2006, see Tuğal (2007).

12. See the Introduction for the multilayered and contested meaning of the term milli.

Chapter 6

1. Note that the AKP and its supporters had not become Islamic modernists openly, but their practices and policies went in this direction. Actually, many of the party's supporters and leaders still rejected Islamic modernism theologically.

2. Already in the 1990s, there were conservatives reacting against the word "Islamist" (Saktanber 2002, 213). What was new in 2006 was that people who used to call themselves Islamist were no longer comfortable with this title.

3. As Azak (2000) notes, such usage of *inşallah* was common among Islamic activists in the 1990s throughout Turkey.

4. The *gusül* ablution is a special ablution that purifies the whole body.

5. *Tesbih* literally means rosary. Pious men usually carry tesbih in their pockets, and they count the beads by silently uttering sentences such as *"Allah-u ekber"* after prayers and during the day. This act of counting is called *tesbihat*. Sufi Muslims practice tesbihat much more frequently than others. In 2001, radicals reacted

to tesbihat as it kept people away from politics and the acquisition of textual knowledge.

6. *Zikir* is a collective Sufi ritual where the various names of God are rhythmically repeated.

7. The Ankara School and Yaşar Nuri Öztürk have been fighting for a modernist interpretation of Islam.

8. Yavuz (2003) and Turam (2007) provide a map of Nurcu groups and discuss how the Gülen community fits into the general picture.

9. For institutional convergence between the AKP and the Gülen community, see Turam (2007, chapter 6).

10. Said Nursi is the original founder of the Nurcu community (Mardin 1989), which split into several groups after his death. For the Nurcu groups today, the main inspirational text is his *Epistles of Light* (*Risale-i Nur*).

11. Regarding the *besmele*, see the Introduction, endnote 13.

12. I did not directly observe such radical generational changes in dress patterns among the conservative population. These were either the exaggerated worries of some hard-liners, or the pious families of the district had done their best to prevent me from speaking to the innovators in their families—which is quite possible given the restricted number of women I could contact.

13. The municipality had started to increase the number of female professionals already in 2000, when it was under the control of the Virtue Party.

14. Changes in women's bodies, clothes, and behaviors (and the changing representation of these) are indices of political transformation in the context of other (even nonreligious) hegemonic projects as well (e.g., see Bonnell 1997, chapters 2 and 3).

15. These different expectations from the researcher may be due either to the commodification I analyze throughout this chapter or to my changing position from a graduate student to an assistant professor.

16. Gramsci himself had noticed this contradictoriness about the consciousness, but not about the everyday practices, of people.

Conclusion

1. These three key countries in the Middle East (Turkey, Egypt, and Iran) are thereby differentiated from the fourth key state, Saudi Arabia, which based its capital accumulation project on an Islamically conservative monarchy. These two different models have set the agenda for smaller states in the Middle East. While Morocco and Jordan could also have been included in this analysis as cases that have approximated a passive revolution (Robinson 1998), the focus here has been restricted to the three countries above because of their role as trendsetters for secular and Islamic movements.

2. This is where I depart from Przeworski's account, which fails to account for the way social democrats interacted with the radicals after they became reformists.

3. For a study of such tendencies of marginalization among autonomist groups, see Leach (2005).

4. In the United States, where radicalism has poorly interacted with party politics in the twentieth century, similar processes of absorption have unfolded through other institutions such as unions (Kimeldorf 1992, 1999).

5. For example, the Confederation of Revolutionary Worker Unions (DİSK), in which the communists were already marginalized (Samim 1981).

6. The passive revolution in Turkey actually came in two waves, where the absorption of Islamic leadership into these political parties was central. A first wave of radicals was absorbed into the Islamist RP-FP, followed by a second, more decisive wave of absorption to the Islamic neoliberal AKP. This integration into legal parties incorporated Islamic revolutionaries into secular capitalism.

7. However, it remains questionable whether the Italian Communist Party's extensive control over municipalities (as well as unions and cooperatives) was meant to set up exemplary communist localities or to better integrate leftist opposition to the capitalist system (Pizzorno 1997; Sidoti 1993).

8. Regarding the development of Islamic knowledge, the Sufi communities and the Islamist party emphasized hand manuals of ritual, the Kur'an, stories about the Prophet's life, along with his sayings. The radical circles preferred the Kur'an and writings from contemporary Islamists from all over the world.

9. Secularization and desecularization can be read through these political lenses rather than as spontaneous processes contingent upon modernization (Berger 1999; Greeley 1989; Liliane 1991; Tschannen 1991; Yamane 1997). When we take this political angle, questions regarding which aspects of life are secularizing (or desecularizing) and at what pace come to be seen in a different light. The impact of religion on life is an effect of religious and secular hegemonic projects. For a similar perspective, see Gorski (2000) and Smith (2003). Asad's (2003) position is also somewhat similar to my position.

10. This emergent tolerance was not extended to all. The municipality and the local government did their best to prevent the construction of an Alevi house of worship (*Cemevi*) using legal excuses.

11. Whereas space is a strong determinant in the constitution of hegemony, not all revolutionary projects have an explicit agenda about transforming space. For example, the transformation of space has been a weak component of revolutionary Marxist politics. An important exception to this is the activities of a movement of city planners, geographers, and architects who worked for a new socialist spatial organization in the Union of Soviet Socialist Republics between 1917 and 1925 (Soja 1989, 89). Starting with Lefebvre, Marxist theorists have written on the spatial aspects of revolutionary leftist projects. Castells (1983) and Harvey (1973, 1989), most prominently, have argued that alternative political projects also need to have spatial projects. Nevertheless,

Marxist political projects did not keep pace with these theoretical developments, partially because they were waning as these theoretical contributions matured.

12. See Tuğal (2007) for an analysis of how this religious neoliberal hegemony depends on cash flows from the West, and therefore on global financial stability.

13. Timothy Mitchell (2002) has also underlined the political making of similar cases of rationalization and rise of experts.

14. See Zollner (2007) for the political roots of this moderation in a split within the MB in the 1960s.

15. Examples of the Islamization of official policies include official courts excommunicating people and courts, newspapers, and al-Azhar enforcing Islamic morality.

16. This shift among the top leadership seems to overlap with and reinforce the shift among the key activist body on the ground from students to tradesmen, which Salwa Ismail (2003) has pointed out.

17. Some scholars raise doubts about the extent of this move away from the centrality of piety in the MB's politics (Bayat 2007).

18. The peripheral neighborhoods in Egypt also experience the state and the market, but the encounter is much more informal, extralegal, and repressive when compared to Turkey (Ismail 2006).

19. The rise of a new political elite that enforced the old structures has also characterized the other major passive revolutions: the Italian Risorgimento (Gramsci 1971), Italian fascism (Gramsci 1971; Riley and Desai 2007), and Indian independence (Chatterjee [1986] 2001).

20. It should be noted that some scholarly accounts question the role of these economic and political factors in bringing about the Iranian Revolution (Kurzman 2003, 2004). I suggest that while these factors, in isolation from each other, could not have brought about a revolution, their coincidence (an organic crisis) prepared the conditions for a revolution, the execution of which depended on human (hegemonic) will.

21. The image of the suffering leader (Erdoğan, Qutb, al-Banna) was crucial for Islamist organization in Turkey and Egypt too, but it never became as central to action as in Iran. The death of Khomeini's son (in late 1977) and a newspaper article that insulted him (in early 1978) lit the spark for the student-clerical-bazaari protests that initiated the Iranian Revolution (Keddie [2003] 2006; Kurzman 2004). Later in the process, Khomeini's ingenuity—as well as what people wanted to see in him—brought diverse sectors together.

22. It can be suggested that independent clerics, acting as a sort of civil society in Iran, intermediaries between the state and the population, still realized Islamization throughout these decades. However, unlike in the Turkish and Egyptian cases, the Islamist movement did not add much to this historically already strong civil component

in Iran and maybe even weakened it by incorporating many clerics into the state bureaucracy.

23. Kurzman (2001) argues that Khatami and other Islamic liberal political leaders refrained from tipping the balance of forces in favor of youth movements due to the fear of civil war, which effectively prevented a decisive shift away from Islamic authoritarianism and toward a more complete restoration of formal capitalism and an Islamic liberal regime.

REFERENCES

Books and Articles

Abed-Kotob, Sana. 1995. "The Accommodationists Speak: Goals and Strategies of the Muslim Brotherhood of Egypt." *International Journal of Middle East Studies* 27: 321–39.

Abrahamian, Ervand. 1989. *The Iranian Mojahedin*. New Haven, CT: Yale University Press.

———. 1991. "Khomeini: Fundamentalist or Populist?" *New Left Review* 186:102–19.

Abrahamsen, Rita. 1997. "The Victory of Popular Forces or Passive Revolution? A Neo-Gramscian Perspective on Democratisation." *Journal of Modern African Studies* 35:129–52.

Adelkhah, Fariba. 2000. *Being Modern in Iran*. New York: Columbia University Press.

Aksoy, Asu, and Kevin Robins. 1994. "Istanbul between Civilization and Discontent." *New Perspectives on Turkey* 10:57–74.

Aktar, Ayhan. 2000. *Varlık Vergisi ve "Türkleştirme" Politikaları*. Istanbul: İletişim.

Albayrak, Sadık. 1989. *Türk Siyasi Hayatında MSP Olayı*. Istanbul: Araştırma Yayınları.

———. 1990. *MSP Davası ve 12 Eylül*. Istanbul: Araştırma Yayınları.

Amir-Ebrahimi, Masserat. 2006. "Conquering Enclosed Public Spaces." *Cities* 23: 455–61.

Anderson, Benedict. 1983. *Imagined Communities: Reflections on the Origin and Spread of Nationalism*. London: Verso.

Anderson, Perry. 1976. "The Antinomies of Antonio Gramsci." *New Left Review I* 100: 5–78.

Arat, Yeşim. 2005. *Rethinking Islam and Liberal Democracy: Islamist Women in Turkish Politics*. Albany: State University of New York Press.

Arjomand, Said Amir. 1988. *The Turban for the Crown: The Islamic Revolution in Iran.* Oxford: Oxford University Press.

———. 2001. "Perso-Indian Statecraft, Greek Political Science and the Muslim Idea of Government." *International Sociology* 16:455–73.

Arrighi, Giovanni. 1990. "The Three Hegemonies of Historical Capitalism." *Review* 13:365–408.

Asad, Talal. 2003. *Formations of the Secular: Christianity, Islam, Modernity.* Stanford, CA: Stanford University Press.

Ashraf, Ahmad. 1990. "Theocracy and Charisma: New Men of Power in Iran." *International Journal of Politics, Culture and Society* 4:113–52.

———. 1993. "The Crisis of National and Ethnic Identities in Contemporary Iran." *Iranian Studies* 26:159–64.

Atacan, Fulya. 2005. "Explaining Religious Politics at the Crossroad: AKP-SP." *Turkish Studies* 6:187–99.

Ates, Davut. 2005. "Economic Liberalization and Changes in Fundamentalism: The Case of Egypt." *Middle East Policy* 12:133–44.

Auyero, Javier. 2001. *Poor People's Politics: Peronist Survival Networks and the Legacy of Evita.* Durham, NC: Duke University Press.

Ayubi, Nazih. 1991. *Political Islam: Religion and Politics in the Arab World.* London and New York: Routledge.

———. 1994. *Overstating the Arab State: Politics and Society in the Middle East.* London: I.B. Tauris.

Azak, Umut. 2000. "İslami Radyolar ve Türbanlı Spikerler." In *İslam'ın Yeni Kamusal Yüzleri*, ed. Nilüfer Göle, 93–109. Istanbul: Metis Yayınları.

Baiocchi, Gianpaolo. 2005. *Militants and Citizens: The Politics of Participatory Democracy in Porto Alegre.* Stanford, CA: Stanford University Press.

Bakhtin, Mikhail. 1981. *The Dialogic Imagination: Four Essays.* Austin: University of Texas Press.

———. [1929] 1984. *Problems of Dostoevsky's Poetics.* Minneapolis: University of Minnesota Press.

Barthes, Roland. [1967] 1977. "The Death of the Author." In *Image, Music, Text*, 142–48. New York: Hill and Wang.

Başer, Alev Erkilet. 1999. *Ortadoğu'da Modernleşme ve İslami Hareketler.* Istanbul: Yöneliş.

Bayat, Asef. 1997. *Street Politics: Poor People's Movements in Iran.* New York: Columbia University Press.

———. 2007. *Making Islam Democratic: Social Movements and the Post-Islamist Turn.* Stanford, CA: Stanford University Press.

Beinin, Joel. 2001. *Workers and Peasants in the Modern Middle East.* Cambridge: Cambridge University Press.

Bellah, Robert N., Richard Madsen, William M. Sullivan, Ann Swidler, and Steven M. Tipton. 1985. *Habits of the Heart: Individualism and Commitment in American Life*. Berkeley and Los Angeles: University of California Press.

Berger, Peter L., ed. 1999. *The Desecularization of the World: Resurgent Religion and World Politics*. Washington, DC: Ethics and Public Policy Center; Grand Rapids, MI: W.B. Eerdmans Publishing Company.

Donnell, Victoria E. 1997. *Iconography of Power: Soviet Political Posters under Lenin and Stalin*. Berkeley and Los Angeles: University of California Press.

Bora, Tanıl. 1999. "Istanbul of the Conqueror: The 'Alternative Global City' Dreams of Political Islam." In *Istanbul Between the Global and the Local*, ed. Çağlar Keyder, 47–58. Lanham, MD: Rowman & Littlefield.

Bora, Tanıl, and Kemal Can. 1991. *Devlet, Ocak, Dergâh: 12 Eylül'den 1990'lara Ülkücü Hareket*. Istanbul: İletişim.

Bourdieu, Pierre. [1972] 1977. *Outline of a Theory of Practice*. Cambridge: Cambridge University Press.

———. 1979. *Algeria 1960: The Disenchantment of the World: The Sense of Honour: The Kabyle House or the World Reversed: Essays*. Cambridge: Cambridge University Press.

———. [1979] 1984. *Distinction: A Social Critique of the Judgement of Taste*. Cambridge, MA: Harvard University Press.

Brenner, Neil. 2004. *New State Spaces: Urban Governance and the Rescaling of Statehood*. Oxford: Oxford University Press.

———, ed. 2003. *State/Space: A Reader*. Malden, MA: Blackwell Publishers.

Bromley, Simon. 1994. *Rethinking Middle East Politics: State Formation and Development*. Cambridge, MA: Polity.

Buğra, Ayşe. 1998a. "Class, Culture, and State: An Analysis of Interest Representation by Two Turkish Business Associations." *International Journal of Middle East Studies* 30:521–39.

———. 1998b. "The Immoral Economy of Housing in Turkey." *International Journal of Urban and Regional Research* 22:304–16.

———. 2002. "Political Islam in Turkey in Historical Context: Strengths and Weaknesses." In *The Politics of Permanent Crisis: Class, Ideology and State in Turkey*, ed. Neşecan Balkan and Sungur Savran, 107–44. New York: Nova Science Publishers.

Burawoy, Michael. 1979. *Manufacturing Consent: Changes in the Labor Process under Monopoly Capitalism*. Chicago: University of Chicago Press.

———. 1998. "The Extended Case Method." *Sociological Theory* 16:4–33.

———. 2000. "Introduction: Reaching for the Global." In *Global Ethnography: Forces, Connections, and Imaginations in a Postmodern World*, ed. Michael Burawoy, Joseph A. Blum, Sheba George, Zsuzsa Gille, Teresa Gowan, Lynne Haney, Maren

Klewiter, Steven H. Lopez, Seán Ó Riain, and Millie Thayer, 1–40. Berkeley and Los Angeles: University of California Press.

———. 2003. "Revisits: An Outline of a Theory of Reflexive Ethnography." *American Sociological Review* 68:645–79.

———. 2004. "For a Sociological Marxism: The Complementary Convergence of Antonio Gramsci and Karl Polanyi." *Politics and Society* 31:193–261.

Burawoy, Michael, Alice Burton, Ann Arnett Ferguson, Kathryn J. Fox, Joshua Gamson, Leslie Hurst, Nadine G. Julius, Charles Kurzman, Leslie Salzinger, Josepha Schiffman, and Shiori Ui. 1991. *Ethnography Unbound: Power and Resistance in the Modern Metropolis.* Berkeley and Los Angeles: University of California Press.

Burke III, Edmund. 1998. "Orientalism and World History: Representing Middle Eastern Nationalism and Islamism in the Twentieth Century." *Theory and Society* 27:489–507.

Çakır, Ruşen. 1994. *Ne Şeriat, Ne Demokrasi: Refah Partisini Anlamak.* Istanbul: Metis.

Çakır, Ruşen, and Fehmi Çalmuk. 2001. *Recep Tayyip Erdoğan: bir Dönüşüm Öyküsü.* Istanbul: Metis.

Çarkoğlu, Ali. 2006. "The New Generation Pro-Islamists in Turkey: Bases of the Justice and Development Party in Changing Electoral Space." In *The Emergence of a New Turkey: Islam, Democracy and the AK Party*, ed. Hakan Yavuz, 160–81. Salt Lake City: University of Utah Press.

Çarkoğlu, Ali, and Binnaz Toprak. 2006. *Değişen Türkiye'de Din, Toplum ve Siyaset.* Istanbul: TESEV.

Cassandra. 1995. "The Impending Crisis in Egypt." *The Middle East Journal* 49:9–27.

Castells, Manuel. 1983. *The City and the Grassroots: A Cross-Cultural Theory of Urban Social Movements.* Berkeley and Los Angeles: University of California Press.

Castoriadis, Cornelius. 1997. *World in Fragments: Writings on Politics, Society, Psychoanalysis, and the Imagination.* Stanford, CA: Stanford University Press.

Çavdar, Gamze. 2006. "Islamist New Thinking in Turkey: A Model for Political Learning?" *Political Science Quarterly* 121:477–97.

Cem, İsmail. 1976. *TRT'de 500 Gün.* Istanbul: Gelişim.

Chatterjee, Partha. [1986] 2001. *Nationalist Thought and the Colonial World: A Derivative Discourse.* Minneapolis: University of Minnesota Press.

———. 2004. *The Politics of the Governed: Reflections on Popular Politics in Most of the World.* New York: Columbia University Press.

Çınar, Alev. 1997. "Refah Party and the City Administration of Istanbul: Liberal Islam, Localism and Hybridity." *New Perspectives on Turkey* 16:23–40.

———. 2005. *Modernity, Islam, and Secularism in Turkey: Bodies, Places, and Time.* Minneapolis: University of Minnesota Press.

Çınar, Menderes. 2006. "Turkey's Transformation under the AKP Rule." *Muslim World* 96:469–86.

Cizre, Ümit. 2008. "Introduction: The Justice and Development Party: Making Choices, Revisions, and Reversals Interactively." In *Secular and Islamic Politics in Turkey: The Making of the Justice and Development Party*, ed. Ümit Cizre, 1–14. London: Routledge.

Cohen, Jean L., and Andrew Arato. 1992. *Civil Society and Political Theory*. Cambridge, MA: MIT Press.

Colas, Alejandro. 2004. "The Re-Invention of Populism: Islamist Responses to Capitalist Development in the Contemporary Maghreb." *Historical Materialism* 12:231–60.

Cook, Michael. 2000. *Commanding Right and Forbidding Wrong in Islamic Thought*. Cambridge: Cambridge University Press.

Coşkun, Zeki. 1995. *Aleviler, Sünniler ve Öteki Sivas*. Istanbul: İletişim.

Crehan, Kate. 1997. *The Fractured Community: Landscapes of Power and Gender in Rural Zambia*. Berkeley and Los Angeles: University of California Press.

Davis, Mike. 2006. *Planet of Slums*. London: Verso.

Davison, Andrew. 1998. *Secularism and Revivalism in Turkey: A Hermeneutic Reconsideration*. New Haven, CT: Yale University Press.

de Certeau, Michel. [1974] 1984. *The Practice of Everyday Life*. Berkeley and Los Angeles: University of California Press.

Denoeux, Guilain. 1993. *Urban Unrest in the Middle East: A Comparative Study of Informal Networks in Egypt, Iran, and Lebanon*. Albany: State University of New York Press.

Derlugian, Georgi. 2005. *Bourdieu's Secret Admirer in the Caucasus*. Chicago: University of Chicago Press.

de Tocqueville, Alexis. [1835/1840] 2000. *Democracy in America*. Chicago: University of Chicago Press.

Doherty, Joseph S. 2007. *The Islamic Bourgeoisie and the Social Imaginary: The Case of MÜSİAD*. Master's thesis, Boğaziçi University.

Duran, Burhanettin. 2008. "The Justice and Development Party's 'New Politics': Steering toward Conservative Democracy, a Revised Islamic Agenda or Management of New Crises?" In *Secular and Islamic Politics in Turkey: The Making of the Justice and Development Party*, ed. Ümit Cizre, 80–106. London: Routledge.

Eickelman, Dale F., and James P. Piscatori. 1996. *Muslim Politics*. Princeton, NJ: Princeton University Press.

Eisenstadt, Schmuel N. 2001. "The Civilizational Dimension of Modernity: Modernity as a Distinct Civilization." *International Sociology* 16:320–40.

el-Ghobashy, Mona. 2005. "The Metamorphosis of the Egyptian Muslim Brothers." *International Journal of Middle East Studies* 37:373–95.

Elias, Norbert. [1939] 2000. *The Civilizing Process: Sociogenetic and Psychogenetic Investigations*. Cambridge, MA: Blackwell Publishers.

Erbakan, Necmettin. 1991. *Adil Ekonomik Düzen*. Ankara: Semih Ofset Matbaacılık.

Erder, Sema. 1996. *Ümraniye: Istanbul'a bir Kent Kondu*. Istanbul: İletişim.

———. 1997. *Kentsel Gerilim*. Ankara: Umag.

———. 1999. "Where Do You Hail from? Localism and Networks in Istanbul." In *Istanbul: Between the Local and the Global*, ed. Çağlar Keyder, 161–71. Lanham, MD: Rowman & Littlefield.

Esposito, John L., and John O. Voll. 1996. *Islam and Democracy*. Oxford: Oxford University Press.

Evans, Peter. 1995. *Embedded Autonomy: States and Industrial Transformation*. Princeton, NJ: Princeton University Press.

———. 2001. *Livable Cities? Urban Struggles for Livelihood and Sustainability*. Berkeley and Los Angeles: University of California Press.

Evans, Peter, Dietrich Rueschemeyer, and Theda Skocpol, eds. 1985. *Bringing the State Back In*. Cambridge: Cambridge University Press.

Fandy, Mamoun. 1994. "Egypt's Islamic Group: Regional Revenge?" *The Middle East Journal* 48:607–25.

Fischer, Michael. 1980. *Iran: From Religious Dispute to Revolution*. Cambridge, MA: Harvard University Press.

———. 1982. "Islam and the Revolt of the Petit Bourgeoisie." *Daedalus* 111:101–26.

Foran, John. 1993. *Fragile Resistance: Social Transformation in Iran from 1500 to the Revolution*. Boulder, CO: Westview Press.

Foucault, Michel. 1977. *Discipline and Punish: The Birth of the Prison*. New York: Pantheon Books.

———. 1980. *Power/knowledge: Selected Interviews and Other Writings, 1972–1977*. Brighton, UK: Harvester Press.

———. [1969] 1984. "What Is an Author?" In *Foucault Reader*, 101–20. New York: Pantheon Books.

Gamson, William. 1975. *The Strategy of Social Protest*. Homewood, IL: Dorsey Press.

———. 1988. "Political Discourse and Collective Action." *International Social Movement Research* 1:219–44.

Gardiner, Michael. 1992. *The Dialogics of Critique: M.M. Bakhtin and the Theory of Ideology*. London: Routledge.

Gellner, Ernest. 1991. "Civil Society in Historical Context." *International Social Science Journal* 43:495–510.

Gibbs, Terry. 2006. "Business as Unusual: What the Chávez Era Tells Us About Democracy under Globalisation." *Third World Quarterly* 27:265–79.

Ginzburg, Carlo. 1980. *The Cheese and the Worms: The Cosmos of a Sixteenth-Century Miller*. Baltimore, MD: Johns Hopkins University Press.

Göçek, Müge F. 1999. "To Veil or Not to Veil: The Contested Location of Gender in Contemporary Turkey." *Interventions* 1:521–35.

Godazgar, Godazgarm, and Laleh Fathi. 2005. "On the Boundaries of the State and the State of Boundaries in Iran." *Social Compass* 52:115–29.

Goffman, Erving. 1959. *The Presentation of Self in Everyday Life*. New York: Anchor Books.

Göle, Nilüfer. 1996. *The Forbidden Modern: Civilization and Veiling*. Ann Arbor: University of Michigan Press.

———. 2000. "Snapshots of Islamic Modernities." *Daedalus* 129:91–119.

Gorski, Philip S. 2000. "Historicizing the Secularization Debate: Church, State, and Society in Late Medieval and Early Modern Europe, Ca. 1300 to 1700." *American Sociological Review* 65:138–67.

———. 2003. *The Disciplinary Revolution: Calvinism and the Rise of the State in Early Modern Europe*. Chicago: University of Chicago Press.

Gramsci, Antonio. 1971. *Selections from the Prison Notebooks of Antonio Gramsci*. London: Lawrence and Wishart.

Greeley, Andrew. 1989. *Religious Change in America*. Cambridge, MA: Harvard University Press.

Hafez, Mohammed M. 2003. *Why Muslims Rebel: Repression and Resistance in the Islamic World*. Boulder, CO: Lynne Rienner Publishers.

Hafez, Mohammed, and Quintan Wiktorowicz. 2004. "Violence as Contention in the Egyptian Islamic Movement." In *Islamic Activism: A Social Movement Theory Approach*, ed. Quintan Wiktorowicz, 61–88. Bloomington: Indiana University Press.

Hall, Stuart. 1985. "Signification, Representation, Ideology: Althusser and the Post-Structuralist Debates." *Critical Studies in Mass Communication* 2:91–114.

———. 1986. "On Postmodernism and Articulation." *The Journal of Communication Inquiry* 10:45–60.

Hardt, Michael, and Antonio Negri. 2000. *Empire*. Cambridge, MA: Harvard University Press.

———. 2005. *Multitude: War and Democracy in the Age of Empire*. New York: Penguin Books.

Harvey, David. 1973. *Social Justice and the City*. Baltimore, MD: Johns Hopkins University Press.

———. 1989. *The Urban Experience*. Baltimore, MD: Johns Hopkins University Press.

———. 2005. *A Brief History of Neoliberalism*. Oxford: Oxford University Press.

Hawkins, Kirk A., and David R. Hansen. 2006. "Dependent Civil Society: The Círculos Bolivarianos in Venezuela." *Latin American Research Review* 41:102–32.

Hefner, Robert. 2001. "Public Islam and the Problem of Democratization." *Sociology of Religion* 62:491–514.

Heper, Metin. 1985. *The State Tradition in Turkey*. Huntingdon, UK: Eothen Press.

Heper, Metin, and Şule Toktaş. 2003. "Islam, Modernity, and Democracy in Contemporary Turkey: The Case of Recep Tayyip Erdoğan." *Muslim World* 93:157–85.

Huntington, Samuel P. 1968. *Political Order in Changing Societies.* New Haven, CT: Yale University Press.

———. 1996. *The Clash of Civilizations and the Remaking of World Order.* New York: Simon & Schuster.

Işık, Oğuz, and Melih Pınarcıoğlu. 2001. *Nöbetleşe Yoksulluk: Gecekondulaşma ve Kent Yoksulları: Sultanbeyli Örneği.* Istanbul: İletişim.

Ismail, Salwa. 1998. "Confronting the Other: Identity, Culture, Politics, and Conservative Islamism in Egypt." *International Journal of Middle East Studies* 30: 199–225.

———. 1999. "Religious 'Orthodoxy' as Public Morality: The State, Islamism and Cultural Politics in Egypt." *Critique: Critical Middle Eastern Studies* 8:25–47.

———. 2003. *Rethinking Islamist Politics: Culture, the State, and Islamism.* London: I.B. Tauris.

———. 2006. *Political Life in Cairo's New Quarters: Encountering the Everyday State.* Minneapolis: University of Minnesota Press.

Jenkins, J. Craig, and Charles Perrow. 1977. "Insurgency of the Powerless: Farm Worker Movements (1946–1972)." *American Sociological Review* 42:249–68.

Jessop, Bob. 2006. "Gramsci as a Spatial Theorist." In *Images of Gramsci: Connections and Contentions in Political Theory and International Relations,* ed. Andreas Bieler and Adam D. Morton, 27–43. London: Routledge.

Kamali, Masoud. 2001. "Civil Society and Islam: A Sociological Perspective." *Archives Europeennes de Sociologie* 42:457–82.

Karbassian, Akbar. 2000. "Islamic Revolution and the Management of the Iranian Economy." *Social Research* 67:621–40.

Karib, Zafer. 1975. *1975 Türkiyesinde Niçin MSP?* Istanbul: İhya.

Kasaba, Reşat. 1997. "Kemalist Certainties and Modern Ambiguities." In *Rethinking Modernity and National Identity in Turkey,* ed. Reşat Kasaba and Sibel Bozdoğan, 15–36. Seattle: University of Washington Press.

Keddie, Nikki R. 1991. "The Revolt of Islam and Its Roots." In *Comparative Political Dynamics: Global Research Perspectives,* ed. Dankwart A. Rustow and Kenneth P. Erickson, 292–308. New York: HarperCollins Publishers.

———. [2003] 2006. *Modern Iran: Roots and Results of Revolution.* New Haven, CT: Yale University Press.

Kelsay, John. 2002. "Civil Society and Government in Islam." In *Islamic Political Ethics: Civil Society, Pluralism, and Conflict,* ed. Sohail H. Hashmi, 3–37. Princeton, NJ: Princeton University Press.

Kepel, Gilles. 1985. *The Prophet and the Pharoah: Muslim Extremism in Egypt.* London: Al Saqi Books.

———. 2002. *Jihad: The Trail of Political Islam.* Cambridge, MA: Harvard University Press.

Keyder, Çağlar. 1987. *State and Class in Turkey: A Study in Capitalist Development.* London: Verso.

———, ed. 1999. *Istanbul: Between the Local and the Global.* Lanham, MD: Rowman & Littlefield.

Keyder, Çağlar, and Ayşe Öncü. 1994. "Globalization of a Third World Metropolis: Istanbul in the 1980s." *Review* 17:383–421.

Keyman, Fuat, and Ziya Öniş. 2007. "Globalization and Social Democracy in the European Periphery: Paradoxes of the Turkish Experience." *Globalizations* 4:211–28.

Khajehpour, Bijan. 2000. "Domestic Political Reforms and Private Sector Activity in Iran." *Social Research* 67:577–98.

Khosrokhavar, Farhad. 2000. "Toward an Anthropology of Democratization in Iran." *Critique: Critical Middle Eastern Studies* 16:3–29.

———. 2004. "The Islamic Revolution in Iran: Retrospect after a Quarter of a Century." *Thesis Eleven* 76:70–84.

Kienle, Eberhard. 1998. "More Than a Response to Islamism: The Political Deliberalization of Egypt in the 1990s." *Middle East Journal* 52:219–35.

Kimeldorf, Howard. 1992. *Reds or Rackets?: The Making of Radical and Conservative Unions on the Waterfront.* Berkeley and Los Angeles: University of California Press.

———. 1999. *Battling for American Labor: Wobblies, Craft Workers, and the Making of the Union Movement.* Berkeley and Los Angeles: University of California Press.

Kimmel, Michael. 1989. "'New Prophets' and 'Old Ideals': Charisma and Tradition in the Iranian Revolution." *Social Compass* 36:493–510.

Koğacıoğlu, Dicle. 2004. "Progress, Unity, and Democracy: Dissolving Political Parties in Turkey." *Law & Society Review* 38:433–62.

Kuran, Timur. 2004. *Islam and Mammon: The Economic Predicaments of Islamism.* Princeton, NJ: Princeton University Press.

Kurzman, Charles. 1998. "Liberal Islam and Its Islamic Context." In *Liberal Islam: A Source Book*, ed. Charles Kurzman, 3–26. Oxford: Oxford University Press.

———. 2001. "Student Protests and the Stability of Gridlock in Khatami's Iran." *Journal of South Asian and Middle Eastern Studies* 25:38–47.

———. 2003. "The Qum Protests and the Coming of the Iranian Revolution, 1975 and 1978." *Social Science History* 27:287–325.

———. 2004. *The Unthinkable Revolution in Iran.* Cambridge, MA: Harvard University Press.

Laclau, Ernesto. 1977. *Politics and Ideology in Marxist Theory: Capitalism, Fascism, Populism.* London: New Left Books.

———. 2005. *On Populist Reason.* London: Verso.

Laclau, Ernesto, and Chantal Mouffe. 1985. *Hegemony and Socialist Strategy: Towards a Radical Democratic Politics.* London: Verso.

Leach, Darcy K. 2005. *The Way Is the Goal: Collectivist Democracy in German New Social Movement Organizations*. PhD Dissertation thesis, University of Michigan.

Lefebvre, Henri. [1947] 1991. *Critique of Everyday Life*. London: Verso.

Lefort, Claude. 1986. *The Political Forms of Modern Society: Bureaucracy, Democracy, Totalitarianism*. Cambridge, MA: MIT Press.

Leiken, Robert S., and Steven Brooke. 2007. "The Moderate Muslim Brotherhood." *Foreign Affairs* 86:107–21.

Lenin, Vladimir Ilich. [1902] 1969. *What Is to Be Done? Burning Questions of Our Movement*. New York: International Publishers.

Lerner, Daniel. [1958] 1967. *The Passing of Traditional Society: Modernizing the Middle East*. New York: The Free Press.

Lewis, Bernard. 1961. *The Emergence of Modern Turkey*. Oxford: Oxford University Press.

———. 1988. *The Political Language of Islam*. Chicago: University of Chicago Press.

———. 1993. *Islam and the West*. Oxford: Oxford University Press.

Lia, Brynjar. 1998. *The Society of the Muslim Brothers in Egypt: The Rise of an Islamic Mass Movement 1928–1942*. Reading, UK: Ithaca Press.

Liliane, Voye. 1991. "Secularization in a Context of Advanced Modernity." *Sociology of Religion* 60:275–88.

Linz, Juan and Alfred Stepan. 1996. *Problems of Democratic Transition and Consolidation: Southern Europe, South America, and Post-Communist Europe*. Baltimore, MD: Johns Hopkins University Press.

Mahmood, Saba. 2005. *Politics of Piety: The Islamic Revival and the Feminist Subject*. Princeton, NJ: Princeton University Press.

Mann, Michael. 1986. *The Sources of Social Power*. Cambridge: Cambridge University Press.

Mardin, Şerif. 1983. "Religion and Politics in Modern Turkey." In *Islam and the Political Process*, ed. James Piscatori, 138–59. Cambridge, MA: Royal Institute of International Affairs.

———. 1989. *Religion and Social Change in Modern Turkey: The Case of Bediüzzaman Said Nursi*. Albany: State University of New York Press.

McAdam, Doug, Sidney Tarrow, and Charles Tilly. 2001. *Dynamics of Contention*. Cambridge: Cambridge University Press.

McCarthy, John D., and Mayer Zald. 1977. "Resource Mobilization and Social Movements: A Partial Theory." *American Journal of Sociology* 82:1212–41.

Melucci, Alberto. 1996. *The Playing Self: Person and Meaning in the Planetary Society*. Cambridge: Cambridge University Press.

Migdal, Joel S. 2001. *State in Society: Studying How States and Societies Transform and Constitute One Another*. Cambridge: Cambridge University Press.

Mitchell, Richard P. 1969. *The Society of the Muslim Brothers*. Oxford: Oxford University Press.

———. 2002. *Rule of Experts: Egypt, Techno-Politics, Modernity.* Berkeley and Los Angeles: University of California Press.

Moaddel, Mansoor. 2004. "The Future of Islam after 9/11." *Futures* 36:961–77.

———. 2005. *Islamic Modernism, Nationalism, and Fundamentalism: Episode and Discourse.* Chicago: University of Chicago Press.

Morris, Aldon D. 1984. *The Origins of the Civil Rights Movement: Black Communities Organizing for Change.* New York: The Free Press.

Müller, Marion G., and Esra Özcan. 2007. "The Political Iconography of Muhammad Cartoons: Understanding Cultural Conflict and Political Action." *Political Science & Politics* 40:287–92.

Nairn, Tom. 1997. *Faces of Nationalism: Janus Revisited.* London: Verso.

Nasr, Seyyed Hossein. 1998. "Religion and Global Affairs: Secular States and Religious Oppositions." *SAIS Review* 18:32–37.

Nasr, Vali. 2005. "The Rise of 'Muslim Democracy.'" *Journal of Democracy* 16:13–27.

Nettl, J. P. 1968. "The State as a Conceptual Variable." *World Politics* 20:559–92.

Nielsen, Greg. 2002. *The Norms of Answerability: Social Theory Between Bakhtin and Habermas.* Albany: State University of New York Press.

Nomani, Farhad, and Sohrab Behdad. 2006. *Class and Labor in Iran: Did the Revolution Matter?* Syracuse, NY: Syracuse University Press.

Norton, Augustus, ed. 1995–1996. *Civil Society in the Middle East.* Leiden, Netherlands: Brill.

Oberschall, Anthony. 1973. *Social Conflict and Social Movements.* Englewood Cliffs, NJ: Prentice-Hall.

Öniş, Ziya. 2006a. "Globalization and Party Transformation: Turkey's Justice and Development Party in Perspective." In *Globalizing Democracy: Party Politics in Emerging Democracies*, ed. Peter Burnell, 122–40. London: Routledge.

———. 2006b. "The Political Economy of Turkey's Justice and Development Party." In *The Emergence of a New Turkey: Islam, Democracy and the AK Party*, ed. Hakan Yavuz, 207–34. Salt Lake City: University of Utah Press.

———. 2007. "Conservative Globalists versus Defensive Nationalists: Political Parties and Paradoxes of Europeanization in Turkey." *Journal of Southern Europe and the Balkans* 9:247–61.

Öniş, Ziya, and Fuat Keyman. 2003. "A New Path Emerges." *Journal of Democracy* 14:95–107.

Özdalga, Elizabeth. 1999. "Education in the Name of 'Order and Progress': Reflections on the Recent Eight Year Obligatory School Reform in Turkey." *Muslim World* 89:414–38.

———. 2002. "Necmettin Erbakan: Democracy for the Sake of Power." In *Political Leaders and Democracy in Turkey*, ed. Metin Heper and Sabri Sayarı, 127–46. New York: Lexington Books.

Özdamar, Mustafa. 1977. *Yaşı ve Başıyla Mim Sin Harekati*. Istanbul: Çığır.

Özel, İsmet. 1978. *Üç Mesele*. Istanbul: Düşünce Yayınları.

Özyürek, Esra. 2006. *Nostalgia for the Modern: State Secularism and Everyday Politics in Turkey*. Durham, NC: Duke University Press.

Parla, Taha. 1985. *The Social and Political Thought of Ziya Gökalp, 1876–1924*. Leiden, Netherlands: E. J. Brill.

———. 1992. *Türkiye'de Siyasal Kültürün Resmi Kaynakları (V3): Kemalist Tek-Parti İdeolojisi ve CHP'nin Altı Oku*. Istanbul: İletişim.

———. 1995. *Türkiye'nin Siyasal Rejimi*. Istanbul: İletişim.

Parsa, Misagh. 1989. *Social Origins of the Iranian Revolution*. New Brunswick, NJ: Rutgers University Press.

Patton, Marcie J. 2006. "The Economic Policies of Turkey's AKP Government: Rabbits from a Hat?" *Middle East Journal* 60:513–36.

Petras, James, and Henry Veltmeyer. 2003. "Whither Lula's Brazil? Neoliberalism and 'Third Way' Ideology." *The Journal of Peasant Studies* 31:1–44.

Pizzorno, Alessandro. 1997. "Opposition in Italy." *Government and Opposition* 32: 647–57.

Polanyi, Karl. 1944. *The Great Transformation*. New York: Farrar & Rinehart.

Poulantzas, Nicos. 1974. *Fascism and Dictatorship: The Third International and the Problem of Fascism*. London: New Left Books.

Przeworski, Adam. 1985. *Capitalism and Social Democracy*. Cambridge: Cambridge University Press.

Putnam, Robert D. 1995. "Bowling Alone: America's Declining Social Capital." *Journal of Democracy* 6:65–78.

Qutb, Sayyid. 1970. *Social Justice in Islam*. New York: Octagon Books.

———. 1993. *Milestones*. Indianapolis, IN: American Trust.

Rahman, Fazlur. 1966. *Islam*. Chicago: University of Chicago Press.

Rahman, Maha Abdel. 2002. "The Politics of 'UnCivil' Society in Egypt." *Review of African Political Economy* 29:21–36.

Ray, Raka, and Seemin Qayum. 2003. "Grappling with Modernity: Calcutta's Respectable Classes and the Culture of Domestic Servitude." *Ethnography* 4:520–55.

Refah Partisi. 1994. *Adil Düzen: 21 Soru/21 Cevap*. Ankara: Refah Partisi.

Riesebrodt, Martin. 1993. *Pious Passion: The Emergence of Modern Fundamentalism in the United States and Iran*. Berkeley and Los Angeles: University of California Press.

Riley, Dylan J., and Manali Desai. 2007. "The Passive Revolutionary Route to the Modern World: Italy and India in Comparative Perspective." *Comparative Studies in Society and History* 49:815–47.

Robinson, Glenn E. 1997. "Can Islamists Be Democrats? The Case of Jordan." *Middle East Journal* 51:373–88.

————. 1998. "Defensive Democratization in Jordan." *International Journal of Middle East Studies* 30:387–410.

Rubin, Michael. 2007. "Will Turkey Have an Islamist President?" *American Enterprise Institute Middle East Outlook* 1:1–10.

Rutherford, Bruce K. 2006. "What Do Egypt's Islamists Want? Moderate Islam and the Rise of Islamic Constitutionalism." *Middle East Journal* 60:707–31.

Saktanber, Ayşe. 2002. *Living Islam: Women, Religion and the Politicization of Culture in Turkey.* London: I.B. Tauris.

Samim, Ahmet. 1981. "The Tragedy of the Turkish Left." *New Left Review* 126:60–85.

Sanasarian, Eliz. 1995. "Ayatollah Khomeini and the Institutionalization of Charismatic Rule in Iran, 1979–1989." *Journal of Developing Societies* 11:189–205.

Sarıbay, Ali Yaşar. 1985. *Türkiye'de Modernleşme, Din, ve Parti Politikası: Milli Selâmet Partisi Örnek Olayı.* Istanbul: Alan.

Scott, James C. 1985. *Weapons of the Weak: Everyday Forms of Peasant Resistance.* New Haven, CT: Yale University Press.

————. 1998. *Seeing Like a State: How Certain Schemes to Improve the Human Condition Have Failed.* New Haven, CT: Yale University Press.

Serajzadeh, Seyed Hossein. 2002. "Croyants Non-Pratiquants: la Religiosite de la Jeunesse Iranienne et Ses Implications Pour la Theorie de la Secularisation." *Social Compass* 49:111–32.

Sevilgen, Gündüz. 1979. *MSP'de Dört Yıl.* Ankara: İstiklal Matbaası.

Shafaee, Seyed Masoud Mousavi. 2003. "Globalization and Contradiction between the Nation and the State in Iran: The Internet Case." *Critique: Critical Middle Eastern Studies* 12:189–95.

Shafir, Gershon. 1995. *Immigrants and Nationalists: Ethnic Conflict and Accommodation in Catalonia, the Basque Country, Latvia, and Estonia.* Albany: State University of New York Press.

Sidoti, Francesco. 1993. "Italy: A Clean-up After the Cold War." *Government and Opposition* 28:105–14.

Singerman, Diane. 1995. *Avenues of Participation: Family, Politics, and Networks in Urban Quarters of Cairo.* Princeton, NJ: Princeton University Press.

Sirman, Nükhet. 1990. "State, Village and Gender in Western Turkey." In *Turkish State, Turkish Society*, ed. Andrew Finkel and Nükhet Sirman, 21–51. London: Routledge.

Sivan, Emmanuel. 1985. *Radical Islam: Medieval Theology and Modern Politics.* New Haven, CT: Yale University Press.

Skocpol, Theda. 1979. *States and Social Revolutions.* Cambridge: Cambridge University Press.

————. 1982. "Rentier State and Shi'a Islam in the Iranian Revolution." *Theory and Society* 11:265–83.

Smelser, Neil. 1963. *Theory of Collective Behavior.* New York: The Free Press.

Smith, Christian. 2003. "Introduction: Rethinking the Secularization of American Public Life." In *The Secular Revolution: Power, Interests, and Conflict in the Secularization of American Public Life*, ed. Christian Smith, 1–96. Berkeley and Los Angeles: University of California Press.

Smith, Dorothy. 1987. *The Everyday World as Problematic: A Feminist Sociology.* Boston, MA: Northeastern University Press.

———. 1998. "Bakhtin and the Dialogic of Sociology: An Investigation." In *Bakhtin and the Human Sciences: No Last Words*, ed. Michael Mayerfeld Bell and Michael Gardiner, 63–77. London: Sage.

Snow, David A., and Robert D. Benford. 1988. "Ideology, Frame Resonance, and Participant Mobilization." *International Social Movement Research* 1:197–217.

———. 1992. "Master Frames and Cycles of Protest." In *Frontiers in Social Movement Theory*, ed. Aldon Morris and Carol M. Mueller, 133–55. New Haven, CT: Yale University Press.

Snow, David, E. Burke Rochford Jr., Steven K. Worden, and Robert D. Benford. 1986. "Frame Alignment Processes, Micromobilization, and Movement Participation." *American Sociological Review* 51:464–81.

Soederberg, Susanne. 2001. "From Neoliberalism to Social Liberalism: Situating the National Solidarity Program within Mexico's Passive Revolutions." *Latin American Perspectives* 28:104–23.

Soja, Edward. 1989. *Postmodern Geographies: The Reassertion of Space in Critical Social Theory.* London: Verso.

Stark, Jan. 2005. "Beyond 'Terrorism' and 'State Hegemony': Assessing the Islamist Mainstream in Egypt and Malaysia." *Third World Quarterly* 26:307–27.

Steinberg, Marc. 1998. "Tilting the Frame: Considerations on Collective Action Framing from a Discursive Turn." *Theory and Society* 27:845–72.

———. 1999. *Fighting Words: Working-class Formation, Collective Action, and Discourse in Early Nineteenth-Century England.* Ithaca, NY: Cornell University Press.

Sunar, İlkay, and Sabri Sayarı. 1986. "Democracy in Turkey: Problems and Prospects." In *Transitions from Authoritarian Rule: Prospects for Democracy*, ed. Guillermo O'Donnell, Philippe C. Schmitter, and Laurence Whitehead, 165–86. Baltimore, MD: Johns Hopkins University Press.

Swidler, Ann. 2001. *Talk of Love: How Culture Matters.* Chicago: University of Chicago Press.

Tarhanlı, İştar. 1993. *Müslüman Toplum, "Laik" Devlet: Türkiye'de Diyanet İşleri Başkanlığı.* Istanbul: AFA.

Tepe, Sultan. 2006. "A Pro-Islamic Party? Promises and Limits of Turkey's Justice and Development Party." In *The Emergence of a New Turkey: Democracy and the AK Parti*, ed. M. Hakan Yavuz, 107–35. Salt Lake City: University of Utah Press.

Tilly, Charles. 1978. *From Mobilization to Revolution*. Reading, MA: Addison-Wesley.

Tschannen, Olivier. 1991. "The Secularization Paradigm: A Systematization." *Journal for the Scientific Study of Religion* 30:395–415.

Tuğal, Cihan. 2002. "Islamism in Turkey: Beyond Instrument and Meaning." *Economy and Society* 31:85–111.

———. 2006. "The Appeal of Islamic Politics: Ritual and Dialogue in a Poor District of Turkey." *The Sociological Quarterly* 47:245–73.

———. 2007. "NATO's Islamists: Hegemony and Americanization in Turkey." *New Left Review* 44:5–34.

———. 2008. "The Greening of Istanbul." *New Left Review* 51:64–80.

———. Forthcoming. "Transforming Everyday Life: Islamism and Social Movement Theory." *Theory and Society*.

Turam, Berna. 2004. "The Politics of Engagement between Islam and the Secular State: Ambivalences of 'Civil Society.'" *British Journal of Sociology* 55:259–81.

———. 2007. *Between Islam and the State: The Politics of Engagement*. Stanford, CA: Stanford University Press.

Turner, Brian S. 1974. *Weber and Islam: A Critical Study*. London: Routledge and Kegan Paul.

Valibeigi, Mehrdad. 1993. "Islamic Economics and Economic Policy Formation in Post-Revolutionary Iran: A Critique." *Journal of Economic Issues* 27:793–812.

van Appeldoorn, Bastiaan. 2003. "The Struggle over European Order: Transnational Class Agency in the Making of an 'Embedded Neo-Liberalism.'" In *State/Space: A Reader*, ed. Neil Brenner, 147–64. Malden, MA: Blackwell Publishers.

Wacquant, Loïc. 2008. *Urban Outcasts: A Comparative Sociology of Advanced Marginality*. Cambridge: Polity.

Walton, John, and Charles Ragin. 1990. "Global and National Sources of Political Protest: Third World Responses to the Debt Crisis." *American Sociological Review* 55:876–90.

Weber, Max. [1922] 1978. *Economy and Society: An Outline of Interpretive Sociology*. Berkeley and Los Angeles: University of California Press.

———. [1904–1905] 1992. *The Protestant Ethic and the Spirit of Capitalism*. London: Routledge.

Wertsch, James. 1991. *Voices of the Mind: A Socio-Cultural Approach to Mediated Action*. Cambridge, MA: Harvard University Press.

White, Jenny. 2002. *Islamist Mobilization in Turkey: A Study in Vernacular Politics*. Seattle: University of Washington Press.

Wickham, Carrie R. 2002. *Mobilizing Islam: Religion, Activism, and Political Change in Egypt*. New York: Columbia University Press.

Wiktorowicz, Quintan. 2001. *The Management of Islamic Activism: Salafis, the Muslim Brotherhood, and State Power in Jordan*. Albany: State University of New York Press.

———, ed. 2004. *Islamic Activism: A Social Movement Theory Approach*. Bloomington: Indiana University Press.

Williams, Raymond. 1973. *The Country and the City*. Oxford: Oxford University Press.

Wolf, Eric R. 1982. *Europe and the People Without History*. Berkeley and Los Angeles: University of California Press.

Wright, Erik Olin. 1985. *Classes*. London: Verso.

Yamane, David. 1997. "Secularization on Trial: In Defense of a Neosecularization Paradigm." *Journal for the Scientific Study of Religion* 36:109–22.

Yavuz, M. Hakan. 2003. *Islamic Political Identity in Turkey*. Oxford: Oxford University Press.

———. 2006. "Introduction: The Role of the New Bourgeoisie in the Transformation of the Turkish Islamic Movement." In *The Emergence of a New Turkey: Islam, Democracy and the AK Party*, ed. Hakan Yavuz, 1–19. Salt Lake City: University of Utah Press.

Yeldan, Erinc. 2006. "Neoliberal Global Remedies: From Speculative-Led Growth to IMF-Led Crisis in Turkey." *Review of Radical Political Economics* 38:193–213.

Zahid, Mohammed, and Michael Medley. 2006. "Muslim Brotherhood in Egypt and Sudan." *Review of African Political Economy* 33:693–708.

Zald, Mayer N. 1996. "Culture, Ideology, and Strategic Framing." In *Comparative Perspectives on Social Movements: Political Opportunities, Mobilizing Structures, and Cultural Framings*, ed. Doug McAdam, John D. McCarthy, and Mayer N. Zald, 261–74. Cambridge: Cambridge University Press.

Zebardast, Esfandiar. 2006. "Marginalization of the Urban Poor and the Expansion of the Spontaneous Settlements on the Tehran Metropolitan Fringe." *Cities* 23: 439–54.

Zeghal, Malika. 1999. "Religion and Politics in Egypt: The Ulema of Al-Azhar, Radical Islam, and the State (1952–94)." *International Journal of Middle East Studies* 31:371–99.

Zollner, Barbara. 2007. "Prison Talk: The Muslim Brotherhood's Internal Struggle During Gamal Abdel Nasser's Persecution, 1954 to 1971." *International Journal of Middle East Studies* 39:411–33.

Zubaida, Sami. 1989. *Islam, the People and the State: Political Ideas and Movements in the Middle East*. London: Routledge.

Newspapers

Hürriyet
Milliyet
The New York Times

Sabah
The Washington Post
Die Welt
Yeni Şafak
Zaman

INDEX

Abdullah, 180

Absorption: into AKP, 5, 147–171, 238–239; in civil society, 243–250; of collective imaginary, 241–243; of dual power, 239–241; economic, 246–250; habitual, 243–245; into Western hegemony, 179–191; of Islamist radicals, 5, 12; of leadership, 236–239; into RP, 77–80, 126–127, 242; spatial, 245–246

Ahmet, 171–172

AKP. *See* Justice and Development Party (AKP)

Alevis, 273n11

Ali, 113–114

Alternative capitalism, 141–144

ANAP. *See* Motherland Party (ANAP)

Anatolian tigers, 132

Anderson, P., 24–25

Arato, A., 24–25

Articulation, as political theory, 23–24

Asad, Muhammad, 195

Associational activity, 31

Atatürk, Mustafa Kemal: attitudes toward, 90; charisma of, 37–38; controversial statue of, 85; cult of, 274n12; suppressing Islam, 5

Authority, and political society, 27

Bahri, 150

Banna, Hasan al-, 252–253

Bekir, 69–70

Body politics, 118–120

Bourdieu, P., 29

Burawoy, M., 30

Çağlar, Cavit, 130

Capitalism, internalization of, 217–225

Çarşaf, 93–94, 212

Cemaat, 273n4

Census (2000), 91–92

Center left, 36–37

Center right, 36–37, 151–152

Cevat, 103–105

CHP. *See* Republican People's Party (CHP)

Christianity, 156, 202

Civilizing mission, of the state, 90–94

Civil society: absorption in, 243–250; constituents of, 271n26; and everyday life, 29; Islamization of, 49, 102–114; linked to political society, 26–28, 33, 262–263; and relations to economy, 30–31; and space, 30; theory of, 22–23; uncoupled from political society, 144

Coffeehouses, 119

Cohen, J., 24–25

Co-local networks, 41, 120–124, 215–216

Constructionists, 133

Consumerism, 113–114

Crescent Foundation, 142

Dar-ul harp, 95, 275n4

Demir, 65, 164–165

Demirel, Süleyman, 38

Democratic Left Party (DSP), 81–82

Democratic Society Party (DTP), 186